Contents

The surest sign that intelligent life exists elsewhere in the universe is that it has never tried to contact us.

— Bill Watterson

1. Embarking on a Galactic Voyage

In the vast tapestry of the cosmos, human curiosity stands as one of our most defining traits. From the time we gazed up at the night sky and imagined constellations, to today, sending probes to the farthest reaches of our solar system, the desire to understand our universe has propelled civilization forward. At the heart of that quest lies a singular question: Are we alone? With recent technological advancements, what was once limited to the realm of science fiction is now a serious field of study. The Majestic Universe: Recognizing Signs of Alien Terraformation invites you on a journey to explore the extraordinary possibility of alien life shaping planets in ways unlike our own. This book explores the scientific potential of extraterrestrial terraforming and the unseen influences possibly at play in the cosmic neighborhood around us. With groundbreaking insights and detailed research, Dennis Joseph Evans unravels the observable hints that may point to civilizations beyond our own party to the majesty of the universe, and together, let's grasp the essence of our shared cosmic journey.

2. Foundations of Terraforming

2.1. The Concept of Terraforming

Terraforming, the theoretical process of altering the environment of a celestial body to make it more Earth-like and potentially habitable for human life and other forms of terrestrial biology, stands as a monumental concept that stretches the imagination beyond our current limitations. At its core, terraforming embodies the ultimate expression of human innovation and determination, encapsulating our drive to not only explore the cosmos but to adapt and reshape our surroundings to meet our needs.

The concept of terraforming pivots on several foundational scientific principles, which are interrelated and essential for understanding how we could modify a planet's atmosphere, temperature, surface, or ecology. These principles include planetary engineering—understanding and manipulating the physical and chemical attributes of celestial bodies—and ecological engineering, which involves creating sustainable biospheres that could support diverse life forms. The idea is not merely to replicate Earth but to create an environment that can support life through a series of carefully calibrated adjustments.

One of the most striking examples of terraforming in scientific discussions often revolves around Mars. The red planet, with its vast expanses of dusty plains and frozen polar caps, represents a tantalizing target for terraforming efforts. Scientists speculate that if we could increase Mars' atmospheric density and temperature—potentially through the introduction of greenhouse gases or the deployment of massive reflectors in orbit—then liquid water could once again exist on its surface. Such changes could catalyze the development of a biosphere capable of supporting human colonization.

The concept also extends beyond Mars. Venus, for example, presents a radically different challenge; its thick atmosphere is composed predominantly of carbon dioxide and possesses crushing surface pressures along with extremely high temperatures. The theoretical approach to terraforming Venus is equally complex, with ideas ranging from introducing genetically engineered organisms that could metabolize carbon dioxide, to constructing giant solar shades that would reduce solar input and cool the planet.

While terraforming is often depicted as a straightforward, if ambitious, engineering problem, the true complexity emerges when considering the stability of these environments. Creating a sustainble ecosystem is not merely about temperature and atmosphere; it's also about fostering a balanced interplay of biotic and abiotic factors. The introduction of non-native species or alterations to atmospheric compositions could have unpredictable repercussions, highlighting the need for a deep understanding of planetary ecosystems.

On Earth, human history provides numerous instances of unintentional terraforming—where human activity has irrevocably altered landscapes and ecosystems, often with devastating results. These historical precedents serve as cautionary tales for future terraforming endeavors. The ethical implications of these undertakings cannot be overlooked. What gives humanity the right to alter another world, even if it is barren? What are the moral implications of possibly extinguishing unique forms of alien life that could exist in the untouched depths of a distant world?

Contemplating these issues ultimately leads to an examination of our own ecological missteps as we have reshaped Earth's landscapes, often prioritizing short-term benefits over long-term sustainability. This reflection is paramount as we consider our place in the cosmos and our responsibility toward alien worlds we may one day encounter.

Furthermore, the idea of terraforming is deeply intertwined with the search for extraterrestrial life. Detecting signs of past or ongoing terraforming efforts by an alien civilization could revolutionize our understanding of life beyond Earth. Scientists speculate that if advanced alien species possess the technological know-how and ethical considerations akin to our own, they might have transformed inhospitable planets into lush, habitable environments. Lunarscapes dotted with technology lost to the ages might provide breadcrumbs of this cosmic endeavor, tantalizingly hinting at civilizations that dared to shape their worlds.

In essence, terraforming is a multifaceted concept that embodies the collision of dreams, ethics, technology, and our relentless quest to become stewards of the universe. While the technological feasibility of such an undertaking remains, for now, a distant reality filled with uncertainties, the dreams and dilemmas surrounding terraforming invite profound questions about humanity's future among the stars and the intricate relationships we might forge with alien worlds, should we dare to reach out and reshape them. As we stand on the precipice of a new era of exploration and potential colonization, the challenge remains: can we learn from our past to ethically and sustainably engage with the universe we seek to understand and inhabit? The pursuit of terraforming beckons us toward an adventure that is as much about self-discovery as it is about reshaping distant planets into new homes.

2.2. Terraforming in Science Fiction

Science fiction has long served as a conduit for exploring humanity's deepest desires, fears, and aspirations concerning the cosmos. From the imaginative landscapes conjured by visionary writers to the complex technological constructs depicted in their narratives, the realm of science fiction allows us to grapple with concepts that are often too daunting or too far removed from reality to consider in a purely scientific context. One of the most compelling themes in science fiction is terraforming—the idea of transforming inhospitable celestial bodies into vibrant, life-sustaining environments. This subchapter delves into the rich tapestry of terraforming as envisioned in science fiction, examining its implications and the relationship between these fantastical narratives and our scientific pursuits.

One of the earliest and most influential portrayals of terraforming can be found in the works of H.G. Wells, especially in "The War of the Worlds," which offers a glimpse into the Martian imagination and their possibly terraformed ambitions for Earth through invasion.

The Martians, with their advanced technology and ruthless nature, serve as a stark contrast to humanity's own ambitions, prompting readers to reflect on the nature of progress, survival, and the moral implications of one civilization imposing its will upon another. The themes of colonization and terraforming intertwine here, presenting a cautionary tale of what happens when one species seeks to dominate another world without considering ethical consequences.

Moving forward to the mid-20th century, the works of authors such as Arthur C. Clarke and Kim Stanley Robinson introduced more sophisticated narratives surrounding terraforming. Clarke's "Rendezvous with Rama" expands on the idea of alien civilizations that manipulate entire systems, leading to an awareness of the universe's vast complexity and the potential of diverse approaches to terraforming. In contrast, Robinson's "Mars Trilogy" presents an elaborate vision of how humanity might take up the mantle of terraforming Mars. Through a careful exploration of ecological systems, social dynamics, and human psychology, Robinson not only depicts the technological feats required to change a planet's landscape, but also delves into the philosophical quandaries surrounding our responsibility toward such an undertaking. His characters grapple with the ecological and ethical dilemmas that arise from attempting to engineer a thriving biosphere on Mars, questioning whether it is humanity's place to alter another world at all.

Parallel to these literary explorations, graphic novels and cinematic representations have continued to expand upon the concept of terraformation. Films like "Total Recall" and "The Martian" depict how humans could either adapt alien environments through terraforming or survive in their unaltered states. These narratives reflect our collective fascination with the possibilities of colonization, pushing the boundaries of what we wish to explore as well as what we might inadvertently destroy. The idea of creating lush environments on barren worlds serves as a metaphor for hope, potential, and the human spirit's resilience, while also forcing us to confront the possible consequences of such actions.

Moreover, the concept of terraforming in science fiction allows for reflection on humanity's own ecological practices. Many narratives treat terraforming as an ethical dilemma, showcasing the unintended consequences of technological advancement—be it climate change on Earth or the destruction of native aliens in alien habitats. The thinning lines between hero and villain, explorer and conqueror, are central themes that echo in modern discourses about ecological responsibility and the rights of alien lifeforms. As we are now discovering the ramifications of our actions on Earth, it is crucial to consider similar possible repercussions in our extraterrestrial ambitions. The insights gleaned from science fiction narratives help ground our theoretical approaches in real ethical concerns and serve as important forays into public discourse on interstellar exploration.

The hypnotic allure of terraforming transcends mere speculation; it taps into our innate desire to reshape our environment. Tales of epic terraforming set against the backdrop of distant worlds resonate powerfully with audiences, often invoking wonder at the potential for interconnectedness and equity among civilizations. This complexity invites comparisons with socio-political realities; the technological prowess depicted in science fiction often reflects humanity's own struggles with power dynamics, environmental stewardship, and community.

Continuing into the present day, science fiction has expanded its scope to include the complexities of alien life forms and their own potential for terraforming. The works of authors like N.K. Jemisin and Ann Leckie explore how alien civilizations might modify their environments or those of other worlds, showcasing not just the technical aspects, but the cultural and philosophical motivations behind such actions. The possibility that formerly unexplored alien systems may hold civilizations engaging in their own forms of terraformation elevates the conversation surrounding the search for extraterrestrial intelligence. These narratives postulate a universe where life is diverse, vibrant, and modified, reshaping our understanding of what constitutes habitability.

In closing, terraforming in science fiction serves as a fundamental mechanism through which humanity can engage with its ambitions and anxieties regarding outer space exploration. It generates a captivating interplay between imaginative narratives and the burgeoning realities of planetary science and ecological conservation. As technological advancements continue to blur the lines between science fiction and science fact, we are not only inspired by these literary constructs but also called upon to heed the warnings that arise from them. The narrative arcs of terraforming challenge us to reflect on our potential role as cosmic stewards, shaping not only our destiny among the stars, but the very future of life itself as we understand it. In this grand tale of cosmic ambition and ethical contemplation, the lessons learned from our fictional explorations serve as guideposts for the journeys yet to come.

2.3. Earth's Terraforming History

The story of Earth's terraforming history is one intricately interwoven with the threads of human endeavor, ambition, and regrettable missteps. While the term "terraforming" itself is relatively modern, the concept evokes an ancient quest—to shape and mold our environment. This subchapter seeks to unravel the evolutionary narrative of Earth as a living testament to transformational forces—both seen and unseen—that have influenced and driven humanity from our primeval beginnings to the sophisticated civilization we navigate today.

In examining Earth's terraforming history, it is essential to delineate between two forms of terraforming: anthropogenic alterations, where human action has directly impacted the landscape, and the natural processes over eons that have shaped our planet's climate, biodiversity, and habitability. The story connects humankind's ingenious capacity to reshape landscapes while also cautioning against the unintended consequences of these alterations.

At its core, human history is marked by a relentless pursuit of altering nature to fit our needs. The earliest evidence of terraforming can be traced back to prehistoric societies, where early humans adopted agriculture, initiating the first wave of environmental alteration.

Through the domestication of plants and animals, they effectively began reshaping ecosystems—selecting which species thrived and which receded. From this nascent act of cultivation sprouted the seeds of more expansive transformation, as agricultural practices expanded and gave rise to urbanization, leading to substantial and often irreparable changes in the landscape.

This transformative journey acquired momentum with the advent of the Industrial Revolution in the 18th and 19th centuries. The shift from agrarian societies to industrial powerhouses escalated the scale of terraforming efforts on Earth. Urban expansion carved vast swaths of forests into asphalt and steel, leading to habitat fragmentation and connectivity losses amongst wildlife. The extraction of natural resources such as timber, minerals, and fossil fuels collided dramatically with Earth's ecological balance. The smoke and soot that billowed from chimneys were more than just signs of burgeoning industrial activity; they signaled profound alterations in atmospheric composition, resulting in the contemporary climate change crisis—a clear echo of terraforming gone awry.

Humanity's increasingly sophisticated engineering feats further facilitated substantial landscape transformations. Aggrandizing challenges of the modern era—be they the artificial management of rivers for flood prevention or the invention of irrigation systems—demonstrate our ability to modify entire hydrological cycles. Large dams reshaping river courses and desert irrigation systems epitomize humanity's ingenious interventions. However, with these interventions has come a harsh reality: the ecological ramifications of upsetting natural systems lead to unforeseen consequences, including species extinction and loss of soil fertility.

The technological advancements of the 20th and 21st centuries have further intensified our ability to tame nature's wildness. With urbanization came not just concrete jungles, but also agriculture intensified through genetic modifications and chemical inputs. In the quest for higher yields and greater efficiencies, ecosystems have been altered to favor a few selected species to the detriment of local biodiversity.

Here, an intricate balance of progress and ecological degradation emerges, a delicate dance poised between the benefits reaped and the downfalls incurred.

However, Earth's terraforming history is not confined to human fingerprints alone. Natural processes, too, have played pivotal roles in shaping our planet and its environments. Geologic activity, for example, through plate tectonics, has been instrumental in transporting materials and creating diverse habitats. Volcanic eruptions have renewed landscapes, enabling the growth of rich soils that support burgeoning wildlife after initial devastation. The climatic shifts over millennia—from ice ages to periods of warming—have rewritten the script of Earth's habitability and its biota. Each of these transformations, whether natural or anthropogenic, contribute layers to the ongoing evolution of life on our planet.

The reflection on Earth's terraforming history invites a broader contemplation of ethical considerations surrounding our role in reshaping environments. As we gaze outward to the cosmos, the lessons gleaned from our own history prompt serious introspection about the responsibilities that accompany terraforming endeavors on other planets. The history of terraforming on Earth serves as a microcosm, a lens through which we can explore our existential questions regarding our place as custodians of our planet and potential modellers of alien worlds.

Moreover, the modern discourse surrounding climate change has ushered in a renewed urgency in examining the realities of terraforming —not just as a concept, but as a potential necessity, as Earth endures mounting pressures from human-induced alterations. Scientists are now more than ever investigating geoengineering measures to mitigate climate change: from carbon capture technologies to ocean fertilization and mankind's ambitious dream of reversing the damage done.

As we brace ourselves for future explorations beyond our planet, understanding Earth's terraforming history is paramount. It must inform our strategies, guiding efforts to safeguard alien ecosystems while also reflecting on the implications of our actions. This historical narrative shapes not only our technological ambitions but also constructs a framework of moral accountability. The responsibility we bear to respect and care for both Earth and any potential habitable worlds we encounter is a lesson rooted deeply in the story of humanity itself.

In this light, Earth's terraforming history offers an edifice that supports our exploration aspirations. As we seek to unlock the secrets of the universe and ponder the possibility of transforming other worlds, we must remember the duality of our legacy: a capacity for monumental change, rich with ingenuity, standing alongside a cautionary tale that underscores the balance required in shaping life, wherever it may be found.

2.4. Current Scientific Understanding

The current scientific understanding of alien terraformation stems from a convergence of astrophysics, planetary science, biology, and technology, pushing our grasp of the cosmos into new paradigms. As humanity stands on the brink of a new era marked by extraordinary advancements in our collective knowledge and capabilities, the quest to decipher the universe's mysteries, particularly in relation to the existence of extraterrestrial life capable of modifying planetary environments, has become increasingly relevant.

At the heart of this exploration lies the question of whether intelligent civilizations may have engaged in terraforming activities on other worlds—seemingly inhospitable planets that might have been transformed into life-sustaining environments. Our journey into this labyrinth of possibilities begins with the ongoing research into exoplanets—those celestial bodies that orbit stars beyond our solar system—which have captivated the attention of astronomers since the first confirmed detections in the 1990s. Exoplanet studies have evolved significantly with the deployment and advancement of space telescopes like Kepler and TESS (Transiting Exoplanet Survey Satellite), which have provided vast datasets that enhance our understanding of potential habitability indicators such as atmospheric components, temperature ranges, and surface conditions.

The scientific understanding of atmospheric characteristics plays a key role in identifying exoplanets that might exhibit signs of terraformation. Strikingly, numerous exoplanets have been detected with atmospheric compositions that diverge significantly from Earth-like attributes. The presence of gases such as carbon dioxide, methane, and ammonia in unusual ratios can act as potential indicators of significant geological activity or biological processes. For instance, observed discrepancies in expected ratios of these gases may hint at artificial manipulation—an anomaly that could suggest the presence of an intelligent species engaging in atmospheric engineering, thereby altering the conditions to sustain a biosphere.

Scientists have also turned their attention to planetary dynamics, exploring how shifts in orbits, axial tilts, and gravitational interactions may impact a planet's climate and habitability. The study of celestial mechanics reveals that a planet's distance from its star significantly influences its temperature and radiation exposure, categories essential for determining habitability. Additionally, interactions with neighboring celestial bodies can lead to catastrophic events that could simultaneously create moments of opportunity—altering a planet's trajectory toward a more habitable state or catalyzing its transformation.

Apart from individual studies of planets, an integrated understanding of stellar evolution is critical in comprehending the broader context of terraformation. The life cycle of stars, which includes phases ranging from their formation to eventual demise, determines the long-term stability of the conditions necessary for life as we know it. For example, habitable zones—regions around stars where conditions might be just right for liquid water—are greatly influenced by the star's size, age, and energy output. As stars age and evolve, their changing luminosity can precipitate climatic transformations on surrounding planets, potentially fostering environments conducive to life or initiating cycles of destruction.

The search for extraterrestrial intelligence (SETI) remains a pivotal aspect of understanding potential alien activities. Researchers have employed an array of techniques to listen for signals emitted by extraterrestrial civilizations. Recent initiatives have expanded the methodologies for signal detection to include monitoring for fast radio bursts and other unusual cosmic phenomena, providing new avenues to search for the hallmarks of intelligent life. The possibilities of extraterrestrial civilizations attempting communication or leaving behind an echo of their existence through engineered signals underscore the complexities of our detection frameworks.

Importantly, while current scientific understanding reveals a tapestry of compelling evidence hinting at the potential for alien terraformation, we remain cautious in our interpretations. The scientific community acknowledges the phenomenon of pareidolia, the tendency of humans to see patterns or ascribe meaning where none may exist. Consequently, steps must be taken to substantiate claims regarding alien activity with rigorous empirical methodologies and comprehensive analysis.

Moreover, the advancements in technology over recent years have catalyzed a paradigm shift in our ability to gather, analyze, and synthesize data relating to planetary science. Innovations in spectroscopy, for instance, allow scientists to dissect the light spectra from distant planets, identifying chemical signatures in their atmospheres that may signal unusual activities—whether natural or artificial. This utility extends to identifying unexpected climatic shifts, assessing changes in temperature, pressure, and chemical balances that could indicate a planet undergoing transformation.

Another vital component of the current scientific discourse is the understanding of planetary protection practices, which shape our approach toward planetary exploration and the ethical implications surrounding potential contamination of pristine environments. The protocols set by international treaties aim to preserve extraterrestrial ecosystems and prevent the irreversible changes that could ensue from human exploration. Thus, our understanding of alien terraformation must also consider our own responsibilities as potential cosmic stewards, evaluating the implications of exerting influence on other worlds.

The future of scientific understanding in relation to alien terraformation is one of boundless curiosity and exploration. Enhanced capabilities—like the upcoming James Webb Space Telescope—promise to revolutionize our approach to exoplanet studies and offer unprecedented insights into the characteristics of distant worlds. As technology becomes increasingly intertwined with interstellar research, the prospects of uncovering the truth about whether we share the universe with technologically advanced civilizations become ever more tantalizing.

In this journey to grasp the nuances of cosmic terraformation, we are propelled not just by a quest for knowledge, but by the profound questions it invites about our existence, morality, and the interconnectedness of life across the universe. The current scientific understanding of alien terraformation ultimately serves as a springboard for further inquiry, exploration, and reflection, as we navigate the celestial pathways leading to our place in the grand cosmic narrative. Together, we shall uncover the majestic possibilities that the universe harbors, acknowledging the fundamental beauty of this quest to engage with the unknown.

2.5. Ethical Considerations

The exploration of ethical considerations in the context of potential extraterrestrial terraformation is a pursuit that transcends scientific curiosity, straddling the delicate line between aspiration and moral responsibility. As we embark on our quest to decipher the cosmos and possibly encounter alien worlds that exhibit signs of artificial influence, we must critically evaluate the implications of our actions and motivations. The foundation of this ethical discourse rests on several core questions: What right do we possess to alter environments beyond our own? How does our historical relationship with Earth inform our approach to these new frontiers? And, importantly, what are the moral ramifications of the existence of extraterrestrial civilizations and their potential rights?

At the crux of ethical discussions surrounding terraformation is the principle of stewardship—an acknowledgment that as intelligent beings capable of manipulating environments, we hold a responsibility toward other worlds. This principle is rooted in our understanding of ecological interdependence; ecosystems are intricately balanced, and introducing new variables, be they biological or mechanical, can have consequential impacts that extend beyond immediate intents. Before we consider terraforming another planet, we must grapple with the potential ecological repercussions. What if our interventions, fueled by well-meaning ambitions, inadvertently annihilate the indigenous life forms—even those of which we are currently unaware? This introduces a layer of moral complexity, where the destruction of alien biospheres for our benefit raises profound questions about our role in the universe as predators or protectors.

To effectively engage with the ethical dimensions of terraforming, it is imperative to draw parallels with human interactions across history. Humans have often approached land and natural resources with a mindset that prioritizes exploitation over conservation. The consequences of colonization efforts, resource extraction, and environmental degradation on Earth have taught us harsh lessons about the fragility of ecosystems. This history serves as a cautionary tale; applying the same practices in extraterrestrial contexts could yield catastrophic consequences that reverberate across physical and moral landscapes. Learning from past transgressions compels us to adopt a posture of humility, ensuring that the pursuit of knowledge does not eclipse our obligation to protect the unknown inhabitants of other worlds.

Furthermore, the question of consent arises with profound implications. Should we encounter an intelligent alien civilization, the ethical ramifications of engaging with them become even more pronounced. Not only do we need to consider how our actions impact their environments, but we must also assess how our intentions align with their aspirations. The possibility of mutual terraforming agreements or collaborations could open up new vistas of existence. Yet, the mere act of presuming to alter a planet—regardless of whether life as we understand it exists—is fraught with notion that humanity holds dominion over all realms. This echoes a colonial mindset and reinforces power dynamics that can lead to exploitation. An ethical framework for engagement must prioritize equity, ensuring that if hypothesized extraterrestrial life forms exist, they exercise agency over their environments.

The potential ramifications of terraforming extend into the philosophical realm, where we must confront existential questions about life and our position in the cosmos. Do we have the right to play God—and to impose our will upon lifeless planets? The perspective that life, in any form, has an intrinsic value demands that we carefully evaluate the necessity and justification for transforming worlds rather than simply repurposing them for our benefit. The move toward a more thoughtful approach rests on the acknowledgment that humanity's narratives of advancement should not come at the expense of other forms of existence.

International cooperation and consensus-building emerge as critical components of establishing ethical guidelines for extraterrestrial exploration. The diverse methodologies and ideologies across cultures can forge a comprehensive framework that governs our ventures beyond Earth. Effective discourse necessitates an evolving dialogue that engages scientists, ethicists, policy-makers, and the public in a shared vision for interstellar responsibility. Treaties and accords aligned with frameworks such as the Outer Space Treaty—which emphasizes the peaceful use of space and the protection of celestial bodies—offer preliminary guidelines, though they require refinement to address the specific realities of potential terraforming scenarios.

As we explore the cosmos and uncover its hidden enigmas, the call for ethical stewardship grows louder. The need for an evolving moral compass guides our engagements with the universe, prioritizing a future juxtaposed against humanity's historical shortcomings. Our scientific explorations have the potential to redefine our understanding of life and existence as we continue to seek understanding beyond the confines of our planet and the ethical frameworks that ground our cosmic endeavors.

Ultimately, the ethical considerations intrinsic to the discussion of terraforming compel us to rise to a higher moral standard—one that values not just human exploration, but the sanctity of life in all forms. As we stand on the threshold of new discoveries, grappling with the knowledge that there is a vast unknown before us, we must tread carefully, ensuring that the call of the cosmos ignites our curiosity while simultaneously invoking our deepest responsibilities. The cosmos holds profound mysteries, and as we seek to unveil them, we must remain vigilant, committed to harmonizing our ambitions with principles of respect, stewardship, and ethical responsibility toward all forms of existence that may inhabit our galaxy and beyond.

3. Signs of Terraforming in the Cosmos

3.1. Unnatural Atmospheric Compositions

The exploration of unnatural atmospheric compositions on celestial bodies is a significant endeavor that opens pathways to understanding the potential for extraterrestrial terraformation. At its essence, this subchapter delves into the rich tapestry of atmospheric chemistry and its implications for identifying signs of alien life, advanced civilizations, or terraforming activities. By analyzing the components and structures of alien atmospheres, scientists can glean insights not only about the potential habitability of these worlds but also about the motives and actions of intelligent beings that may have once resided or presently exist within these alien realms.

To begin unpacking the concept of unnatural atmospheric compositions, it's essential to grasp the established baseline of what constitutes a "normal" atmosphere on Earth compared to what might be expected or observed on other planets. Earth's atmosphere, rich in nitrogen (approximately 78%), oxygen (21%), and trace amounts of other gases like carbon dioxide, argon, and water vapor, has existed in relative balance for eons, supporting life as we understand it. In contrast, the atmospheres of other planets in our solar system, including Mars and Venus, are drastically different, providing pivotal clues to their histories and possible avenues for terraformation.

Examining atmospheres through a cosmic lens unveils a captivating complexity. For instance, Mars currently presents an atmosphere composed of around 95% carbon dioxide, with only negligible traces of oxygen and water vapor. This starkly different composition from Earth raises questions about the red planet's past. Was there a time when Mars had a thicker atmosphere more conducive to liquid water and, therefore, to life? The answer may lie buried within the planet's geological history.

Researchers scrutinize isotopic ratios of elements like carbon and oxygen within Martian samples to decipher its evolutionary path. The presence of methane in the Martian atmosphere serves as another tantalizing clue, invoking scientific studies to explore its potential biological origins, whether as a result of geological processes or even the activities of microbial life. These observations pose compelling questions: Could the methane point toward a self-regulating biosphere, or is it merely a remnant of Mars' turbulent geological past? As scientists analyze such atmospheric phenomena, they begin to unravel the enigma of Martian terraformation—both natural and artificial influences throughout history.

Venus, on the other hand, serves as an example of an atmosphere that presents significantly pronounced similarities to Earth's in terms of being a thick gas envelope yet is plagued by dangerous extremes, consisting of roughly 96.5% carbon dioxide and a similar composition of sulfuric acid clouds. This harsh environment calls into question whether a civilization could have existed there once, or whether advanced alien species may have viscerally altered its climate through active terraforming efforts. The hellish conditions surface poignant inquiries into the methods that could have been utilized to induce atmospheric change on such a scale; were vast geoengineering projects implemented, and if so, for what purposes?

In considering these heavenly bodies, it becomes necessary to tackle the implications of atmospheric anomalies that might transcend natural geological evolution and reflect the hands of intelligent design. The detection of gases such as phosphine, detected in the clouds of Venus, has sparked a wealth of discussions about potential biological processes. Phosphine is associated with anaerobic life on Earth, and its observation in an environment hostile to surface life raises myriad possibilities. Could it indicate the existence of unknown life forms, and might these indicate a civilization once capable of advanced atmospheric manipulation?

The scientific community contemplates that if intelligent life holds the capability to terraform a planet, they would likely modify the atmospheric composition not merely to create habitable conditions, but to sustain their technological needs and ensure their long-term survival. For instance, the introduction of gases like oxygen through synthetic biological systems or other technological means could lead to a revitalization of an alien environment, supporting not only biological life but higher échelons of technological development.

Moreover, the search for extraterrestrial atmospheric compositions extends beyond our solar system, with astronomers or planetary scientists deploying space-borne telescopes, like the James Webb Space Telescope, that have revolutionized our ability to analyze the constituents of exoplanet atmospheres. The study of exoplanet atmospheres through transmission spectroscopy, for example, allows scientists to identify chemical signatures indicative of atmospheric processes. Discovering a plethora of gases, such as water vapor, carbon dioxide, methane, or ammonia in abnormal ratios or co-occurring in unexpected manners, could serve as an indirect detection of an alien civilization's manipulations.

Such inquiries usher forth profound implications when considering Earth-like exoplanets within the habitable zones of their stars, where conditions may favor life. In regions such as TRAPPIST-1 or Proxima Centauri, the presence of unusual atmospheric traits warrant attention and scrutiny. Researchers evaluate possible metallic or gaseous aerosols that diverge significantly from expected terrestrial standards, contemplating whether deviations reflect the fingerprints of advanced engineering or perhaps hints of unintended engineered side-effects.

However, the interpretations of atmospheric anomalies must be approached with caution. Given the variety of planetary processes, both geologic and atmospheric, that can yield abnormal gas concentrations —volcanic activity, geological outgassing, or even external impacts —signaling intelligent life based solely on atmospheric analysis can be a tricky endeavor. Rigorous, multidisciplinary efforts emerge as the cornerstone of deciphering the complexities of unnatural atmospheric compositions, which may at once display characteristics of exceptional complexity arising from geological processes or serve as pathways to divine extraterrestrial ingenuity.

In conclusion, unnatural atmospheric compositions represent a crucial frontier in our exploration of the cosmos for signs of life and potential terraformation. As we collect more data and refine our technologies, the possibility of unlocking the secrets held within these alien atmospheres beckons like a wisp through the bounded coil of the universe. Every discovery carries the thrill of and responsibility to consider—if we do find evidence of civilizations that once navigated their environments through such alterations, can we align our exploration of these worlds with a renewed commitment to ethical stewardship? Ultimately, the implications of our findings may compel us to reflect on how we engage not only with celestial frontiers but also the greater questions of existence within the vast tapestry of the universe.

3.2. Geoengineering Markers

The concept of geoengineering markers delights the imagination, presenting a tapestry woven with the threads of hope and intrigue about the potential interactions between advanced civilizations and their environments. As humanity stands at a juncture where terraforming celestial bodies has ascended from the realm of science fiction to tangible scientific inquiry, the examination of how such monstrous endeavors might manifest across the cosmos becomes imperative. Specifically, geoengineering markers could provide crucial insights into whether civilizations beyond our own are capable of, or have indeed engaged in, the manipulation of their planetary spheres in pursuit of habitability or sustainability.

To appreciate geoengineering markers thoroughly, one must first understand the premise of geoengineering itself. Defined as climate intervention strategies intended to alter Earth's physical environment intentionally to mitigate the effects of climate change or to promote ecological resilience, these ambitious initiatives mirror some of the most speculative and profound possibilities that advanced civilizations may employ on other planets. They may range from altering atmospheric composition to sustaining energy flows, effectively transforming inhospitable environments into biodiverse ecosystems capable of supporting life.

Geoengineering markers, therefore, embody tangible evidence of such interventions. To identify these markers, scientists must explore multiple layers of planetary data, including atmospheric composition, geological structures, hydrology, and climatic conditions. Unusual deviations from natural variations within these domains may signify an overarching influence—one that could be the work of an intelligent agency attempting to steer its environment towards a more hospitable state.

For instance, if we were to uncover planets exhibiting distinct atmospheric signatures that deviate drastically from expected ratios, this could serve as a possible geoengineering marker. Atmospheric compositions heavily imbalanced with greenhouse gases, or conversely, normative conditions juxtaposed with significant oxygen concentrations where life had never purportedly existed, may hint at advanced civilizations engaging in extreme measures to promote life-sustaining environments. Such transformations could range from deploying technologies capable of sequestering carbon dioxide en masse to the introduction of synthetic biological entities that perform specific ecological roles.

Investigating altered geological structures similarly augments the search for geoengineering markers. Evidence of planetary-scale alterations in sedimentation patterns or thermal anomalies suggestive of geothermal manipulation could point toward intelligent interventions. For example, the installation of massive solar panels or orbital reflectors intended to moderate climate could yield heat patterns dramatically different from unaltered planetary norms. If detected, such engineering configurations would stand as powerful geoengineering markers and a testament to civilizations striving to enhance or desperately sustain life.

Hydrology, another critical parameter, can act as an evocative geoengineering marker. The presence of large artificial oceans or lakes, advanced water recycling systems, or an orchestrated reworking of natural river systems may pertain to the sophisticated planetary engineering efforts of alien civilizations. Identifying fluid dynamics that do not conform to natural expectancies could beckon the inference that a planet has undergone significant intervention, rendering it potentially more amenable for sustaining extraterrestrial life.

Temperature and climatic patterns—key attributes embodying the essence of a planet's habitability—represented in telemetry could serve as critical geoengineering markers. If we encountered celestial bodies with sustained temperature gradients leading to favorable conditions for liquid water, alongside signals of atmospheric changes or altered albedo effects, we may be witnessing the aftereffects of immense geoengineering campaigns. In this context, present-day models of climate manipulation on our own planet can serve as analogs for interpreting data from such cosmic phenomenologies.

Additionally, the recent exploration of exoplanets within habitable zones brings new vigor to identifying geoengineering markers beyond our solar system. As telescopic technology has advanced, the ability to detect variations in light spectra, identify exoplanetary atmospheres, and analyze geological surfaces for signs of alien activity has enhanced. Discoveries of unusual atmospheric characteristics—such as the disproportionate presence of exotic gases in combination with constituents typically associated with biological activity—could be viewed as indicators of sophisticated efforts to reshape environmental conditions.

The quest for geoengineering markers also interlaces with the broader narrative of planetary protection and ethical considerations. The pursuit of terraforming and geoengineering opportunities raises significant questions about how we manipulate other worlds and the moral obligations inherent to altering ecosystems that might teem with their own forms of life. This duality—hope and ethical accountability—demands an ongoing dialogue among the scientific community, policymakers, ethicists, and the public to foster an understanding that extends beyond mere curiosity, emphasizing a responsible approach to interstellar engagement.

In conclusion, geoengineering markers stand as compelling signposts in our exploration of the cosmos, hinting at a broader narrative of intelligent influences threading through the fabric of space-time. The quest to unravel these enigmatic clues beckons researchers to merge empirical methodologies with imaginative inquiries. These markers do not solely inform us about the possible existence of other intelligent lifeforms but compel us to reflect on our aspirations as stewards of this universe. As we navigate the cosmos in search of signs of terraforming, geoengineering, and alien interventions, we challenge the depths of our scientific understanding. In doing so, we embrace a future rich with the promise of discovery amidst the astonishing complexity that defines the universe itself.

3.3. Altered Planetary Dynamics

As we delve into the intricate interplay of cosmic forces, it becomes abundantly apparent that the dynamics governing celestial bodies are not static but rather a tapestry of continual change. Altered planetary dynamics offers a lens through which we can examine how these forces may be influenced—intentionally or unintentionally— by advanced civilizations undertaking terraforming activities across the universe. Understanding this concept proffers insights into how civilizations might adapt and reshape worlds to foster habitability, while simultaneously grappling with overarching questions about the nature of existence and the potential complexity of life itself.

At the heart of altered planetary dynamics lies the gravitational dance of celestial bodies in their orbits. This dance is not only dictated by the mass and distribution of existing planets, moons, and stars but is also susceptible to external forces, including potential modifications imposed by technological entities. Gravitational interactions among celestial bodies play a paramount role in determining the conditions on a given planet, including its climate, axial tilt, and orbital stability. Consider the moon's influence on Earth: its gravitational pull affects tides and stabilizes axial tilt, mitigating drastic climate fluctuations over millennia. As we contemplate extraterrestrial civilizations, we can theorize their capabilities in creating or eliminating gravitational interactions, thereby effecting significant planetary changes.

For instance, advanced civilizations may possess the technological prowess to engineer massive constructs within their solar systems—akin to artificial moons or asteroids—that would intentionally alter a planet's rotational dynamics or climate patterns. Such undertakings could stabilize or destabilize a planet, preventing catastrophic events or fostering conditions ripe for life. Imagine a civilization injecting a series of asteroids into a planetary orbit, influencing climatic conditions in a desirable manner. This engineering feat could open new avenues for developing habitats that could flourish in once-hostile environments, turning celestial bodies into vibrant ecosystems.

Moreover, the concept of creating artificial suns or orbiting reflectors to modify a planet's solar exposure epitomizes how intentional manipulation could lead to altered planetary dynamics. For instance, a terraforming endeavor may revolve around deploying solar sails that redirect photons, adjusting the amount of heat and light a distant planet receives. Such interventions could warm up cold planets or cool down scorching ones, establishing a foundation for biological processes that underpin life.

Climatic patterns also fall within the domain of altered planetary dynamics. These patterns are influenced not only by physical geography but also by atmospheric composition, which acts as the backdrop for climate systems. The introduction of new gases from terraforming endeavors could signal a pivotal transformation in a planet's atmospheric dynamics. Consider a scenario in which an advanced civilization produces compounds to thicken the atmosphere of a barren world, initiating greenhouse sensations to raise the temperature, allowing for precipitation, and, consequently, enabling the presence of liquid water. Such a realm, once inhospitable, may burgeon with life as plants and organisms evolve in response to their engineered surroundings.

The pursuit of planetary stability also leads to considerations of how to counter catastrophic events. Natural disasters that may arise from planetary dynamics—such as meteor strikes, volcanic eruptions, or gravitational disruptions—pose substantial hazards that advanced civilizations might wish to circumvent. These civilizations could theoretically harness the forces of nature using technologies to deflect potential impacts, mitigate extreme weather, or even stimulate geological activity to revitalize dormant landscapes. In doing so, they solidify their role not just as inhabitants of a planet, but as intentional architects of its future.

Perspective shifts further when we consider the interconnectedness of planets within a star system. The gravitational interactions that unfold among multiple celestial bodies can be dysregulated by the activities of an intelligible civilization. Asteroids, moons, and even comets become vectors through which alterations ripple through an entire system. For instance, redirecting asteroid belts or manipulating the orbits of moons could lead to unparalleled tectonic upheaval, potentially reshaping multiple planets within the same system, facilitating introductions of atmospherics conducive to thriving life forms.

The implications of altered planetary dynamics extend beyond thermodynamic processes. An advanced civilization's understanding of materials science and bioengineering may allow them to synthesize organisms that could actively participate in planetary systems. Genetically altered microorganisms might be programmed to adapt to hostile environments, altering soil compositions, fixing nitrogen levels, or stabilizing ecosystems disrupted by systematic interventions. Such an act of intentional design could lead to cascading effects, triggering a harmonious integration of life forms that fosters sustainability in the becoming realm.

Existing under the umbrella of cosmic possibility, we encounter the dilemma of proving intentionality behind altered planetary dynamics. Scientists strive to differentiate between organic transformations that reveal intelligent agency and those resulting purely from untoiled natural processes. Therefore, the frameworks established within astrophysics, combined with geological and ecological evidence, could serve as vital indicators—seeing beyond the visible to collapse narratives of coincidental occurrences into realms of designed interventions.

Consider the insights gathered from planetary exploration missions. Data concerning geological signatures on planets and moons, like Enceladus and Europa, reveal clues drawn from icy crusts, suggesting subsurface oceans teeming with the possibility of life. Missions focused on exploring these worlds may confront indicators of deliberate manipulation—perhaps while searching for life forms residing beneath the ice, we might discover artifacts—beacons of hope or remnants of civilizations that transcended their planets.

In contemplating the universality of altered planetary dynamics, we ignite a greater quest not merely for knowledge but for understanding our place within this cosmic landscape. Can we, as humanity, assert that we are the sole architects of our destiny, or is the potential of progressing alongside other intelligent beings an opportunity? The notable shifts in perspective compel the mind to inquire whether our unfolding narrative blends into the broader context of existence within the universe—will we one day be seen as builders and caretakers of worlds alongside others who mirror our innovative spirit?

Ultimately, the exploration of altered planetary dynamics challenges us to reflect upon profound questions that extend far beyond scientific inquiry—it invites us to examine the very essence of life, its myriad forms, and the boundless creativity that undergirds the quest for understanding in the universe. In recognizing the potential for dynamic transformation across the expanse of space, we may yet discover a universe richly interconnected by the endeavors and aspirations of innumerable civilizations questing to carve their legacies among the stars.

3.4. Unexpected Climatic Shifts

As we explore the concept of unexpected climatic shifts in the context of potential extraterrestrial terraformation, we uncover the intricate layers that define a planet's atmosphere, hydrosphere, and surface conditions. Such shifts can be indicative of both natural processes and advanced civilizations' interventions, elevating our understanding of how life could flourish—or falter—in environments that are initially inhospitable. The examination of these unexpected climatic transitions compels us to broaden our perspective on planetary dynamics and the possible footprints left by intelligent agencies across the cosmos.

Understanding sudden climatic anomalies starts with recognizing that planetary conditions are often characterized by equilibrium —this balance is subject to myriad forces, both celestial and terrestrial. However, when we encounter climatic shifts that defy natural expectations, scientists can interpret these occurrences as potential indicators of active terraforming efforts. Advanced civilizations may harness technologies that manipulate atmospheric conditions and ecosystems, prompting changes that could create habitable environments where none existed before.

Take, for instance, the intriguing case of Mars. While this planet is presently known for its frigid and arid conditions, anomalous evidence of past climate stability suggests that it may have once showcased a warmer and wetter environment. Geological features, such as river valleys, lakes, and mineral deposits, indicate episodes where liquid water flowed upon its surface—a clear anomaly considering the current understanding of Martian conditions. Researchers are left pondering whether these unexpected shifts occurred due to cyclical planetary dynamics, such as changes in axial tilt or volcanic activity, or whether they are reflections of a terraforming initiative undertaken by intelligent beings who sought to create a habitable realm.

In examining unexpected climatic shifts, one crucial aspect is the role of greenhouse gas emissions. On Earth, the rapid alterations in climate due to anthropogenic activities have led to an increase in global temperatures, resulting in notable shifts within our ecosystems. If similar greenhouse gases—possibly introduced through deliberate actions—are detected on celestial bodies like Venus, we may be witnessing deliberate environmental engineering by an advanced civilization seeking to warm the planet or provide additional greenhouse shielding. This serves as a clear reminder that the building blocks of life can exist even under perceived adverse conditions.

Moreover, planetary atmospheres are dynamic systems subject to change through interactions with external factors. External inputs, such as the impacts of comets or asteroids, can trigger unexpected climatic shifts by introducing new materials or altering a planet's axis of rotation. For instance, if a comet rich in volatile compounds were to collide with a barren planet, it could significantly affect atmospheric pressure and composition—potentially paving the way for subsequent biological development, and akin to earlier ideas of 'panspermia' where life is delivered to habitable zones through external sources. This brings forth the critical inquiry: could extraterrestrial civilizations have mastered the navigation of celestial bodies to induce beneficial climatic shifts through calculated impacts?

Looking beyond our solar system, understanding climatic shifts on exoplanets opens new frontiers for exploration. Researchers utilize advanced telescopes to analyze the light spectra emitted from distant celestial bodies, providing insights into atmospheric compositions. Unusual ratios of gases, such as the co-occurrence of methane and oxygen, may indicate recent climatic changes that deviate from what would be expected in unaltered settings. If such atmospheric compositions were the result of intentional manipulation, it signifies a civilization's attempt to foster conditions amenable to sustaining life. We observe how terraforming could range from efforts aimed at creating sustainable biospheres to unintended consequences resulting from complex interactions among their artificial ecological systems.

As we build our understanding of unexpected climatic shifts, the analysis expands to consider ecological responses. In many cases, sudden changes force rapid adaptations within biological systems, with invasive species or engineered organisms thrust into ecosystems at an unprecedented pace. Such patterns could reveal the outcomes of terraforming efforts designed to integrate new life forms. Examining how ecological systems respond to these shifts not only informs our comprehension of adaptation and resilience but also poses profound questions regarding the responsibilities of intelligent beings wielding the power of planetary transformation.

Furthermore, the recognition of climate change as a prevailing theme on Earth offers a metaphorical parallel to how we conceptualize extraterrestrial environments. The current insights into eco-consciousness espoused by humanity reflect the urgency to protect not only our planet but also hypothetical alien biospheres. What ethical considerations spring forth from unexpected climatic shifts as we engage with uninhabited worlds? An exploration of these considerations will inevitably rouse deep philosophical inquiries about our role in the cosmos as both observers and participants.

In sum, the study of unexpected climatic shifts serves as a vital tool in our quest to discern the fingerprints of extraterrestrial terraforming. These shifts hold the potential to speak volumes about a planet's history—shedding light on both the natural forces at play and the possible interventions by intelligent life forms. As we venture deeper into our cosmic exploration, it becomes critical to remain vigilant, discerning the extraordinary amidst the ordinary, as we decode the ongoing saga of life's resilient dance against the backdrop of time and space. This inquiry lights a path forward as we strive to understand our connections with the myriad worlds across the universe—a pursuit laden with intrigue, responsibility, and the unyielding human spirit of discovery.

3.5. Newly Discovered Patterns in Exoplanets

Newly discovered patterns in exoplanets represent a critical advancement in our understanding of the cosmos and the potential for extraterrestrial civilizations to engage in terraforming activities. The insights gathered from ongoing observations and studies of these distant worlds have begun to elucidate not only their characteristics but also the intriguing possibilities of intentional modifications made by intelligent life. As astronomers employ increasingly sophisticated instruments to probe the depths of space, they unveil a myriad of patterns that suggest complexity and order, fostering a renewed interest in the search for life beyond Earth.

Central to this quest is the identification of exoplanetary systems that mirror the conditions necessary for habitability. The search has yielded remarkable findings, with thousands of confirmed exoplanets cataloged since the inception of the Kepler mission in 2009. Many of these planets reside within the circumstellar habitable zone—often termed the "Goldilocks Zone"—where temperatures allow for the existence of liquid water. This zone expands the definition of habitability beyond our solar system and establishes a foundation upon which the possibility of terraforming can be structurally examined.

Recent discoveries have unveiled patterns that diverge from our conventional understanding of planetary formation and development. Contrary to long-held assumptions that exoplanets had stable trajectories and environments similar to our own, astronomers have observed irregularities that bring forth the notion of dynamic systems influenced by external factors or deliberate interventions. Some exoplanets exhibit unusual atmospheric compositions characterized by unexpected ratios of gases, hinting at the possibility of engineering activities. Such findings compel scientists to reevaluate existing models of planetary growth and adaptation, recognizing that intelligent manipulation could lead to environments conducive to life.

The study of exoplanet atmospheres is particularly revealing. Scientists utilize transmission spectroscopy, a technique that analyzes the light spectra filtered through a planet's atmosphere as it transits its host star. This method has unveiled a plethora of atmospheric signatures—ranging from water vapor to carbon dioxide and methane —each bearing testament to the processes at play. Importantly, anomalies in gas compositions, such as the simultaneous presence of both oxygen and methane, can imply biological activity or technological influence, as these gases typically react and would not coexist without the ongoing replenishment through natural or artificial means. Such atmospheric markers may indeed reflect terraforming endeavors that signal the hand of a civilization working to modify its environment for sustainability.

In addition to atmospheric assessments, researchers are increasingly focused on surface features that could imply unintended climatic perturbations or deliberate alterations. For example, identifying structures or geological formations on exoplanets that suggest terraforming—such as large-scale irrigation systems, architectural remnants, or casings of technological constructions—may act as significant indications of intelligent life having engaged with their planetary sphere. These manifestations, if discovered, would fundamentally alter our understanding of life in the universe, suggesting that civilizations might actively shape their worlds rather than passively adapt to them.

Among the more astonishing discoveries are the signs of exoplanetary migration patterns which can provide vital clues about a planet's history. Recognition that some exoplanets have altered their orbits significantly within their systems challenges our geological perceptions and postulates a new narrative around planetary habitation. Actions taken by advanced civilizations—should they possess the wherewithal to modify or redirect celestial bodies—could have lasting ramifications on adjacent planets, fostering an ecosystem of interdependence and transformation. This scenario raises critical questions regarding the technological and moral implications of such interventions.

Furthermore, the study of binary star systems—where two stars orbit a common center—has uncovered distinct patterns in how planets form and sustain themselves in such dynamic environments. The gravitational complexities inherent to these arrangements could feasibly prompt advanced civilizations to engineer or terraform planets in response to their stars' interactions. Such strategic adaptations might involve altering a planet's axial tilt or atmospheric conditions to create equilibrium or mitigate the extremes expected from stellar fluctuations.

Another set of remarkable patterns emanates from the exploration of larger celestial structures such as planetary rings or asteroid belts. Anomalies within these structures might indicate artificiality —the presence of orchestrated systems designed to create energy harnessing capabilities or stabilize a planet's climate. For instance, manipulating ring systems could reflect an advanced understanding of gravitational forces as they pertain to climate control, while simultaneously enriching planetary surfaces with essential minerals to create habitable conditions.

Moreover, the recent paradigm shift toward recognizing the role of moons and satellites in harboring potential life has opened new pathways of consideration. Many exoplanets orbit gas giants with extensive moons, which may exhibit conditions suitable for terraforming. These moons might harbor subsurface oceans heated by tidal forces, representing perfect candidates for extraterrestrial biodiversity. In this framework, alien civilizations could be engaged in fostering life on multiple celestial bodies, displaying a multifaceted approach to cosmic engineering.

The implications of these newly discovered patterns extend beyond mere scientific curiosity. They compel us to reflect on the nature of existence and what it means to be alive in a universe that brims with possibilities. As we draw connections between observable patterns and the actions of potential alien civilizations, we confront profound questions about our role within this grand cosmic tableau. Are we simply passive observers, or do we carry the potential to one day influence worlds, akin to those we seek? Such reflections lead us to engage the ethical dimensions at play, as our understanding of exoplanets and extraterrestrial terraforming continues to unravel.

In conclusion, the discovery of newly identified patterns in exoplanets signifies a critical chapter in the ongoing quest for knowledge about the universe and its myriad inhabitants. As we refine our observational tools and deepen our understanding of planetary dynamics, we inch closer to addressing the fundamental queries about life beyond Earth and the potential for terraforming across the cosmos. Each revelation invites us to question not only the existence of civilizations capable of shaping worlds, but also our place within this far-reaching narrative—a narrative steeped in curiosity, responsibility, and the unbridled human spirit dedicated to exploring the majestic universe that surrounds us.

4. Identifying Alien Intentions

4.1. Why Aliens Would Terraform

In contemplating the motivations behind why an advanced extraterrestrial civilization might engage in terraformation, we enter a realm rich with both scientific inquiry and philosophical speculation. At the core of this exploration lies a fundamental understanding: intelligent beings, driven by various needs, aspirations, and challenges, may actively seek to reshape inhospitable worlds into environments that sustain life, not only for themselves but potentially for myriad forms of existence. The reasons for engaging in such monumental endeavors can be broadly categorized into survival, exploration, expansion, ecological balance, cultural expression, and the inherent drive of conscious beings to innovate and adapt.

Survival sits atop the hierarchy of motivations. For a civilization facing catastrophic extinction risks—whether borne from natural disasters, resource depletion, or cosmic events—terraforming could emerge as an essential strategy for ensuring the species' longevity. If a homeworld becomes increasingly uninhabitable due to climate change, pollution, or celestial threats, the capacity to terraform another planet could offer a lifeline. The imperative to create habitable conditions elsewhere would drive technological innovation as these civilizations seek to replicate or even enhance the environmental conditions of their original home. This notion resonates deeply with Earth's ongoing struggles with climate change and sustainability, reaffirming the relevance of cosmic perspectives on our terrestrial existence.

Exploration represents another compelling motivation. Advanced civilizations could be driven by a profound desire to explore and understand the universe. This pursuit may manifest not just in the quest for knowledge but as a tangible effort to manipulate environments for scientific study. By transforming barren landscapes into biological testbeds, alien engineers could experiment with ecosystems, studying their development and interactions. In this sense, terraforming serves as an experiment in interstellar biology—an effort to grasp how life evolves in radically altered environments and how various organisms interact within engineered systems. The potential knowledge gained from such explorations could lead to breakthroughs that enhance their original world or even aid in the preservation of endangered forms of life.

The desire for expansion further fuels terraforming ambitions. In the grand narrative of life's evolution, expansion manifests as a defining characteristic—whether across territories on Earth or throughout different stars systems. An alien civilization might seek to establish new domains that mitigate overcrowding and allocate resources more effectively, paving the way for the sustainable development of its population. Terraforming provides a means through which societies can project their aspirations into the cosmos, expanding their habitats while flourishing amidst newfound landscapes that embody their legacy.

Ecological balance enters the fray as a significant consideration. Intelligent beings may recognize the interconnectedness of ecosystems and the importance of environmental stewardship, causing them to protect their environments through active transformation. A civilization cognizant of the detrimental effects previously wrought by its industrial development may prioritize ecological restoration and resilience. Active terraforming would signify an effort to rehabilitate deathly ecosystems into vibrantly interwoven habitats, harnessing technological prowess to mitigate issues like soil depletion and pollution—transforming not just landscapes but also their own cultural narratives around environmental care.

Cultural expression inevitably shapes the motivations behind terraforming efforts as well. Civilizations enculturated in artistic endeavors may see the alteration of worlds as a canvas upon which to express themselves. Terraforming can, therefore, embody not just a practical endeavor but also a highly symbolic act. The intricate designs of a constructed atmosphere, engineered ecosystems, or elaborate aesthetic features may serve to define the identity and legacy of a civilization. Much like the art forms and architectural achievements seen throughout human history, the commitment to transforming alien worlds could echo profound narratives of creativity, lineage, and the fundamental drive to create.

Additionally, the intricate interplay between technology and necessity may inspire the push toward terraforming. As technological advances accumulate, civilizations may find themselves compelled to push the boundaries of possibility and achievement to both sustain their populations and explore their aspirations. The need for new energy sources, advanced agricultural systems, and atmospheric engineering would fuel innovation, echoing our own Earth's pathway toward resource allocation. Intelligent civilizations might explore innovative solutions to life's challenges by utilizing engineering techniques that do not merely pull from existing principles but also unveil newly imagined possibilities.

Furthermore, the decision to terraform may encompass a broader, almost philosophical understanding of life itself. The exploration of what constitutes a 'habitable' environment could broaden as these civilizations expand their scopes beyond conventional biological frameworks, seeking not only their own survival but the enrichment of life in myriad forms. If humanity learns anything from biology, it's that adaptation is the key to survival; similarly, advanced civilizations may seek to cultivate a diversity of living organisms, allowing for a more vibrant ecological tapestry in their newly engineered worlds.

Discussion of why aliens would terraform would be incomplete without examining the potential ethical implications accompanying such actions. Engaging in terraformation raises complex questions about the value of uninhabited environments, the rights of potential alien life forms that may exist within those biospheres, and the moral responsibilities of altering cosmic ecosystems. If civilizations were to thoughtfully consider these implications—through treaties akin to the Outer Space Treaty that emphasize peaceful exploration and preservation—they may nurture a paradigm that not only respects their quest for habitation but acknowledges the rights of other forms of existence.

In summary, the motivations for why aliens might engage in terraformation are multifaceted and deeply human-like in their complexities. Many of the underlying drivers resonate with our own perceived needs—survival, exploration, expansion, ecological balance, cultural expression, and the inevitable push toward innovation. Each of these motivations paints a broader picture of intelligent life's possible relationship with the cosmos, revealing an inherent desire not just to survive but to flourish and share the interconnected tapestry of existence in ways that reflect a commitment to life and innovation beyond individual worlds. As we endeavor to understand our role in this cosmic narrative, we may also glean insights from these reflections that guide our future interactions and ethical considerations in a universe filled with possibilities.

4.2. Analyzing Alien Motivations

In the vast expanse of the cosmos, contemplating the motivations of advanced extraterrestrial civilizations prompts profound inquiries into their nature, objectives, and potential actions. The prospect of alien terraformation—intentional alterations made to inhospitable worlds—leads us to examine a range of reasons why such civilizations might engage in these monumental endeavors. Rooted in survival, exploration, ecological stewardship, cultural expression, and the intrinsic nature of conscious beings, these motivations reflect not only their relationship with their environments but also resonate deeply with our understanding of humanity's own aspirations.

Survival remains the preeminent driver behind the act of terraforming. Intelligent species, much like humanity, may confront existential threats from natural disasters, dwindling resources, or cataclysmic planetary changes. Terraformation could thus be perceived as a method of preserving life—a way to expand into new environments where future generations can thrive. For instance, if an advanced civilization's home planet were ravaged by climate change or made uninhabitable due to solar upheaval, the necessity to terraform another world could become paramount. In such scenarios, terraformation is not merely an option but a matter of survival—a lifeline for the continued existence of sentient beings.

Closely tied to survival is exploration, a fundamental characteristic of intelligent life. The urge to explore and understand the universe can yield motivations for terraforming as well. Such civilizations may seek to adapt barren landscapes into vibrant ecosystems to facilitate experimentation and study. In contrast to passive observation of distant worlds, terraforming may represent a proactive approach to engagement, allowing these civilizations to learn from transformed environments. By conducting ecological experiments on terraformed planets, they could harvest valuable insights that benefit their original homeworld—even forging connections with diverse forms of life existing beyond their own.

Additionally, the impulse toward expansion tends to fuel motives behind terraforming. Similar to humanity's drive to colonize and settle new territories throughout history, advanced civilizations may extend their reach into the cosmos seeking new habitats. Overpopulation, technological advancements, and resource scarcity may compel such species to pioneer terraforming as a viable means of creating space and ensuring sustainable living conditions. Terraforming would thus reflect not only physical expansion but also a broader desire for shared lineage—an endeavor to embed their identity within the interstellar tapestry of life.

Equally important is the recognition that ecological balance may dictate the motivations behind terraforming practices. As intelligent life evolves, a heightened awareness of environmental interdependence often emerges. Civilizations that have evolved alongside ecological degradation may recognize the need to restore balance through terraforming efforts. These initiatives could involve engineering processes to rehabilitate degrading biospheres and deploy technologies designed to balance existing ecosystems. Such motivations reflect the extent to which intelligent species may engage in stewardship of their worlds, acting as custodians of their environments rather than mere exploiters of resources.

Moreover, cultural expression adds depth to the motivations surrounding terraforming. Civilizations may view the act of reshaping the world as a profound testament to their identities and cultural heritage. Just as art has been an essential component of human expression, drawing upon the very elements of our surroundings, terraforming might serve as a canvas upon which an advanced civilization manifests its ideals, creative aspirations, or collective memory. Environmental alterations may serve to ensure legacy—building upon the narrative of the species while simultaneously attuning habitats to their values.

Finally, the dimension of technological innovation must not be overlooked. Advanced civilizations may relish the challenge presented by terraforming, pushing technological boundaries to explore new horizons. Each terraformed world represents a potential testament to their ingenuity and potential. Supposing civilizations possess capacities for extreme engineering, they may view terraforming as an opportunity to leverage technologies for sustainable development. These civilizations would be compelled by their ambitions, reinvigorating their creative pursuits.

While examining these motivations, we ultimately encounter a crucial ethical terrain explaining the implications of terraforming endeavors. The intersection of aspiration and responsibility must guide such initiatives, inviting dialogues around the moral ramifications of altering other worlds. As humanity transitions into an era of extraterrestrial exploration, reflections on our ethical obligations toward uninhabited environments become paramount. Should we encounter alien civilizations, as stewards of planetary integrity, we must consider how motivations align with recognition of the intrinsic value of all forms of life.

In concluding our analysis of alien motivations, it becomes clear that the reasons for engaging in terraformation transcend mere survival and reach into the realms of exploration, ecological stewardship, cultural expression, and technological prowess. Each motivation underscores the complexity of intelligent life as they navigate the cosmos, irrevocably shaping their environments while also crafting their legacy amid the stars. Exploring these aspects fosters renewed inquiry into our aspirations as humanity reaches toward the universe, shaping our own understanding of motivation, purpose, and potential as we ponder the overarching narrative of existence.

4.3. Historical Evidence in Mythology

The notion of tracing historical evidence in mythology serves as a fascinating intersection between human imagination and the potential realities of extraterrestrial influences across time. Mythologies, spanning diverse cultures and epochs, often contain narratives that reflect humanity's deepest inquiries about existence, nature, and the cosmos. They offer rich tapestries woven with symbols, allegories, and characters that speak to our understanding of alien encounters, celestial events, and the interplay between the divine and the earthly. This subchapter dives into the mythological narratives that may harbor echoes of ancient terrestrial or extraterrestrial terraformers, suggesting a historical recognition of advanced civilizations or events that radically altered the state of life on Earth.

Central to this exploration is the understanding that mythology often functions as a means of interpreting the unknown. In many cultures, myths arose in response to profound questions about creation, the nature of deities, the origins of humanity, and the cosmos itself. For example, creation myths, such as those found in various Indigenous cultures and religious texts, often recount how the world was formed and populated, hinting at the possibility of deliberate acts of design. As humanity engaged with the natural world, these narratives may reflect encounters with beings that possessed capabilities far beyond those of ordinary humanity—beings capable of influencing or transforming ecosystems through their actions.

Consider the ancient Mesopotamian narratives of the Anunnaki, deities often depicted as beings possessing advanced knowledge and technologies. Some alternative interpretations posit that these figures were not simply mythological constructs but representations of extraterrestrial beings that visited Earth and actively engaged with ancient populations. Such interpretations suggest an even more profound relationship between humanity and these beings, positing that rather than conferring wisdom purely in theological terms, the Anunnaki directly influenced various aspects of civilization, including agriculture, architecture, and urban planning. Viewed through the lens of terraforming, these myths can take on a new dimension—many tales may serve as allegorical recountings of technological and ecological intervention facilitated by advanced civilizations.

Similarly, the Polynesian tale of Maui, a demigod credited with creating islands, highlights the theme of transformative agency over natural landscapes. Maui's exploits—fishing up islands from the ocean floor, slowing down the sun, and altering climates—may symbolize human attempts to understand ecological manipulation from a mythological perspective. Such stories encapsulate humanity's desire to engage with the natural world and exert influence or control over it, reflecting an enduring curiosity about the capacity to reshape environments, echoing modern discussions surrounding asteroid mining, climate modification, and terraforming.

Furthermore, the myth of Phaethon from Greek mythology, the son of Helios, who attempted to drive the sun's chariot, contains themes of environmental instability caused by mismanaged power. According to the myth, Phaethon's reckless driving led to significant climatic changes on Earth, resulting in devastation. This narrative serves as a powerful allegory for the consequences of unchecked technological advancement and modification of the ecological balance—an echo of discussions in contemporary society surrounding climate change and environmental mismanagement, linking ancient myth to pressing current phenomena.

One cannot overlook creation stories featuring giant beings or gods dynamically reshaping landscapes, as seen in many indigenous cultures around the world. The Iroquois creation story features a woman falling from the sky onto the back of a turtle, which subsequently transforms into North America. These rich tales often embody values of respect for natural cycles, intertwining reverence for beings that shape worlds. Such narratives may serve as reflections of an ancient understanding of systems thinking, revealing people's recognition of interdependence and adaptation necessary for survival—a reminder of our current responsibility to reflect on how we as humans may influence ecosystems.

Moreover, narratives of floods—such as the biblical flood involving Noah or the story of Utnapishtim from the Epic of Gilgamesh—reveal a recurring theme of cataclysmic events acting as agents of change. Flood myths almost universally signify transformation, representing opportunities for rebirth and recreation of worlds. From a terraforming perspective, these floods could be interpreted as allegorical references to ancient technological endeavors or natural transformations that reshaped landscapes as civilizations strove to create harmonious environments. If we consider these stories as encoded memories of significant shifts or interventions in Earth's ecosystems, it becomes possible to view them through the lens of historical evidence of terraforming.

The historical significance of these myths unfolds as we pursue their implications for extraterrestrial influences and the idea of an advanced civilization possessing the capacity for significant environmental interventions—actions taken intentionally or perhaps mistakenly with widespread effects. Additionally, the possible existence of cultural memories that persist through generations might encourage our modern quest for understanding how to engage with our own environment responsibly. This connection illuminates the cyclical nature of humanity's aspirations and cautions against the mistakes of the past, urging stewardship as we contemplate our own role in the cosmos alongside any potential non-human architects.

In conclusion, the exploration of historical evidence in mythology as it pertains to potential extraterrestrial terraformation unveils a rich tapestry that entwines humanity's collective imagination with the quest for understanding our place in the universe. These mythological accounts showcase humanity's enduring desire to explain our existence and environment, echoing themes of technological prowess, environmental stewardship, and transformative agency. As we continue to delve into the myths of the past, we recognize a profound connection to the ongoing conversation about life beyond Earth and how we might navigate our cosmic responsibilities, ensuring that our legacies honor those narratives rooted in the ancient struggle for balance, resilience, and understanding. Through this lens of mythology, we grasp not just the allegorical interpretations of our history but also the ethical imperatives that guide our future interactions with the universe at large.

4.4. Communication Attempts

In our quest to understand the cosmos and the potential for interaction with intelligent life, the question of communication attempts stands as a fundamental pillar of inquiry. The need to bridge the vast distances across space fuels our search for signs of extraterrestrial life, revealing not just our scientific curiosity but our innate desire to connect with others. The exploration of communication attempts encompasses a spectrum of theoretical frameworks, historic dialogues, and emerging technologies that intersect with our understanding of the cosmos and our role within it.

A cornerstone of communication attempts is the acknowledgement of distances involved in our search for extraterrestrial intelligence (SETI). When we consider the vastness of space and the millions of potential planets that could harbor life, the sheer logistics of establishing contact becomes daunting. Each star system lies light-years away from another, and even at the speed of light, transmissions take years to reach their intended destinations. This delay necessitates a paradigm shift in how we conceptualize communication across these cosmic expanses. How, then, do we formulate messages intended for unknown recipients who may possess entirely different forms of intelligence, languages, technologies, and even ways of perceiving reality?

Historically, our communication attempts have been marked by the desire to send messages outwards, as exemplified by the Arecibo Message—a binary-encoded radio message sent into space in 1974, targeting the globular star cluster M13. This iconic act encapsulated humanity's desire to proclaim existence, share fundamental knowledge about our species, and send our hopes and dreams into the cosmos. The message contained essential information: our numerical system, the structure of DNA, our solar system, as well as an illustration of human figures. It was not only a scientific endeavor but a symbolic representation of our yearning for connection with other intelligent beings.

As we explore potential communication attempts further, we must also consider the signals that might already be surrounding us. The phenomenon of fast radio bursts (FRBs) has radically transformed our understanding of the possible nature of cosmic communications. These mysterious, brief bursts of radio waves emanating from remote galaxies have generated extensive debate among scientists regarding their origins. Are they natural astrophysical processes, or might they be created by alien technologies? The hunt for answers surrounding FRBs illustrates the lengths to which researchers go to discern signals in the noise of the universe.

In addition to directed, one-off communications, there exists the compelling question of whether alien civilizations might employ recurring patterns or rhythmic signals. Pulsars—rapidly rotating neutron stars emitting beams of radiation at regular intervals—serve as both cosmic lighthouses and potential markers of extraterrestrial engineering. If intelligent beings were to harness pulsar signals for communication, it leads to profound inquiries about their purpose and the methods that intelligent species might employ to encode meaning within these signals. By analyzing potential patterns, scientists and researchers work to decipher whether any observed phenomena signal an underlying intelligence, revealing the sophistication or perhaps simplicity of their message systems.

The emergent technologies of radio astronomy and advanced observatories have recently allowed astronomers to pursue an increasingly nuanced understanding of the universe. Instruments like the Square Kilometer Array (SKA) facilitate the capture of vast amounts of data and communication attempts in unprecedented detail. This leap in data analysis fosters hope in breaking through the barriers of noise to uncover potential communications or signs of intelligent life meticulously buried within cosmic chatter. The role of collaboration between national and international observatories fuels this endeavor, merging expertise and perspectives toward a common goal.

As we navigate the complexities of communication attempts, ethical considerations also come to the fore. The ramifications of sending messages into the universe must account for the potential responses, intentional or otherwise, that such acts may initiate. If we were to make contact with another civilization, questions of the cultural differences and potential dangers arise. What implications would there be for humanity if every signal sent out were answered? At what cost does our curiosity to explore the cosmic dialogue risk inadvertently inviting those who may not have benign intentions? These questions echo the historical narratives of human contact with distant cultures, drawing parallels that intertwine our understanding of communication with our responsibilities as cosmic citizens.

Furthering our understanding of communication attempts also involves speculative frameworks regarding what forms of communication intelligent life may pursue. Light-based communication methods, such as lasers, offer a compelling approach; not only are they highly directed and rapid, but they also could traverse vast distances with limited degradation. The theoretical framework of using modulated laser signals to convey messages sparks dialog about the potential universality of light communication as a method of dialogue not just in our limited scope of understanding but transcending beyond terrestrial limits toward cosmic engagement.

As we forge ahead in our quest to unravel the grand cosmic puzzle, we remain grounded in our innate curiosity about who, if anyone, is out there. Each attempt to communicate becomes an echo of our shared humanity, resonating with the age-old desire for connection. The technologies, ethical considerations, and scientific approaches that guide us illuminate a pathway where the symphony of the universe serves as both the backdrop and canvas of existence—a tapestry replete with the potential for dialogue, discovery, and wonder as we aim to understand our place among the stars. The weave of communication attempts and the cosmic questions they evoke invites an abiding fascination with what the universe might hold—and what connections await our discovery in the vast expanses beyond.

4.5. Energy Signatures and their Significance

The examination of energy signatures within the context of extraterrestrial terraformation unveils a fascinating interplay of science and speculation, offering a profound lens through which we can understand the potential actions and capabilities of advanced civilizations. Energy signatures, defined as the specific patterns of energy emission —ranging from light and heat to various forms of radiation—can provide crucial evidence of not only natural processes but also intentional manipulation. This subchapter delves into the significance of energy signatures, their implications for terraforming, and the broader cosmic inquiry into the existence of intelligent life.

Energy signatures serve as the universal language of the cosmos, expressing the myriad ways matter and energy interact within celestial bodies. As we study the universe, these signatures become vital indicators in the search for extraterrestrial life and the intriguing possibility of terraforming efforts. By deciphering the wavelengths of light emitted from distant planets and their atmospheres, scientists can draw conclusions about their compositions, temperatures, and potentially even the presence of life.

The identification of energy signatures begins with the fundamental principles of spectroscopy—analyzing how light interacts with matter. When light emitted or absorbed by an object passes through a prism or is observed through a spectrometer, it splits into a spectrum. Each element has a unique spectral fingerprint that reveals its presence. This technique allows astronomers and planetary scientists to ascertain the compositions of distant worlds, scrutinizing their atmospheres and discerning whether unusual ratios of gases might point toward artificial influences.

Particularly compelling within this context are the energy signatures associated with waste heat—unintended byproducts of technological activity. An advanced civilization engaged in terraforming would likely produce significant energy as it customized environments for habitability. This scenario raises the question: can we detect the waste heat as a telltale indicator of alien engineering? On Earth, industrial activities produce heat emissions that alter local climates, and similar phenomena could emerge on other worlds. By identifying excess thermal energy signatures emanating from a planetary body, scientists may find indirect evidence that intelligent life is engaged in extensive environmental manipulation.

In addition to waste heat, the deliberate modulation of energy signatures can manifest through technological means designed to affect climate or ecological states. For instance, deploying artificial satellites to alter light patterns, managing energy flow through solar reflectors, or utilizing orbital structures to change planetary albedo would create distinct energy signatures detectable from afar. Anomalies in expected radiation patterns could alert researchers to the presence of advanced engineering, hinting at civilizations striving to terraform inhospitable locations.

One of the most captivating prospects lies in the transmission of energy signals directly aimed at other civilizations. The quest for extraterrestrial intelligence (SETI) has involved scanning the skies for deliberate signals, such as radio waves or laser pulses, that may signify intelligent life. If a civilization possesses the capacity to engineer worlds, it would potentially have the technological means to communicate their intentions through energy modulation—sending out patterns or messages encoded in light matched to specific wavelengths detectable by advanced telescopes. The discovery of such deliberate signals would fundamentally alter our understanding of the cosmos and our place within it.

As we delve deeper into the concept of energy signatures, it is important to acknowledge their interrelationship with other scientific disciplines. The study of planetary geology and atmospheres, combined with cutting-edge astrophysics, enhances our understanding of how energy signatures inform us about the history and evolution of celestial bodies. The dynamics of a planet's geology, including tectonic movements or volcanic activity, can manifest changes in atmospheric composition or surface features. By studying the energy profiles of these interactions, researchers can construct narratives revealing the natural and unnatural forces shaping a world.

The implications of energy signatures extend beyond mere observation; they cultivate ethical considerations that echo throughout humanity's narrative. In seeking out evidence of terraforming or technological engagement on other worlds, we must consider the rights and existence of potential life forms that may inhabit those environments. The dilemma of interpreting energy signatures as tools of transformation poses relevant questions: do we possess the moral authority to alter the course of life on another world? Furthermore, our exploration of energy signatures invites larger reflections on stewardship: how do we navigate our inquisitive impulses while respecting and preserving other ecosystems?

Moreover, the implications of identifying energy signatures suggest that our search for extraterrestrial life can lead us toward broader inquiries about existence itself. Recognizing energy as the foundational currency of life raises philosophical questions concerning the fundamental nature of intelligence, engineering, and the patterns that arise within the cosmos. The pursuit of understanding energy signatures compels humanity to engage with its past—reminding us of our own journey, the impact of our technologies, and the choices we must confront in determining our legacy among the stars.

In conclusion, the exploration of energy signatures and their significance in the context of alien terraformation presents a rich tapestry that intertwines science with speculation. The quest for detecting these signatures propels our investigation of technological manipulation, uncovering possibilities that may reveal advanced civilizations engaging with their environments. Through the lens of energy signatures, we assess our relationship with the cosmos—extending questions not only toward understanding life beyond Earth but also contemplating our ethical duties and responsibilities as we venture into an expansive universe. The journey toward capturing and interpreting energy signatures stands as a pivotal chapter in unraveling the enigmatic narratives that the cosmos has to offer, directing us toward our shared aspirations for exploration, discovery, and a deeper understanding of the intricate interplay that defines existence itself.

5. Instruments of Discovery

5.1. Telescopic Technologies

The evolution of telescopic technologies has profoundly transformed our ability to observe the universe, unlocking mysteries and expanding the horizons of astronomy. Telescopes, in their various forms, have served as the windows through which humanity peeks into the cosmos, enabling us to investigate celestial phenomena, monitor atmospheric compositions of distant planets, and gather evidence that could indicate the existence of extraterrestrial life or the potential for terraforming. This subchapter explores the historical development, advancements, and future prospects of telescopic technologies, examining their implications for detecting signs of alien terraformation.

The journey of telescopic innovation began in the early 17th century with the invention of the refracting telescope by Galileo Galilei. His early observations of celestial bodies significantly changed humanity's understanding of the universe, revealing moons orbiting Jupiter and the phases of Venus—indications that not everything revolved around Earth. The rudimentary design of the telescope, which utilized lenses to magnify distant objects, marked the inception of a momentous shift in astronomy, igniting a wave of future developments.

As the centuries progressed, advancements in optics led to the creation of larger and more effective telescopes. The introduction of new materials, such as glass, allowed for improved lens crafting, sharpening the clarity of images. The invention of the reflecting telescope by Isaac Newton further enhanced observational capabilities by reducing chromatic aberrations—a significant limitation of refracting telescopes. This innovative design, which utilized mirrors to collect and focus light, paved the way for astronomers to build larger instruments that could collect more light from distant celestial sources.

By the 19th century, the construction of telescopes reached new heights with the creation of the Great Melbourne Telescope and the 100-inch Hooker Telescope at Mt. Wilson Observatory. These monumental instruments represented a significant leap in size and power, allowing astronomers to explore fainter and more distant objects than ever before. Coupled with advancements in photography, telescopes could capture detailed images of celestial phenomena, heralding an era of astrophotography that provided invaluable data for scientific analysis.

In the 20th century, the advent of radio telescopes introduced a new dimension to astronomical observation. Pioneered in the late 1930s by scientists like Karl Jansky, radio telescopes enabled researchers to detect radio waves emitted by celestial bodies, allowing for the exploration of the universe beyond the visible spectrum. The discovery of pulsars and cosmic microwave background radiation through radio observations revolutionized our understanding of star formation, the Big Bang, and the nature of the universe itself.

Moreover, space-based telescopes such as the Hubble Space Telescope have brought forth a new era of astronomical observation by circumventing Earth's atmospheric interference. Launched in 1990, Hubble has provided profound insights into the universe, capturing stunning images of galaxies, nebulae, and exoplanets. With its ability to observe in various wavelengths—from ultraviolet to near-infrared—Hubble has not only contributed to our understanding of the cosmos but has also allowed scientists to explore the atmospheric characteristics of distant exoplanets, identifying potential signs of habitability or terraforming.

Looking toward the future, the landscape of telescopic technologies is poised for further transformation, with the upcoming James Webb Space Telescope (JWST) expected to revolutionize our understanding of the universe. Set to launch in the near future, JWST will take observational astronomy to new heights, employing advanced infrared technology to study the formation of stars and galaxies, and to investigate the atmospheres of distant exoplanets. Its capacity to detect chemical signatures in the atmospheres of these worlds may illuminate the presence of potentially life-sustaining compounds or signal alterations indicative of terraforming.

Additionally, terrestrial telescopes are evolving at an exponential rate, incorporating cutting-edge technologies such as adaptive optics to correct atmospheric distortion, allowing for sharper images of distant celestial objects. Moreover, computational advancements, including machine learning algorithms, are facilitating the analysis of vast datasets to identify patterns, anomalies, or even potential signals from extraterrestrial civilizations. These developments herald a new era in which technological sophistication will enable astronomers to delve deeper into planetary atmospheres, searching for unnatural compositions that might suggest past or ongoing terraforming activities.

Telescopic technologies also intersect with interdisciplinary research, merging fields such as planetary science, biology, and engineering. Designing instruments that can withstand extreme environments, such as those found on Mars or other celestial bodies, opens avenues for direct exploration. Telescopes equipped with spectrometric capabilities, capable of analyzing light spectra from atmospheres, can reveal chemical clues suggestive of life or terraforming, effectively bridging our understanding of habitability across the cosmos.

In conclusion, telescopic technologies stand at the forefront of our quest to understand the universe and the potential for alien terraformation. From humble beginnings to the sophisticated instruments of today, telescopes have illuminated our path, revealing cosmic wonders that challenge our understanding of life beyond Earth. As advancements continue to unfold, the intersection of telescopic inquiries and the exploration of extraterrestrial environments promises to deepen our understanding of our place in the cosmos and potentially unveil the signs of civilizations that have sought to reshape their worlds for survival, exploration, and the flourishing of life. The future of telescopic technologies holds great promise for answering fundamental questions about the universe and igniting our enduring curiosity about the existence of extraterrestrial life and the transformative endeavors they may have employed.

5.2. Radio Astronomy Innovations

The field of radio astronomy has undergone remarkable transformations over the past few decades, ushering in innovative techniques and technologies that have revolutionized our understanding of the universe. These advancements position radio astronomy as a critical tool in the quest to identify potential signs of extraterrestrial civilizations and their possible terraforming activities on distant planets. As we embark on this exploration, we will delve into the innovations that have shaped radio astronomy, the challenges that persist, and the exciting prospects that lie ahead.

At the heart of radio astronomy lies the principle of capturing and analyzing radio waves emitted by celestial objects. Unlike optical telescopes that rely on visible light, radio telescopes harness frequencies that enable astronomers to peer deeper into the universe's mysteries. The ability to detect these longer wavelengths provides a window into phenomena that are often obscured or invisible to the naked eye. This capability has proven invaluable for studying cosmic events, from pulsars and quasars to the faint whispers of cosmic microwave background radiation—remnants of the universe's infancy.

One of the most prominent innovations in radio astronomy is the advancement of interferometry techniques, which have drastically improved observational sensitivity and resolution. Interferometry involves linking multiple radio telescopes across vast distances to work in tandem, effectively creating a virtual telescope with a size determined by the distance between them. This method enables astronomers to achieve resolutions that were previously unattainable, allowing for the detailed imaging of celestial structures. Projects such as the Very Large Array and the Atacama Large Millimeter Array (ALMA) exemplify this technique, enabling the study of molecular clouds and star formation in unparalleled detail.

Furthermore, the development of the Square Kilometer Array (SKA), a large-scale radio telescope project currently under construction in South Africa and Australia, promises to push the boundaries of radio astronomy even further. Once fully operational, the SKA will be one of the most powerful radio instruments ever built, capable of collecting vast amounts of data across a wide range of frequencies. Its unprecedented sensitivity and broad frequency coverage will enable scientists to investigate previously unexplored territories in the universe, probing for signals indicative of alien civilizations and the possibilities of terraformation.

A significant aspect of radio astronomy lies in its capacity to listen for signals that could signify the presence of intelligent life. The Search for Extraterrestrial Intelligence (SETI), a field closely associated with radio astronomy, employs radio telescopes to monitor frequencies for anomalous patterns reminiscent of artificial signals. Innovative data processing techniques, including machine learning algorithms, are being developed to sift through the vast amounts of data collected, seeking out signals that stand out from the cosmic background noise. This integration of technology enables researchers to increase the probability of detecting potential communications from other civilizations, as well as identifying signatures of terraforming activities within the atmospheric compositions of distant planets.

Moreover, advancements in radio telescope technology have culminated in the ability to conduct spectrometric analysis—analyzing the spectral fingerprints of molecules in exoplanetary atmospheres. By determining the composition and abundance of gases present in these atmospheres, scientists can glean vital information about planetary conditions and assess whether they might harbor life or exhibit signs of terraforming. This application of radio astronomy illustrates its vital role in the broader discourse surrounding extraterrestrial life, combining observational techniques with chemical analysis to provide insights into potentially habitable environments.

While the progress in radio astronomy is largely promising, challenges remain. The increasing presence of technological interference —particularly from satellites and terrestrial broadcasts—constitutes a considerable obstacle. Interference can contaminate the delicate signals that astronomers aim to detect, necessitating the development of advanced filtering techniques and ongoing efforts to isolate radio observatories from human-made noise. Additionally, the vast amount of data generated by radio telescopes necessitates sophisticated storage and processing capabilities. Researchers must continually innovate to develop efficient algorithms and computing methods that allow for the real-time analysis of incoming data.

The future of radio astronomy is rife with possibilities. The advent of new telescopes and upgraded systems will pave the way for exciting discoveries. For example, the upcoming launch of the James Webb Space Telescope, while primarily focused on infrared observations, will complement existing radio telescope research, offering expanded insights into exoplanetary atmospheric compositions and potential biosignatures.

In a broader context, the synthesis between radio astronomy and other scientific disciplines—such as planetary science, biology, and engineering—will enhance our understanding of the complex interplay of forces at work across the cosmos. This interdisciplinary approach will likely result in innovative strategies to explore, analyze, and interpret the potential for extraterrestrial terraformation.

In conclusion, the innovations in radio astronomy stand as a powerful testament to humanity's relentless quest for understanding and connection. As we harness advancing technologies to explore the universe's vast expanse, we edge closer to answering fundamental questions about life beyond Earth and the potential for other civilizations to shape their environments. The journey of discovery continues, driven by a shared curiosity about the cosmos and the profound possibilities it holds. With each refinement and technological leap, we inch closer to uncovering the cosmic secrets that elude us and, perhaps, to finding signs of those who might have already taken significant strides in reshaping worlds across the universe.

5.3. Space Probes and Satellites

The exploration of space probes and satellites as our vanguard in the quest for extraterrestrial knowledge and the potential for discovering signs of alien terraformation necessitates understanding the intricate technologies and missions that have shaped our view of the cosmos. These instruments serve not merely as tools of observation but as extensions of human curiosity, enabling us to peer into the depths of space and investigate the myriad worlds beyond our own. This subchapter will delve into the historical developments, current efforts, and future aspirations of space probes and satellites, examining their roles in advancing our knowledge of alien life and potential terraforming activities that may occur elsewhere in the universe.

Historically, the dawn of the space age can be traced back to the launch of Sputnik 1 by the Soviet Union in 1957—the first artificial satellite to orbit the Earth. This monumental achievement laid the groundwork for future explorations beyond our planet. Subsequent missions followed suit, with an array of satellites deployed to study Earth, other planets, and even the distant reaches of the solar system. Each mission has contributed to our growing understanding of planetary dynamics, environmental conditions, and the spatial context of celestial bodies within the cosmos.

The design and deployment of space probes represent a critical evolution in our exploration efforts. Unlike satellites, which remain in stable orbits around a planet or celestial body, space probes are engineered for movement, traveling vast distances to gather data from multiple environments. The Mariner missions of the 1960s and 1970s were pivotal in our understanding of Mars and Venus and set a precedence for future exploratory missions. Mariner 4, for example, was the first spacecraft to successfully transmit images of Mars, revealing a world much different than the visions held by scientists at the time —an inhospitable landscape marked by craters and desolation.

As mission capabilities advanced, the Voyager spacecraft epitomized the ambition embodied in space exploration. Launched in 1977, Voyager 1 and 2 embarked on a grand tour of the outer planets, sending back an astonishing wealth of images and data about Jupiter, Saturn, Uranus, and Neptune. These missions not only enriched our understanding of planetary processes and atmospheres but also ignited the imagination with images of distant worlds, unveiling the complexity and beauty of the solar system.

In terms of terraformation, space probes have proven instrumental in gathering data that informs our theoretical understanding of other planets' potential for life and human habitation. The Mars Exploration Rovers, Spirit and Opportunity, launched in 2003, provided groundbreaking evidence supporting past liquid water on Mars' surface, thus bolstering the hypothesis that Mars could have once supported microbial life. Insights gained from these missions prompt reflection on whether intentional terraforming efforts could one day make Mars hospitable to current life forms—expanding humanity's reach into the cosmos.

Space probes such as New Horizons have ventured further into the depths of our solar system, offering first looks at distant bodies like Pluto. Launched in 2006, New Horizons traversed to the Kuiper Belt and sent back stunning images of Pluto's surface, revealing a world characterized by icy plains and complex geology. In doing so, it sparked curiosity about the nature of celestial bodies previously considered fringes of our solar system—not just as targets for exploration but as environments ripe for analysis concerning speculation about alien life and the potential for terraforming in unique conditions.

Furthermore, the burgeoning field of exoplanet exploration has been significantly fueled by satellite missions. The Kepler Space Telescope, launched in 2009, revolutionized our understanding of planetary systems around stars beyond our solar system. By employing the transit method—monitoring changes in brightness as planets pass in front of their stars—Kepler has identified thousands of exoplanets, many of which lie within their stars' habitable zones. These findings have resulted in an explosion of interest regarding the potential for life on exoplanets and the prospects for future terraforming efforts.

Now, with missions such as the Transiting Exoplanet Survey Satellite (TESS), launched in 2018, we are witnessing a new wave of discovery focused on identifying Earth-like candidates. TESS aims to characterize hundreds of exoplanets over a two-year survey, heralding a new era for understanding planetary compositions and atmospheric properties. It is increasingly evident that studying any potential terraforming activities will hinge on our ability to analyze the atmospheres of these distant worlds.

Additionally, satellites play a vital role in monitoring Earth's environment, generating comparisons that inform our understanding of climate systems and the challenges we may face when engaging in possible terraforming elsewhere. Understanding Earth's ecological systems provides essential lessons for managing potential terraformation on other planets. By analyzing atmospheric gases on Earth through satellites like the European Space Agency's Sentinel missions, we gather critical data that contributes to understanding how climate dynamics operate and how they could be (re)engineered on celestial bodies.

The future of space probes and satellites promises exciting advancements poised to bridge gaps in our cosmic understanding. The advent of more sophisticated instruments, such as the James Webb Space Telescope, set for launch, will provide unprecedented insights into exoplanet atmospheres, including the detection of chemical signatures that may signal signs of biosignatures or even terraforming efforts. The interplay between terrestrial and extraterrestrial studies continues to deepen as we navigate ethical considerations, potential collaborations with different scientific disciplines, and innovations in instrumentation.

As we look ahead, there is growing recognition that our engagements with the cosmos must be guided by a sense of responsibility and ethical stewardship. The space probes and satellites we send as emissaries into the universe should reflect our aspirations to learn, understand, and perhaps, engage with distant worlds in the most reverent and conscientious manner possible. The merging of technological advancement with ethical considerations drives the quest for knowledge as we stand at the confluence of curiosity and awareness, striving to uncover the cosmic tapestry woven through exploration, discovery, and the enduring quest to understand our place in it all.

In summary, the evolution and endeavors of space probes and satellites provide profound insights into our pursuit of knowledge about alien worlds and the possibilities of terraformation. These instruments not only extend our reach into the cosmos but also serve as symbols of human ambition and imagination, reflecting the intricate dance between curiosity and responsibility as we navigate the breathtaking complexities of the universe.

5.4. Spectrometric Analysis

The study of spectrometric analysis stands as a cornerstone in the quest to understand the universe and the potential for alien terraformation. This method involves the examination of how light interacts with matter, providing crucial insights into the atmospheric compositions of celestial bodies. By analyzing the light spectra emitted or absorbed by different substances, scientists can deduce the presence of various elements and compounds, which is essential for identifying planets or moons that may harbor life or have undergone significant environmental changes through terraforming.

At its core, spectrometric analysis leverages the principle that different elements and molecules absorb and emit light at characteristic wavelengths. Just as a fingerprint can uniquely identify an individual, the spectrum of light emitted from an object can uniquely signify its chemical makeup. When light travels through a substance, specific wavelengths are absorbed, creating a distinct absorption spectrum that can be detected and analyzed. This data is invaluable, providing scientists with the ability to identify the elemental and molecular compositions of distant planets, and offering critical information about their potential habitability.

The capabilities of spectrometric analysis have been dramatically enhanced with the development of advanced instruments. The advent of high-resolution spectrometers enables astronomers to obtain precise measurements of light signatures, unveiling the rich tapestry of atmospheric chemistry at play in far-off worlds. Space-based observatories like the Hubble Space Telescope and the upcoming James Webb Space Telescope are outfitted with powerful spectrometric instruments that will broaden our ability to analyze the atmospheres of exoplanets.

One prominent application of spectrometric analysis lies in the search for biosignatures—indicators of life that can be detected in the atmospheres of other planets. Specific gas combinations, such as the simultaneous presence of methane and oxygen, coupled with their unusual ratios, could signify biological processes or even technological activities by advanced civilizations. On Earth, these gases coexist due to complex interactions within ecosystems; detecting a similar phenomenon in alien atmospheres may suggest the presence of life capable of performing these functions.

Moreover, understanding the atmospheric chemistry of planets provides insights into their climatic and environmental histories. For example, the analysis of isotopes can yield information about formative processes on planets like Mars or Venus. The isotopic ratios of carbon, hydrogen, and oxygen can help scientists piece together the climatic evolution of these worlds. On Mars, for instance, the presence of water ice and certain mineral deposits indicates that liquid water may have existed in the past, suggesting that the planet could have supported life before undergoing dramatic environmental changes.

The implications of identifying unusual spectral signatures extend beyond merely discovering existing planets. They also delve into the realm of potential terraforming activities. If advanced civilizations possess the means to manipulate planetary atmospheres, they would likely leave behind telltale signs detectable through spectrometric analysis. The deliberate introduction of greenhouse gases or engineered atmospheric components could transform a planet's conditions to make them more conducive to life. By identifying these engineered signatures, scientists can build a more nuanced understanding of how civilizations might adapt inhospitable worlds to support various forms of life.

Furthermore, spectrometric analysis allows scientists to scrutinize exoplanets for signs of alien engineering through the detection of modified chemical pathways that diverge from natural processes. For instance, the introduction of new materials or anomalous gases could signify terraforming projects aimed at creating habitable environments. This pursuit is fraught with challenges, however, as interpreting these signatures requires a sophisticated understanding of both planetary science and astrobiology. Disentangling natural phenomena from artificial influences necessitates advanced modeling techniques and an interdisciplinary approach, unifying knowledge from atmospheric sciences, biology, and chemistry.

As the scientific community evolves its understanding of spectro-metric methodologies, emerging technologies continue to shape the landscape of cosmic discovery. Quantum technologies, for example, promise greater sensitivity and specificity in measurements, thereby enhancing the detection of faint signals emitted from distant celestial bodies. Such advancements could transform our capabilities to monitor and interpret spectral data, ultimately aiding in the identification of planets that may exhibit signs of advanced, potentially terraform-initiating civilizations.

While spectrometric analysis offers unprecedented opportunities, ethical considerations also arise in this endeavor. The pursuit of knowledge about other worlds and potential life forms mandates a sense of responsibility toward the ecosystems we might encounter. Explorers must confront important moral questions about the impact of our inquiries—whether intentional or unintentional—on alien biospheres.

In conclusion, spectrometric analysis acts as a powerful lens for interpreting the chemical signatures left in the wake of celestial processes and potential alien engineering endeavors. Equipped with this knowledge, scientists embark on a transformative journey, cutting through the fabric of the cosmos to unveil the mysteries surrounding life beyond Earth. By synthesizing technological innovations with inter-disciplinary insights, the quest for understanding the atmospheres of other worlds continues to unfold, driving us ever forward in our exploration of the possibilities that lay in the vast expanse of the universe, and the potential for finding signs of alien terraformation or even distant civilizations that may have once roamed the cosmic landscape. The journey ahead is not merely an exploration of the universe but a testament to our enduring drive to seek knowledge and unravel the enigmatic mysteries that define our existence.

5.5. Emerging Technological Frontiers

In an ever-evolving understanding of the universe and its myriad possibilities, the exploration of emerging technological frontiers is a profound and exciting domain. Humanity stands on the precipice of innovation that can revolutionize our grasp of not just our environment, but also the celestial spaces beyond Earth. This chapter serves as a critical canvas where we explore the advanced technologies likely to emerge, shaping future understandings of alien terraforming, extraterrestrial civilizations, and the expansive frontiers awaiting our curiosity.

At the heart of emerging technological frontiers is the continuous evolution of spacecraft design and propulsion methods. Traditional forms of space travel have relied heavily on chemical propulsion systems, which, while effective, impose strict limits on travel speed and efficiency. The introduction of advanced propulsion techniques, such as ion propulsion systems, fusion propulsion, and the speculative concept of warp drives, presents potential pathways to traverse vast distances in space more effectively. These innovations could facilitate closer exploration of exoplanets suspected of harboring life or undergoing terraformation, ultimately enabling humanity to engage with these distant worlds in unprecedented ways.

Moreover, advancements in artificial intelligence and robotics play a pivotal role in expanding our capabilities for exploration. Autonomous and semi-autonomous systems could operate vehicles and probes, perform landings on distant planets, and carry out scientific research, both on the surface and in atmospheric studies. These intelligent systems can analyze vast amounts of data far more rapidly than a human scientist could, detecting patterns that might hint at terraforming activities or unusual atmospheric phenomena. By employing AI, researchers could simulate alien environments and assess potential terraforming strategies for Mars, Venus, or other celestial bodies, allowing us to visualize the complexities of ecological integration on a planetary scale.

The integration of biotechnology represents another frontier in our quest for understanding and potentially terraforming alien worlds. By harnessing synthetic biology, scientists are now exploring the engineering of organisms capable of thriving in extraterrestrial environments. Genetically modified microbes could be designed to metabolize elements abundant on other planets, serving as foundational agents in creating breathable atmospheres or producing essential nutrients for colonization efforts. This biotechnological leap would not only enhance our understanding of life but may also pave the way for sustainable biospheres that can adapt to and thrive in environments previously deemed inhospitable.

In parallel, advancements in materials science are anticipated to revolutionize the development of habitats for future space missions. The exploration of 3D printing with in-situ resources can enable astronauts to construct habitats from materials found on the Moon, Mars, or asteroids—reducing the logistical burdens of transporting materials from Earth. These adaptable habitats could be designed to withstand harsh conditions and dynamically adjust to solar radiation, temperature variations, and atmospheric pressures. Such innovations would also hold implications for terraforming as they enable human presence on alien terrains, augmenting the ecosystem's ability to evolve.

The capabilities of telescopic technologies also continue to reach new heights, contributing significantly to our understanding of alien worlds and their transformations. Emerging telescopes equipped with spectrometric and imaging capabilities can provide critical insights into the atmospheric compositions of exoplanets. By analyzing light spectra and atmospheres from these distant worlds, scientists can decipher the chemical signatures indicative of potential terraform signatures or biological processes. Furthermore, advancements in radio telescope technology enable researchers to engage in investigations of cosmic signals, possibly uncovering evidence of extraterrestrial communications or activities.

As we consider the implications of these technological frontiers, ethical dilemmas arise. With advancements comes the responsibility to approach extraterrestrial exploration with caution and humility. The ability to manipulate environments in the name of terraforming or colonization prompts profound ethical questions regarding our responsibilities as stewards of the universe. Engaging in open dialogues about the moral implications of our technological capabilities will become increasingly imperative as we venture further into space.

The continuous rise of international cooperation in science and technology also fosters an atmosphere of shared exploration. Collaborative efforts—be it through united space missions, data sharing among research institutions, or planetary science coalitions—provide rich resources and insights that deepen our understanding of past discoveries, hypotheses, and future possibilities. The shared pursuit of knowledge emphasizes the interconnectedness of humanity as we extend our curiosity beyond our terrestrial confines.

In conclusion, as we embrace the unfolding realities of emerging technological frontiers, we stand on the threshold of transformative opportunities that can yield deeper insights into the nature of life across the cosmos. From advanced propulsion systems to synthetic biology and collaborative scientific efforts, the possibilities seem boundless. The quest for understanding our universe not only fuels innovation but also beckons us to reflect on the ethical responsibilities that accompany such advancements. The journey forward into the vast, uncharted domains holds the promise of revelations that could reshape our understanding of both our continental legacy and its interconnected thread among the wondrous tapestry of the cosmos. As we chart this trajectory, we must remain committed to honoring these exciting possibilities, fostering the spirit of exploration, under-standing, and ethical stewardship for generations to come.

6. Debating Alien Transformations

6.1. Case Studies: Mars and Beyond

In the exploration of alien terraformation, particularly concerning Mars and beyond, we embark on an intricate journey that intertwines scientific inquiry with visionary speculation. Mars stands at the forefront of this endeavor, embodying both the tantalizing prospects and formidable challenges presented by the terraforming agenda. The red planet's desolate landscapes and historical signs of ancient water flow ignite discourse surrounding the potential for transforming it into a more Earth-like environment—a venture alive with scientific merit and philosophical significance.

One of the most compelling cases for Mars as a candidate for terraforming stems from its intriguing geological history. Recent studies reveal extensive features such as ancient riverbeds, lake sediments, and mineral deposits indicative of past water presence—prime factors suggesting that Mars may have once supported microbial life. These findings nurture the ambition to revitalize its atmosphere, potentially making it hospitable for future human settlers. Terraforming could theoretically involve increasing the atmospheric pressure and temperature through methods such as releasing greenhouse gases like carbon dioxide, thus attempting to create conditions that would facilitate the presence of liquid water on its surface.

Efforts to model the possible pathways toward this ambitious transformation reveal myriad challenges. For instance, the two primary obstacles take the form of Mars' thin atmosphere (approximately 95% carbon dioxide) and its cold temperatures, consistently hovering around −80 degrees Fahrenheit. To alter these realities, solutions ranging from large-scale industrial operations creating greenhouse gases, to constructing orbital mirrors to reflect sunlight down to the Martian surface, have been proposed. Each of these strategies demands advanced technology and a level of precision that challenges current engineering capabilities, posing significant uncertainties in tranches of practicality, ethics, and ecological integrity.

Beyond Mars, the propositions for terraforming extend into the depths of our solar system, challenging conventional perceptions of what constitutes a habitable environment. Notably, Venus—often labeled Earth's 'sister planet'—offers a radically different canvas for terraforming aspirations. Encased in a thick atmosphere of carbon dioxide and sulfuric acid clouds, along with extreme surface pressures and temperatures, the endeavors to transform Venus for human habitation conjure ambitious ideas. Approaches, including the notion of constructing solar shades to reduce temperature or the potential use of engineered microorganisms capable of metabolizing carbon dioxide, highlight the expansive creativity that guides these discussions.

Astrobiological factors play a crucial role in the framework of terraforming Mars and other celestial bodies. If we examine Mars' potential to support life through the lens of ecological sustainability, one must interrogate how introducing Earth organisms impacts the native Martian environment, even as it presently stands devoid of confirmable life forms. The ethical implications of this consideration promote dialogues surrounding the right to alter a planet and the responsibilities that emerge within this so-called 'interplanetary stewardship.'

The exploration of terraforming further extends into the exoplanetary domain, where scientists encourage the ongoing examination of distant worlds. The search for potentially habitable exoplanets—with characteristics resembling those conducive to life—fuels scientific inquiry. Using techniques like transit photometry or radial velocity measurements, researchers can identify exoplanets residing within the habitable zone of their stars, where conditions might likewise allow for terraformation efforts. The ambition to reshape these remote celestial bodies to facilitate life encapsulates not only human aspirations but also a greater continuum of discovery, as we engage in identifying whether advanced civilizations elsewhere might have undertaken similar endeavors.

However, the discussion around terraforming is not without skepticism. Critics emphasize the formidable challenges associated with the unpredictability of ecological consequences that could ensue from such radical interventions. What if, in our efforts to create a habitable world, we inadvertently trigger irreversible transformations to the ambient ecosystems? Case studies of anthropogenic impacts on Earth serve as cautionary tales; the lessons learned from our neglect of Earth's ecological systems are instructive when considering our potential impact on other worlds.

In addressing these complexities, scientific dialogues advocating for responsible stewardship and ethical reflection emerge as guiding principles. Identifying the markers of terraforming, understanding the intrinsic value of alien ecosystems, and re-orienting our ambitions around the preservation of cosmic diversity will shape our plans moving forward. The exploration of terraforming—both within our solar system and beyond—thus calls for an engaged and contemplative approach to ensure that our cosmic aspirations do not inadvertently lead to harm, but rather enhance the tapestry of life that we seek to affirm across the universe.

As we synthesize the lessons learned from Mars and beyond, we stand poised at the intersection of exploration, innovation, and philosophy. The unfolding narrative of terraforming presents a dual opportunity and challenge—opening doors to new realms where human ingenuity can thrive, while simultaneously demanding an acute awareness of the responsibilities that accompany such transformative agendas. The rich tapestry of case studies across Mars and its extraterrestrial peers encourages us to dream boldly but also to tread carefully, ensuring that as we venture into the unknown, we do so with reverence, respect, and ethical commitment to the universe that surrounds us. The cosmic odyssey towards terraforming and the exploration of life beyond our planet beckons—a journey laden with promises that can reshape our understanding of existence itself.

6.2. Challenges in Proving Terraforming

The complexities surrounding the concept of proving terraforming —specifically in the context of potential alien activity—encompass a spectrum of challenges that intersect scientific rigor, technological limitations, ethical considerations, and a burgeoning public interest. To crystallize our understanding of terraforming's implications, we must first appreciate that the concept itself is deeply intertwined with the myriad phenomena observable across the cosmos, urging us to navigate a labyrinth of scientific exploration while simultaneously grappling with the philosophical ramifications of our findings.

Foremost among the challenges encountered in proving terraforming is the contentious nature of scientific skepticism. The realm of astro-biology has historically faced scrutiny due to its speculative roots and the limitations inherent in our current understanding of life. Assertions regarding the existence of engineered environments hinge on the ability to gather and interpret data that reliably signals intelligent design rather than natural processes. When scientists propose the existence of terraformed worlds, they must differentiate between geological and environmental anomalies that might suggest biological processes from those that could simply reflect the cosmic randomness of physics. The challenge of isolating genuine markers of alien engineering from mere geological happenstance is monumental, often leading to cautious interpretations within the scientific community.

Evidence of terraforming, if it exists, may lie hidden behind the veil of uncertainty. The rigorous standards of scientific validation require repeatable experiments and observations, which cannot easily be transposed onto cosmic phenomena. For example, while Mars exhibits features that may suggest ancient water flow—an element crucial for life—proving that such features were influenced by intelligent intervention would require direct evidence of engineering processes. As a result, the scientific dialogue surrounding terraforming often oscillates between fervent speculation and reticent indifference, hindering consensus around its viability as a conceptual framework.

Furthermore, advances in technology inform the capabilities we possess for investigation; yet, limitations persist. Our observational technologies constantly improve—enabling us to detect chemical signatures on distant exoplanets and monitor atmospheric variations on planets within our own solar system—but they often grapple with inherent constraints such as distance, atmospheric interference, and the spanning light-years that separate us from potential subjects of study. Not every celestial body can be meticulously analyzed, leading to gaps in our understanding that fuel skepticism over proposed terraforming activities.

The challenge extends to the realm of ethical considerations, complicating our dialogue surrounding terraforming. Should we uncover definitive evidence of advanced civilizations engaging in terraforming, we are compelled to confront the moral implications of such actions. The potential existence of extraterrestrial life evokes pressing questions about the rights of alien ecosystems and the responsibilities we bear as custodians of our homeworld and any others we encounter. Terraforming—not merely a scientific endeavor but also one that carries profound ethical weight—demands a careful re-examination of our motivations and the possible consequences of interfering in natural processes on extraterrestrial bodies.

With an ever-expanding public interest in extraterrestrial life and terraforming activities, the role of media becomes a double-edged sword. Media outlets often sensationalize discoveries, shaping public perception around speculative findings while sometimes overshadowing the nuanced, cautious narratives of the scientific community. While enthusiasm for the potential of life beyond Earth fuels interest and investments in space exploration, it can also distort expectations, leading to public disillusionment if extraordinary claims lack corresponding proof. This relationship between scientific discourse and media representation highlights an ongoing tension that must be navigated delicately to promote informed discussions around tackling the complexities of terraforming.

As we delve deeper, we must also recognize how challenges in proving terraforming can ripple through the policies governing space exploration. As the discourse surrounding terraforming gains traction, policymakers must grapple with the ethical, legal, and regulatory frameworks that would govern any attempts to alter environments on celestial bodies. The establishment of guidelines responsive to the rights of potential alien life, the integrity of uninhabited ecosystems, and the custodianship models will be essential for ensuring sustainable practices in the face of remarkable discoveries.

In summary, the challenges in proving terraforming culminate from a confluence of scientific scrutiny, technological limitations, ethical considerations, public fascination, and the resultant impact on policy. As we navigate this intricate landscape, our inquiries into the cosmos must proceed with both intellectual rigor and ethical awareness, encouraging collaboration among scientists, ethicists, policymakers, and the public. Embracing this multidimensional approach will serve to enrich our understanding of not only the potential for alien terraforming but also the overarching mysteries that define our existence in this majestic universe. The collective undertaking positions us as seekers, prompting us to refine our quest for knowledge while respecting the unknown realms that lie beyond our comprehension.

6.3. Scientific Skepticism

The exploration of scientific skepticism within the scope of understanding and identifying signs of alien terraformation invites both challenge and introspection, as it underscores the complex nature of interpreting cosmic phenomena through rigorous scientific methodologies. Scientific skepticism operates as a vital mechanism within the scientific method, compelling researchers to question theories, scrutinize evidence, and uphold high standards of proof before reaching conclusions that might seem extraordinary. In the context of extraterrestrial terraformation—an inherently speculative domain— skepticism plays an indispensable role in ensuring rigorous inquiry and responsible interpretation of the data collected.

To appreciate the nuance of scientific skepticism, we must acknowledge that its foundations rest on systematic investigation and empirical evidence. When confronting claims of alien life or terraforming, scientists are tasked with establishing criteria that can differentiate between the potential markers of intelligent design and the natural geological processes that occur across celestial bodies. The prevailing question becomes: what constitutes sufficient evidence for claims that intelligent civilizations have successfully manipulated other worlds?

Consider, for instance, the debate surrounding Mars as a candidate for past or ongoing terraforming efforts. Researchers have detected mineral deposits, dry riverbeds, and other geological features that suggest the historical presence of liquid water—an essential ingredient for life as we understand it. Yet, the skepticism arises not from the potential of these findings, but rather from the interpretation of their significance. Without definitive proof of biological entities or deliberate modifications made by intelligent life, claims of terraforming risk falling prey to assumptions tinged with human bias. This calls for a disciplined and methodical approach to research, demanding rigorous evidence and replication of results.

Furthermore, skepticism extends to theorizing about the presence of extraterrestrial signals. The scientific community has engaged in extensive searches for signals indicative of intelligent life through initiatives like the Search for Extraterrestrial Intelligence (SETI). However, scientists must exercise caution in claiming a signal as evidence of alien engineering. For example, the WOW! Signal, detected in 1977, remains unexplained and has led to fervent speculation about its origins. While it sparked excitement, its ambiguous nature underscores how skeptical principles serve to guard against premature conclusions, reminding us that without confirmatory evidence, any claim stays in the realm of speculation.

In recent years, the advancement of observational technologies has only intensified the inquiry surrounding finding alien life and terraforming. Space telescopes and missions to exoplanets embody the potential for uncovering new worlds and signs of life. However, skepticism must accompany these advancements to ensure that claims of habitability are grounded in empirical measures rather than conjecture. For example, measuring atmospheric compositions in exoplanets might reveal interesting gas signatures, but careful study is required to distinguish between biological processes and abiotic phenomena that could yield similar results. Establishing frameworks for rigorous scientific testing fosters trust in discoveries that hold the potential for expansion in understanding.

While scientific skepticism is fundamental, it also bears the load of philosophical implications that invoke questions about humanity's outlook on existence. As the pursuit of knowledge progresses, it necessitates not only empirical scrutiny but also ethical reflections. As we seek to understand the possibility of terraformation or the existence of extraterrestrial life, we must grapple with the ethical responsibilities associated with such discoveries. How do we engage with potential forms of life that harbor their own ecosystems? What right do we have to interfere in environments, even hypothetically, given our historical missteps concerning ecological stewardship on Earth?

In practical terms, scientific skepticism informs the policies governing space exploration and the search for extraterrestrial intelligence. Conversations within the scientific community regarding the standards for evidence that validate extraordinary claims can reshape regulatory frameworks and treaties that guide interstellar exploration. The ethical principles that arise from discussions surrounding terraforming prompt ongoing dialogue about how humans might navigate future engagements with unknown worlds, advocating for accountability and responsibility.

In conclusion, scientific skepticism serves as the guardian of rigorous inquiry as we explore the mystifying potential of alien terraformation and the existence of extraterrestrial life. It encourages healthy questioning, precise investigations, and interpretation grounded in evidence. The interplay between skepticism and aspiration propels scientific understanding forward, while the philosophical dimensions ensure that we reflect on the ethical implications of our explorations. As we navigate the vast universe beyond our reach, the importance of skepticism in framing our inquiries cannot be overstated—a vital component in the pursuit of knowledge as well as our unwavering attempts to comprehend, appreciate, and respect the intricate tapestry of life across the cosmos.

6.4. Public and Media Response

The public and media response to the burgeoning field of alien terraformation is as multifaceted and dynamic as the scientific inquiries that fuel it. As discoveries in astrobiology, planetary science, and exoplanet studies continue to gain momentum, the imagination of the public has been stimulated, leading to heightened awareness, interest, and speculation about potential extraterrestrial life and the consequences of their activities. This subchapter explores the varied reactions and influences that such studies elicit from both the general public and media narratives, as well as the interplay between scientific endeavors and public perception.

At the heart of public engagement with alien terraformation lies an intrinsic curiosity about existence beyond our planet. Philosophical questions regarding the possibility of extraterrestrial life are often interwoven with broader existential considerations. Are we alone in the universe? If other life exists, what forms might it take, and how could it shape or manipulate its environments? The increasing visibility of projects like the Search for Extraterrestrial Intelligence (SETI) allows everyday citizens to participate in scientific discourse, fostering a sense of involvement in the shared quest to uncover cosmic secrets. Public interest often spikes during significant milestones—such as the detection of potentially habitable exoplanets or discoveries made by missions like Mars Rover—that serve as tangible reminders that the exploration of other worlds is ongoing and accessible.

The media plays a pivotal role in shaping and amplifying public discourse surrounding alien terraformation. Coverage of key scientific announcements often borders on sensationalism, capturing headlines with bold assertions about life on Mars, unusual atmospheric conditions on Venus, or groundbreaking discoveries of exoplanets in habitable zones. Such narratives, while driving interest and promoting scientific literacy, can also lead to misconceptions about the immediacy of contact or the likelihood of finding life. For instance, when the detection of methane on Mars was announced, media outlets rushed to speculate on the implications of potential biological origins, driving a narrative that suggests an immediate connection to alien life rather than grounding the results in careful scientific context. The ensuing excitement was palpable but also contained a whisper of disappointment as more nuanced interpretations emerged.

Public response is frequently influenced by portrayals of extraterrestrial life in popular culture, science fiction, and entertainment media. Films such as "Arrival," "Interstellar," and countless others have captivated audiences, often driving fascination with the possibility of contact and the ethical dilemmas associated with terraforming. These narratives visually and thematically explore the challenges, complexities, and moral considerations that accompany the prospect of altering environments and engaging with alien life. They often evoke emotions, sparking conversations about humanity's role in the universe and the responsibilities that come with technological advancement. As the lines between science and fiction blur, individuals may grapple with both the thrilling possibilities and ethical dilemmas presented by such portrayals.

Social media has emerged as an arena where discussions around alien terraformation thrive. Platforms like Twitter, Reddit, and Instagram enable rapid dissemination of scientific findings, fostering communities of enthusiasts, skeptics, and curious onlookers who engage deeply with ongoing discoveries. Users share content ranging from scientific articles and infographics to memes and speculative theories, creating a vibrant dialogue about our universe. In this dynamic environment, scientific misinterpretations can spread quickly, as can debates among those who champion or criticize the likelihood of terraforming endeavors. Hashtags like #TerraformingMars or #AlienLife foster a sense of community but may also amplify confusion if not accompanied by science-based discourse.

As public enthusiasm for the discussion of alien terraformation grows, so too does the responsibility of scientists to communicate their findings effectively and accurately. The scientific community is faced with the challenge of bridging knowledge gaps and providing clear information to quell misinformation while simultaneously retaining the public's interest and curiosity. Engaging communication efforts, including outreach events, educational programs, and accessible reports from institutions like NASA, play a vital role in demystifying scientific concepts. Creating clear narratives around complex phenomena is paramount, ensuring that public fascination translates into informed interest that appreciates the nuanced reality of astrobiological research.

Ultimately, the public and media response surrounding alien terraformation serves as a reflection of our collective aspirations and anxieties regarding life beyond Earth. The urgent questions echoing through these discussions—What does it mean to be human within a cosmic network? How should we proceed if contact is made? —invite contemplation and discourse that bridges scientific inquiry and philosophical reflection. The resulting dialog heralds a new era where public engagement in the scientific process not only enhances understanding but shapes the trajectories of research and knowledge as humanity endeavors to understand its place in the vast tapestry of the universe. Thus, the interplay between public interest, media narratives, and scientific integrity forms a vital framework within which the debate surrounding alien terraformation unfolds, demanding continual evaluation and reflection as we navigate our uncharted cosmic neighborhood.

6.5. Impact on Science Policies

The rapid evolution of science policies in response to emerging concepts surrounding alien terraformation illustrates how human understanding and ambition intersect with the ethical challenges of cosmic exploration. Policymakers grapple with a landscape intricately woven with scientific discovery, technological advancements, and ethical responsibilities. As humanity inches closer to the possibility of encountering extraterrestrial life or demonstrating the capability for terraforming, the frameworks governing our interactions with the cosmos must adapt to reflect the complexities of these aspirations.

In addressing the impact on science policies, it is imperative to first underscore the inherent responsibilities of governance as new discoveries arise. The potential for detecting signs of alien life—and possible terraforming activities—creates an obligation for sustainable practices in the face of newfound opportunities. Policymakers must engage with the scientific community to develop frameworks that prioritize responsible exploration, echoing the existing protocols governing planetary protection. These protocols are crucial in ensuring that efforts to investigate extraterrestrial environments do not inadvertently harm or disrupt existing ecosystems—whether they harbor life or not.

The ethical dimension complicates the formulation of these policies significantly. How do we safeguard potential extraterrestrial ecosystems? What rights do hypothetical alien life forms possess? A comprehensive policy approach must address these questions while integrating international perspectives, recognizing that space remains a collective heritage of all humanity. The establishment of treaties and agreements, akin to existing frameworks such as the Outer Space Treaty, will foster a cooperative global framework guiding collective space exploration efforts. Effective collaboration will empower diverse stakeholders—scientists, ethicists, policymakers, and the public —to engage in a shared vision of responsible exploration that honors the values of stewardship and respect for other worlds.

Emerging technologies further influence the trajectory of science policies related to terraforming and extraterrestrial life. The capabilities of advanced telescopes, spectrometric analysis, and radio astronomy reshape our understanding of the universe while simultaneously introducing new methods for identifying potential signs of terraformation. Policymakers must ensure that these technologies are cultivated within ethical parameters, striving to strike a balance between innovation and caution. As leaders recognize the ultimate impact of these scientific advancements, they should actively consider public engagement initiatives that promote transparency and foster trust, empowering citizens to navigate the intricacies of cosmic exploration alongside policy decisions.

Moreover, the question of responsibility extends to the potential consequences of actions taken during terraforming endeavors. In contemplating the long-term implications of altering an extraterrestrial environment—whether by human hands or those of advanced civilizations—policies must contemplate the risk of unintended environmental consequences, ecological disruptions, and ethical dilemmas that may arise. This necessitates ongoing dialogues rooted in interdisciplinary research, where scientists work collaboratively with policymakers and ethicists to evaluate the ramifications of our expeditions beyond Earth.

Investment in education and outreach also emerges as a critical component of policy frameworks surrounding alien terraformation. As the public's interest in space exploration and the possibilities of terraforming grows, policies should prioritize educational initiatives that promote scientific literacy and inspire responsible engagement with the cosmos. Therefore, heightened awareness of the ethical implications and societal impacts of terraformation serves to cultivate a generation of informed citizens who can actively participate in critical discussions about humanity's role in shaping life on other worlds.

In conclusion, the impact on science policies related to alien terraformation must be characterized by a balance of scientific rigor, ethical responsibility, and public engagement. Policymakers face the pivotal challenge of evolving frameworks that embrace new scientific discoveries, engage with the complexities of our changing understanding of cosmic life, and uphold a commitment to stewardship and integrity. As humanity pushes the boundaries of exploration and comprehension, novel policies will allow us to honor the inherent interconnectedness of existence while preparing for a future that may reveal the mysteries lying dormant among the stars. The unfolding journey toward understanding alien terraformation necessitates a hybrid approach that reflects both our ambitions and responsibilities, guiding humanity in navigating the intersection between scientific discovery and the ethical imperatives of a shared universe.

7. Theoretical Models of Alien Ecosystems

7.1. Potential Biosphere Adjustments

The universe is a complex and finely tuned system, where life—however fragile—might find a foothold in the most unexpected places. Our understanding of potential biosphere adjustments in extraterrestrial environments is still a developing field, but it offers a fascinating glimpse into how alien worlds could be modified to support life as we know it or even introduce entirely new ecosystems.

At the core of any biosphere adjustment lies the science of ecology, intertwined with astrobiology and planetary science. When envisioning how a biosphere might be adjusted, we draw from a myriad of scientific theories and principles that underline the balance required for life to thrive. The process is dynamic, necessitating an understanding of local conditions and the intricate interactions between different life forms and their environments. In this context, the prospect of biosphere adjustments encompasses a range of possibilities, from climate modification and atmospheric engineering to the transplantation of flora and fauna engineered for alien conditions.

The starting point for any biosphere adjustment is understanding the existing conditions of the target planet, including its atmosphere, temperature, geological makeup, and the presence of water. For instance, Mars, often touted as a prime candidate for terraforming, presents a barren landscape, characterized by a thin atmosphere primarily composed of carbon dioxide and surface temperatures too cold to support liquid water. Adjusting its biosphere would therefore require the introduction of elements capable of transforming these conditions into something more hospitable for life. One theoretical approach involves artificially thickening the atmosphere by releasing greenhouse gases, such as methane or perfluorocarbons (PFCs), to trap heat and raise surface temperatures, promoting the presence of liquid water.

Incorporating engineered flora and fauna into this envisioned Martian biosphere adjustment could accelerate the terraforming process.

Scientists might develop extremophile organisms, microorganisms that thrive in harsh conditions, to play crucial roles in creating a sustainable ecosystem. These organisms could facilitate nutrient cycling, enrich soil, and process atmospheric gases to produce oxygen. The subsequent introduction of terrestrial plants genetically modified to survive in high levels of carbon dioxide and with lower water requirements could further support ecosystem stability, paving the way for herbivores and, eventually, higher trophic levels to establish themselves.

Another example of potential biosphere adjustments can be found in the Venusian context. While current conditions on Venus present a significant challenge due to extreme heat and crushing pressure, concepts for altering its atmosphere involve reducing carbon dioxide levels and introducing thermophilic organisms capable of surviving in acidic conditions. Innovations such as solar shades positioned in orbit to cool the planet, coupled with biotechnologically enhanced plants that convert carbon dioxide to oxygen, could initiate a series of changes resulting in a more hospitable environment.

When considering extraterrestrial biosphere adjustments, the potential interventions must also take into account the ecological principles governing biocompatibility and interdependence. The introduction of a new life form must be carefully calibrated to avoid unintended consequences that could arise from introducing foreign species into a novel ecosystem. Detailed modeling and simulations would be crucial steps in anticipating how organisms interact with one another, their environment, and any existing (or previously existing) life forms that may inhabit the new biosphere.

Given our understanding of terrestrial ecosystems, a holistic approach to biosphere adjustments would prioritize creating diversity to ensure resilience against fluctuations and disturbances. This diversity may involve various trophic levels, incorporating producers, consumers, and decomposers that work synergistically to maintain ecological balance. The design of donor species might be informed by existing organisms on Earth, yet modified to thrive within the unique environmental conditions of the target world, establishing a functional framework capable of supporting a new biosphere.

Furthermore, establishing a sustainable biosphere requires an understanding of how technological implementations can contribute to long-term stability. For instance, energy systems—including solar batteries, biofuels, or engineered bioreactors—could generate energy to power biological processes, allowing human settlers or terraforming automated systems to sustain life over extended periods. Developing sensors and monitoring systems to assess environmental changes in real-time can help assess the success of biosphere adjustments, providing feedback and allowing for adaptive iterations if conditions deviate from the desired outcomes.

Adaptive strategies might serve to mitigate potential risks—ensuring that as an atmosphere is being engineered and species introduced, there is a responsive mechanism to address any harmful ecological consequences. Continuous assessment of soil chemistry, atmospheric composition, and biological interactions can facilitate the necessary fine-tuning throughout the terraforming process, ensuring that the newly architected biosphere can flourish.

In essence, the potential for biosphere adjustments on extraterrestrial worlds encapsulates the biological, ecological, and technological breakthroughs humanity may achieve. Moving toward the realization of these adjustments requires not only scientific ingenuity but also deep ethical reflections on the responsibilities we bear as custodians of other worlds. As we explore the cosmos, adjusting biospheres to foster environments where life can thrive must be approached with respect and foresight—an endeavor rich with promise that resonates deeply with our innate desire for exploration, understanding, and connection across the universe. The quest to alter worlds transcends mere scientific ambition; it embodies a celebration of the inherent interconnectedness shared by all life and reflects humanity's broader purpose within the cosmic tapestry.

7.2. Adaptive Flora and Fauna

In diverse ecosystems, adaptability is often the linchpin of survival, evolution, and ecological balance. This principle holds true whether we discuss Earth's own flora and fauna, or we explore the potential for life on extraterrestrial worlds. Adaptive flora and fauna, as they might exist in the context of alien terraformation, present fascinating possibilities that reflect the intricate interplay of biology, environment, and technology. In contemplating these adaptive beings, we examine the underlying mechanisms that allow life to thrive in changing conditions, envisioning innovative solutions that could be employed to support the establishment of extraterrestrial ecosystems.

At the forefront of adaptive flora and fauna lies the ability of organisms to respond to their surroundings, a feature amplified further in extraterrestrial contexts where environmental conditions can be drastically different from those on Earth. For instance, if we consider the prospect of engineering plant species suited for Martian soil, scientists might explore genetic modifications to enhance resistance to high radiation levels and extreme temperatures. Such adaptations could encompass thicker cuticles to limit water loss, specialized cellular structures to mitigate the effects of solar radiation, and metabolic pathways that allow for efficient nutrient absorption in less than optimal conditions.

Moreover, potential flora might employ unique photosynthetic mechanisms, allowing them to utilize the dim light available on other planets. For example, the introduction of synthetic molecules akin to those used by certain extremophiles on Earth—organisms that thrive in extreme conditions—could grant these extraterrestrial plants a broader spectrum of light absorption. This biological innovation could serve as a cornerstone for establishing viable plant life on alien worlds, promoting the creation of breathable atmospheres and fostering nurturing habitats for higher-level organisms.

The same principles can be applied to the development of adaptive fauna, particularly when considering the physiological and behavioral mechanisms that allow for survival in challenging environments. In contexts such as Mars, where atmospheric pressure is low and temperatures are frigid, hypothetical terrestrial animals may exhibit adaptations such as enhanced insulating layers, including specialized fur or blubber-like structures to retain body warmth. Additionally, physiological adaptations to respiratory systems could enable these creatures to thrive on the limited supplies of oxygen produced by engineered flora, creating symbiotic relationships essential to sustaining life in newly terraformed ecosystems.

Moreover, the possibilities for adaptive fauna extend beyond Earth-derived models, inviting exploration of entirely novel life forms engineered specifically to inhabit alien environments. The manipulation of DNA could yield unique organisms that thrive in varying atmospheric compositions, with some capable of processing carbon dioxide as a primary energy source or utilizing other local resources effectively. The imagined success of such ventures hinges upon a thorough understanding of the underlying genetic foundations that dictate adaptability and resilience in diverse ecological contexts.

As we design and implement adaptive ecosystems on extraterrestrial planets, it becomes crucial to recognize the interdependence of all life forms. The success of a newly engineered biosphere hinges upon the ability of flora and fauna to coexist in an intricate web of relationships that support mutual survival. This principle calls for astute attention to species interactions, nutrient cycling, and the establishment of ecological networks. For example, introducing herbivores that graze on engineered plants could promote optimal growth and nutrient cycling while creating niches for higher trophic levels to thrive, ultimately fostering a rich tapestry of biodiversity.

Incorporating ethological considerations—understanding the behaviors of organisms—in the design of adaptive fauna will further enhance the persistence of these ecosystems. Training organisms to adapt to novel cues, migration patterns, and social structures can lead to enhanced survival rates amidst competing pressures and unpredictability within alien environments. The observation and modeling of existing species on Earth could provide insights into how certain behaviors could be nurtured or adapted for extraterrestrial settings, further promoting coexistence in engineered ecosystems.

As stakeholders across scientific disciplines—biologists, engineers, ethicists, and policymakers—collaborate to create adaptive flora and fauna, they must also consider potential ethical implications. The development and introduction of engineered organisms demand reflection on the long-term consequences of altering ecosystems, including the challenge of ensuring that newly established life does not inadvertently disrupt existing biomes or ecosystems. Integrating ethical frameworks within this process will prove essential in navigating the delicate balance between innovation and stewardship.

In summary, the exploration of adaptive flora and fauna offers a tantalizing glimpse into the potential for life beyond Earth. By leveraging the principles of adaptability and interdependence, scientists can engineer organisms poised to thrive in unfamiliar environments, enabling the creation of vibrant ecosystems on alien worlds. As we pursue terraforming efforts, the thoughtful consideration of ecological interactions and ethical dimensions will remain foundational to ensuring that both flora and fauna flourish, cultivating resilience and harmony within the cosmic tapestry that defines our universe. With careful design and respect for the complexities of life, we may aspire to create thriving alien ecosystems—expanding the definition of life and existence as we forge ahead into an exciting future among the stars.

7.3. Hypothetical Biomes

As humanity's imagination stretches into the cosmos, the concept of hypothetical biomes provokes profound curiosity and speculation. Within this exploration lies the potential for diverse ecosystems that could emerge on various celestial bodies, shaped either through natural processes or deliberate interventions by advanced civilizations. These hypothetical biomes might serve as potential habitats for life, embodying a fusion of ecological principles, evolutionary adaptability, and technological ingenuity.

Envisioning hypothetical biomes begins with an understanding of the fundamental requirements for life: energy, water, and essential nutrients. Each potential biome must navigate unique environmental challenges dictated by the climate, atmosphere, and surface conditions of its host planet or moon. For instance, Mars represents a compelling candidate for terraforming efforts, harboring potential biospheres that could arise from the current barren landscape. Imagine a Martian biome characterized by salt-loving organisms, capable of surviving in highly saline and arid conditions, with adaptations that allow them to extract necessary nutrients from the soil while resisting radiation—a prototype ecosystem that arises from careful engineering and selective evolution.

In considering the potential biomes of distant exoplanets, scientists must examine the characteristics of those worlds, such as their proximity to their stars, atmospheric composition, and surface conditions. Take, for example, an oceanic moon orbiting a gas giant. Such a moon, rich in subsurface liquid water and dynamic geological activity, could give rise to a unique ecosystem that thrives in the depths—a biosphere reliant on chemosynthetic organisms that derive energy from minerals in hydrothermal vents. These organisms would form the basis of a food web, supporting larger fauna that could adapt to the extreme pressures and temperatures found in the ocean depths.

Moreover, the possibilities for plant and animal life in extraterrestrial environments bring forth imaginative scenarios. Hypothetical biomes may showcase flora with unique adaptations to low light conditions, owing to the distance from their star or the dense atmosphere. Vegetation could emerge with reflective surfaces designed to maximize light absorption, while also functioning in ecological partnerships with microorganisms that fix atmospheric nitrogen and assist in nutrient cycling.

The integration of technological solutions into the cultivation of these biomes further expands the scope of what could be achieved. Advanced biotechnological innovations, such as genetically engineered organisms tailored to survive in extreme environments, would facilitate the establishment of robust ecosystems. Utilizing synthetic biology, these organisms could be equipped with resilience traits—capable of repairing cellular damage from radiation, or even utilizing carbon dioxide as a primary energy source, thus creating a self-sustaining cycle of life.

The hypothetical biomes extend beyond mere speculation; they demand meticulous planning and interdisciplinary cooperation. To implement such ecological projects, scientists must combine knowledge from various fields—including ecology, genetics, atmospheric science, and engineering—to construct sustainable systems. This collaborative ethos can ensure the successful integration of different organisms into robust biomes, fostering resilient and adaptive ecosystems that can endure fluctuations and environmental changes.

As we probe deeper into the construction of these hypothetical biomes, ethical considerations also surface. Upon introducing Earth-based organisms into alien environments—whether through terraforming or genetic engineering—the potential consequences must be deliberated with care. Could the introduction of engineered flora disrupt existing ecosystems? How might interactions between these organisms and hypothetical native lifeforms play out? It becomes increasingly apparent that understanding interspecies interactions is paramount to ethical engagement in planetary engineering.

In conclusion, the exploration of hypothetical biomes opens avenues for profound inquiry into the nature of life, potential ecosystems, and the challenges of extraterrestrial habitation. Each biome embodies the intersection of creativity, science, and ethics, demanding a thoughtful approach as humanity navigates its path toward cosmic exploration. The beauty of these hypothetical structures lies in their reflection of our aspirations—crafted not only for survival but for the flourishing of life itself, wherever it may be found among the stars. As we stand on the cusp of uncharted frontiers, these biomes encapsulate the potential for discovery, reverberating with the prospect of life beyond Earth and the unique ecological possibilities awaiting our exploration.

7.4. Sustainable Technological Implementations

In the contemporary quest for knowledge about the cosmos and the prospects of extraterrestrial life, sustainable technological implementations emerge as a critical theme intertwining scientific innovation and ethical stewardship. As humanity's capabilities evolve, so does the responsibility to wield technology in a manner that promotes ecological balance and sustainability, particularly as we consider the intricate mechanics of terraforming other worlds.

At the heart of sustainable technological implementations lies the integration of renewable energy systems. The lessons learned from Earth's ecological challenges call for innovative solutions that minimize environmental impact while maximizing resource efficiency. For instance, harnessing solar, wind, or geothermal energy in the terraforming process could provide the necessary power to run large-scale atmospheric engineering projects. By deploying solar farms or wind turbines on extraterrestrial surfaces, advanced civilizations might accumulate clean energy without depleting local resources. Such strategies reflect an understanding of the importance of renewable energy in ensuring the longevity and stability of engineered biospheres.

Moreover, the utilization of closed-loop ecological systems is paramount. In synthetic biology applications, the design of self-sustaining ecosystems would entail creating networks where waste products from some organisms serve as nutrients for others. This approach mirrors the delicate balance found in Earth's ecosystems, where species interactions underpin the cycles of matter and energy. For instance, introducing specially designed microorganisms that can breakdown pollutants into harmless byproducts would promote environmental health in newly terraformed settings. The resulting biosphere could achieve resilience against ecological disturbances while fostering biodiversity that echoes the richness found in Earth's ecosystems.

Water management also plays an essential role in sustainable technological implementations. For terraforming initiatives, methods of sourcing, recycling, and conserving water must be meticulously planned to address the specific needs of the newly introduced flora and fauna. Innovative solutions such as atmospheric water harvesting —capturing moisture from the air—and advanced irrigation systems modeled on Earth's most efficient agricultural practices could prove invaluable. These strategies would not only support plant growth but also maintain the delicate balance of the newly engineered ecosystems, mitigating risks of drought or soil degradation.

Furthermore, advances in biotechnology offer exciting prospects for developing adaptive species that contribute to sustainability in transformed environments. Genetic modifications could focus on enhancing the resilience of Earth-derived crops to withstand harsh climates, limited water supplies, or elevated levels of carbon dioxide. As these engineered species establish themselves, they would become crucial components of the terraformed biosphere—helping stabilize soils, regulate climate, and enrich local ecosystems through their metabolic processes.

In the context of extraterrestrial environments, sustainable technological implementations must also consider the ethical implications of genomic interventions. The potential effects of introducing engineered species into alien biospheres necessitate careful examination of population dynamics and ecological interactions. Technologies must be developed in tandem with monitoring systems that assess environmental impacts, ensuring that unforeseen consequences are swiftly addressed. By employing rigorous ecological assessments and engaging in adaptive management strategies, terraforming efforts can resonate with a commitment to environmental stewardship.

Moreover, policy frameworks formulated to govern terraforming practices will shape the balanced relationship between technology and sustainability. As we strive for international cooperation in space exploration, protocols must be established for responsible resource usage, ecosystem monitoring, and the prevention of unintended contamination of alien worlds. International agreements could encapsulate a collective commitment to utilizing technology responsibly while fostering sustainable practices as a cornerstone of galactic exploration and colonization.

The pursuit of harnessing sustainable technologies in terraforming alien worlds is ultimately rooted in a broader vision of cohabitation and mutual respect for life in all its forms. As we advance our technological capabilities, the imperative to ensure that our interventions respect the integrity of any existing ecosystems becomes paramount. In navigating the complex relationships among species, habitats, and the technologies we create, we invite a new paradigm where life—both terrestrial and extraterrestrial—can thrive harmoniously.

In closing, the concept of sustainable technological implementations serves as a guiding principle in the exploration of extraterrestrial terraformation. Balancing human ambition with ecological responsibility will ensure that as we journey into the cosmos, we do so not simply as conquerors of nature, but as mindful custodians, dedicated to leaving an indelible mark of stewardship on the worlds we seek to understand and transform.

7.5. Interdependence in Alien Ecosystems

Interdependence in alien ecosystems raises profound questions about the intricate relationships that could exist among the myriad life forms on extraterrestrial worlds. As we contemplate the possibility of terraforming and the establishment of new biospheres, understanding how organisms adapt, interact, and flourish in their environments becomes paramount. Weaving together principles of ecology, evolutionary biology, and astrobiology, we can envision ecosystems on alien planets that—while seemingly foreign—may resonate with the interconnectedness that characterizes life on Earth.

At the forefront of interdependent alien ecosystems lies the dynamic relationship between various species and their environments. Within any ecosystem, organisms rely on one another for food, shelter, nutrient cycling, and various environmental functions. Picture a hypothetical ecosystem on Mars—engineered plants designed to extract nitrogen from the atmosphere may exist alongside nitrogen-fixing microorganisms in the soil. Together, they would collaborate to create fertile ground, providing a harmonious setting for the growth of more complex organisms, such as herbivorous species that thrive on the nutrient-rich flora. This intricate web of interdependence echoes Earth's ecosystems, where the balance between species is essential for existence.

The adaptation of organisms to extreme conditions on alien worlds also deserves attention. For example, if life were to develop on Venus, where temperatures reach scorching heights, we could envision organisms evolving with specialized anatomy and biochemistry. These extremophiles might possess unique proteins that function at elevated temperatures or develop protective mechanisms against high atmospheric pressure. An interdependent community of sulfur-metabolizing bacteria could share their products with plant analogs, leading to a thriving ecosystem that can withstand conditions far more extreme than those on Earth.

When contemplating the composition of these alien ecosystems, the role of primary producers, consumers, and decomposers will be fundamental. Just like on Earth, primary producers—whether they are plant-like or microorganism-based—are likely the backbone of any biosphere, harnessing energy from their surroundings. These organisms may utilize various energy sources, such as light, thermal radiation, or even chemical energy gleaned from mineral-rich environments. When designing sustainable alien ecosystems, the interface between producers and consumers should be closely considered, as the successful transfer of energy across trophic levels shapes the overall resilience of the ecosystem.

The intriguing potential for symbiotic relationships further enhances our understanding of interdependence in these ecosystems. Imagine earth-like creatures evolving to become symbiotic partners with engineered flora. Such organisms could exchange resources, whether it be nutrients, energy, or protection. In the context of a terraformed Mars, we might witness a collaboration between hardy desert plants designed to stabilize soil and small burrowing animals that aerate the soil, scattering seeds as they forage. Together, these organisms could reshape their environment, promoting the emergence of a diverse and thriving biosphere.

Creating adaptable organisms that exhibit beneficial traits in alien ecosystems will hinge on meticulous selection and engineering processes. Through the principles of directed evolution, scientists might strive to craft organisms with specific capabilities that allow them to respond positively to environmental shifts, enhancing their interdependence within the broader ecosystem. By harnessing genetic engineering or synthetic biology, organisms could be designed not only to withstand the prevailing conditions of an alien world but also to contribute actively to the system's stability. This could pave the way for creating resilient ecosystems that could face challenges such as climate instability or invasive alien species.

The ethical implications of establishing such interdependent systems cannot be overstated. As humanity moves closer to terraforming and engaging with alien ecosystems, deep questions arise about our responsibilities as architects of these new worlds. The introduction of Earth life into extraterrestrial environments necessitates careful consideration of potential ecological disruptions, particularly concerning the preservation of unknown native life forms that may exist in these settings. Exploration and terraforming endeavours must echo principles of stewardship, where the goal is not merely to dominate but to foster collaboration among diverse life forms.

Additionally, understanding how to monitor the health and functionality of these interdependent ecosystems is vital. Implementing technology-driven research, such as biosensors and automated monitoring systems, may serve to assess ecosystem dynamics as they evolve. By continuously gathering data on populations, nutrient flows, and energy exchanges, researchers could gain valuable insights into the status of these newly engineered ecosystems. Regular assessments will equip scientists to make informed decisions regarding interventions needed to maintain stability and promote resilience amidst the uncertainties of alien environments.

In summation, the exploration of interdependence in alien ecosystems presents a fascinating inquiry, intricately woven into the more extensive tapestry of humanity's ambitions to terraform and understand alien worlds. The collaborative relationships that may manifest among organisms, environments, and technological interventions can profoundly reshape our understanding of life beyond Earth. As we tread this path, it is imperative to acknowledge the ethical responsibilities that accompany our endeavors, ensuring that we approach cosmic exploration on a foundation of respect, cooperation, and sustainability. While we envision the rich potential for life in alien biospheres, we must remain committed to exploring our interconnectedness with life—both Earth-bound and cosmic—across the majestic universe we seek to understand.

8. Cosmic Architecture: Sculpting Worlds

8.1. Asteroids and Comets in Terraforming

In the quest to understand the intersection of asteroids and comets with the process of terraforming, we are drawn into a fascinating arena filled with potential and implications. These celestial bodies, often viewed as mere remnants of the early solar system, provide tantalizing opportunities for material enhancement and ecological engineering beyond Earth. As we explore their roles, we begin to perceive asteroids and comets not just as obstacles or remnants of cosmic history but as valuable resources and catalysts in the ambitious endeavor of terraforming other worlds.

The foundation of using asteroids and comets in terraforming stems from their composition. Many of these bodies are rich in essential minerals and volatiles, such as water ice, carbon dioxide, nitrogen, and metals—elements critical for creating and sustaining a life-supporting environment. For planets like Mars, where existing resources are scarce, targeting these bodies presents a pragmatic approach to acquiring materials necessary for creating an atmosphere conducive to life. Imagine rolling asteroids into Martian orbit or delivering cometary remnants to the surface, initiating the infusion of vital chemicals that could thicken the atmosphere and introduce water to arid terrains.

This process of resource acquisition involves not only the physical reallocation of material but also advanced methods of propulsion and directed impact. Theoretical models suggest the development of technologies capable of diverting asteroids from their natural trajectories and directing them to desired locations. By utilizing ion engines, nuclear propulsion systems, or gravitational assists, we could orchestrate the journey of asteroids and comets, guiding them into calculated orbits or allowing them to impact surfaces with precision to maximize the beneficial effects of their mineral deposits.

Asteroids and comets also serve potential roles in the development of early biospheres. For instance, organic compounds found in carbonaceous chondrites—meteorites originating from asteroids—could yield the building blocks of life. If transported to a barren world, these bodies could instigate a chain reaction of biogenesis, providing essential genetic material and harnessing conditions heightened by brand new atmospheres.

The introduction of volatiles from these bodies can be a game-changer in terraforming efforts. Water ice from comets, when delivered to planetary surfaces, could initiate the formation of rivers, lakes, or oceans, catalyzing a series of ecological processes that would pave the way for future biological development. Imagine the transformation of the Martian landscape with the arrival of these icy giants, flooding lowlands and encouraging the establishment of organisms that thrive in moist environments. The resultant ecosystems could not only stabilize temperatures through evaporative cooling but also contribute to a regenerative cycle of moisture and nutrients, enriching the environment over time.

Additionally, the gravitational nuances of an asteroid or comet interacting with a planet can yield transformative benefits. These bodies, upon impact, could generate heat from kinetic energy, potentially initiating volcanic activity or hydrothermal systems that enrich local geology. Imagine an asteroid crashing into a desolate Martian plain, creating a caldera filled with water and rich minerals, which subsequently fosters microbial life within a localized ecosystem. Such scenarios highlight how asteroids and comets can trigger environmental changes that might otherwise take eons to develop naturally.

Nonetheless, the utilization of asteroids and comets raises significant ethical and practical considerations. The implication of altering celestial bodies and their trajectories demands meticulous planning, particularly regarding the potential consequences of introducing new materials to environments that may already possess their own delicate balances. Furthermore, the unknown presence of existing life forms—whether microbial or otherwise—that may inhabit these bodies invites profound questions about the rights of alien life.

In the broader context of planetary engineering, coordination across international scientific communities will become paramount. Policies must be agreed upon regarding how to utilize these resources ethically and sustainably, ensuring that the extraterrestrial ecosystems we create respect any form of life that could be impacted.

Engagement with international partnerships will drive the accumulation of knowledge served by our technological endeavors, reinforcing the shared commitment to responsible exploration and preservation of potential extraterrestrial environments.

In conclusion, asteroids and comets represent gateways to the cosmos, holding the keys to unlocking the potential for terraforming and life beyond our terrestrial home. As we continue to unravel the mysteries of the universe, these celestial bodies can catalyze extraordinary transformations, allowing us to craft environments suited for thriving ecosystems. By navigating the challenges and promises of utilizing asteroids and comets, humanity stands poised to embark on a new chapter of exploration and engagement with the cosmic realm, channeling curiosity and innovation into sustainable practices that honor both our aspirations and the delicate fabric of the universe. The journey into deep space remains a collaboration between technology, ethics, and nature, as we sculpt worlds and coalesce connections that transcend the confines of our own existence.

8.2. Orbital Alterations

In the realm of terraforming and the manipulation of extraterrestrial environments, orbital alterations represent a compelling avenue of inquiry, blending astrophysical principles with speculative engineering. The notion of altering the orbits of celestial bodies, particularly planets and their moons, introduces a captivating dimension to the conversation about how we might facilitate habitable conditions on worlds that were once inhospitable. At its core, this concept encompasses gravitational mechanics, advanced technology, and the potential long-term influence of directed alterations on planetary ecosystems.

The foundation of orbital alterations rests on our understanding of celestial mechanics—the branch of physics that governs the motion of celestial objects under the influence of gravitational forces. When considering the alteration of a planet's orbit, one must take into account not only its current trajectory but also the effects of gravitational interactions with other celestial bodies, such as moons or nearby planets. For example, if we consider Mars, changing its orbit to place it within a more favorable distance from the Sun could increase temperatures and bolster the presence of liquid water—two essential factors for supporting life.

The implementation of orbital alterations, however, presents significant challenges. Such endeavors would require monumental engineering efforts—potentially utilizing an array of large-scale kinetic impacts or even the deployment of advanced propulsion systems capable of delivering precise energy outputs to alter trajectories. Spacecraft equipped with propulsion mechanisms could be constructed to navigate alongside a target planet, perhaps employing gravity assists to strategically change its course. This monumental task would necessitate unprecedented levels of coordination, technological innovation, and precision engineering.

Moreover, the implications of orbital alterations extend into the domain of ecological balance. When a planet's orbit is adjusted, the climatic consequences could be far-reaching. Local seasons might shift, atmospheric conditions could change drastically, and resource availability may be affected in unpredictable ways. The resulting environmental flux would especially influence the hypothetical life forms being engineered to thrive in newly established ecosystems. Therefore, any changes to a planet's orbit must be accompanied by proactive measures that take into account the resilience of designed ecosystems against these sudden shifts, allowing for adaptable flora and fauna that can withstand novel conditions.

Beyond Mars, the exploration of orbital alterations dovetails intricately with our understanding of moons—specifically, how they might interact with planetary bodies they orbit. The relationships between planets and their moons can tie into longer-term climate stability and ecological processes. For example, the stabilizing effect that Earth's moon has on its axial tilt contributes to comparatively moderate climates, fostering a balance within terrestrial ecosystems. If we take this knowledge to other celestial bodies, altering a moon's orbit could significantly impact the climate of the planet it orbits, affecting tidal patterns, stabilizing axial tilt, and ultimately shaping the environmental conditions conducive to developing life.

The hypothetical orbital alteration of moons opens up potential avenues for terraforming efforts as well. Consider an exploration of Europa, one of Jupiter's moons, which harbors a subsurface ocean beneath its icy crust. By modifying Europa's orbit, we could potentially increase heat from tidal forces—encouraging geological activity or creating conditions favorable for sustaining life in its ocean. A successful manipulation of such orbital dynamics would manifest profound implications for astrobiology, highlighting the potential interactions between gravity, orbital mechanics, and life-sustaining processes.

Many factors come into play when discussing the ethics of orbital alterations. The ramifications of manipulating the orbits of celestial bodies raise significant philosophical questions: What rights do we have to alter other worlds? Would such alterations interfere with natural processes that may already be nurturing nascent forms of life? As humanity engages with the cosmos, it becomes essential to employ frameworks of stewardship that respect the integrity of celestial environments, ensuring that our ambitions do not result in irrevocable harm to potential ecosystems, unknown life forms, or celestial phenomena.

In conclusion, orbital alterations present an enthralling aspect of our exploration of terraforming possibilities. By contemplating the mechanics of celestial interactions, the engineering challenges ahead, and the ethical nuances involved, we can envision a future where humanity not only reaches for the stars but actively shapes them. The journey ahead beckons a synthesis of scientific rigor, technological innovation, and a deep commitment to responsible stewardship —a balancing act that may ultimately lead to the flourishing of life in the most unexpected corners of the universe. As we chart these ambitious paths through orbits and beyond, we embrace the profound interconnectedness that defines our quest to understand our place in the cosmos.

8.3. Volcanic Activity Management

In the context of managing volcanic activity, it's essential to draw parallels between Earth-based geological processes and the broader implications of the terraforming initiative, particularly when considering the potential for volcanic forces to both facilitate and hinder efforts to create habitable environments on other celestial bodies. Volcanic activity plays a crucial role in shaping planetary landscapes, influencing atmospheric composition, and potentially guiding the quest for sustainable ecosystems.

Volcanic activity on a planet can serve multiple functions in the terraforming process. For example, volcanoes are natural sources of greenhouse gases, such as carbon dioxide and sulfur dioxide, which are critical for thickening atmospheres and creating conditions necessary for maintaining liquid water on a planet's surface. The eruption of gases and minerals can act as a catalyst for developing an Earth-like environment, particularly on planets like Mars, which currently hosts a tenuous atmosphere. By strategically managing volcanic sites, scientists could aim to harness eruptions, directing volcanic gas emissions to build a thicker atmosphere and raise surface temperatures, contributing to the long-term stability of newly engineered environments.

However, the potential for uncontrolled volcanic activity also poses significant risks. Excessive volcanic eruptions could lead to climate destabilization, with ash and gases blocking sunlight and creating cooling effects that negate ongoing terraforming efforts. The prevention of catastrophic volcanic events becomes paramount in planning sustainable interventions. Advanced monitoring systems utilizing satellite observations and ground-based sensors could be deployed to track volcanic activity in real time, enabling scientists to promptly assess risks and develop responsive strategies.

Crucially, understanding the geological history of a planet is vital in predicting volcanic behaviors and their subsequent impact on terraforming initiatives. For instance, analyzing past volcanic activity through geological surveys may reveal patterns of eruptions, dormant periods, and the potential for supereruptions—massive volcanic events capable of expelling vast quantities of ash and gas. Such studies inform the management of volcanic resources and direct efforts to mitigate hazards, ensuring that the terraforming process proceeds in a secure and calculated manner.

The management of volcanic activity must also consider ethical implications, particularly the rights of any existing microbial life that may inhabit a planet's subterranean environments. If evidence suggests that microbial organisms exist in extreme conditions beneath a planet's surface, then terraforming efforts must be designed to preserve these unique ecosystems, avoiding disruption while balancing the introduction of new life forms from Earth. Developing ethical protocols surrounding volcanic resource management will ensure that the presence of microbial life is safeguarded, reflecting a responsible stewardship approach to planetary interventions.

Furthermore, the interplay of energy sources generated by volcanic activity can contribute to terraforming through geothermal energy exploitation. By harnessing the heat from volcanic eruptions, advanced civilizations could facilitate energy production, powering technological initiatives designed to create sustainable ecosystems. This approach reflects a dual benefit of harnessing geothermal power while simultaneously utilizing volcanoes as modification tools.

In summary, volcanic activity management emerges as a critical component in the broader narrative of alien terraforming efforts. By understanding the dynamics of volcanic processes, harnessing their potential benefits, and mitigating associated risks, we position ourselves to create and maintain habitable ecosystems on distant worlds. This journey, however, must be undertaken with sensitivity to existing life forms, ethical responsibilities, and a commitment to advancing human knowledge while maintaining harmony within planetary environments. As we navigate this cosmic endeavor, the lessons gleaned from Earth's geology will serve as both a guide and cautionary tale in our quest to shape the universe and foster the flourishing of life across the stars.

8.4. Cryogenic Applications

The vast potentials tied to cryogenic applications in the context of terraforming and extraterrestrial environments are nothing short of breathtaking. Cryogenics, the science of cooling and using materials at extremely low temperatures, unlocks transformative possibilities for managing planetary ecosystems, launching exploratory missions, and preserving biological materials. As we forge ahead in the quest to comprehend the cosmos and our place within it, understanding cryogenic technologies becomes paramount in preparing for the monumental task of terraforming and sustaining life on other worlds.

Cryogenic applications serve numerous roles in terraforming efforts, with one of the most critical being the manipulation of temperature and preservation of resources. By utilizing cryogenic freezing techniques, scientific missions can transport biological specimens, such as seeds or microorganisms, to extraterrestrial environments while maintaining their viability. This capacity to preserve genetic diversity becomes especially crucial when attempting to introduce Earth organisms into alien ecosystems, reflecting both the need for resilience in newly established biospheres and the possibility of aiding life in adapting to new conditions.

In conjunction with resource preservation, cryogenic techniques hold immense potential for atmospheric engineering and climate control. By managing temperature extremes or inducing localized cooling, it is possible to initiate weather phenomena that could aid in transforming barren landscapes. For instance, strategically deploying cryogenic materials to create temporary impacts could catalyze condensation, potentially generating precipitation in regions where water is scarce.

Such applications showcase how cryogenics can play a critical role in atmospheric management, promoting the establishment of life-sustaining environments.

Another exciting frontier in cryogenic applications revolves around the transportation of materials across the cosmos. As humanity embarks on ambitious explorations, the challenge of carrying resources —whether they are raw materials from asteroids or biological samples to support terraforming—takes on new urgency. Cryogenic systems can facilitate the preservation of these materials, ensuring that they remain stable during long journeys through space. The concept of using cryogenic fuel sources, such as liquid hydrogen or methane, further enhances the potential for efficient propulsion mechanisms to reach distant planets.

Moreover, the feasibility of using cryogenic technology to extract water ice from celestial bodies is an area of intense study. Many moons and asteroids harbor significant amounts of ice that could serve as a vital resource for future terraforming efforts. By applying cryogenic methods to mine and process these ice reserves, scientists could facilitate the creation of liquid water—an essential ingredient for supporting any biosphere.

However, while the prospect of cryogenic applications in terraforming is enticing, ethical considerations emerge that guide the trajectory of these endeavors. The introduction of Earth-based organisms and the manipulation of extraterrestrial environments raise significant philosophical questions. As we utilize cryogenics to enhance our terraforming initiatives, we must remain steadfast in our commitment to ecological integrity, ensuring that any interventions are performed with biological, environmental, and ethical responsibilities at the forefront.

Additionally, the intersection of cryogenics and bioengineering offers a wealth of possibilities. The emergence of synthetic biology and genetic engineering can leverage cryogenic techniques to develop organisms capable of thriving in extraterrestrial settings. Researchers could explore genetic modifications to create extremophiles—organisms that are inherently resilient to harsh conditions—allowing for the successful introduction of adaptive life forms into new environments. As we expand our scientific understanding, the implications of cryogenic applications in engineering life become paramount in guiding the narrative surrounding the future of terraforming.

In summary, cryogenic applications present pivotal opportunities for facilitating and managing the complex processes inherent to terraforming efforts across the cosmos. By harnessing the power of low-temperature technologies, we can preserve vital genetic materials, manipulate atmospheric conditions, transport resources, and establish a foundation for sustainable ecosystems on alien worlds. The promise of these awe-inspiring advancements, however, is tempered by the responsibility we bear as stewards of both Earth and potential extraterrestrial environments. As we tread forward into the uncharted territories of the cosmos, it is essential that we employ cryogenics thoughtfully and ethically, ensuring that our inquiries resonate not just with ambition, but also with respect for the intricate tapestry that we seek to understand and reshape. The cryogenic frontier beckons, a key to unlocking the doorways toward transformed worlds where life may one day flourish amidst the stars.

8.5. Bioengineering on a Planetary Scale

Bioengineering on a planetary scale presents both an unparalleled opportunity and an immense challenge. As scientists begin to explore the potential for reshaping entire ecosystems on extraterrestrial worlds, we encounter a vast landscape of possibilities, innovative strategies, and ethical considerations that raise profound questions about our role as cosmic architects. This exploration requires an intricate understanding of biology, ecology, engineering, and the complex interactions that govern living systems. Such bioengineering could provide solutions to daunting challenges, shape habitable environments, and enable the flourishing of life in inhospitable settings.

At the crux of bioengineering on a planetary scale lies the very essence of adaptation. The success of life on Earth hinges on organisms' ability to respond to changes and thrive under varying environmental conditions. In contemplating the introduction of Earth-based species to alien ecosystems or the development of entirely new organisms specifically engineered to suit extraterrestrial environments, it is essential to incorporate principles of ecology and evolutionary biology. We must ensure that these organisms can establish themselves, interact positively with their new surroundings, and contribute to the overall stability of the ecosystem.

As we define the objectives of such bioengineering efforts, we must consider the specific environmental challenges presented by the target planet. For instance, Mars, with its thin atmosphere and harsh climate, beckons for the introduction of extremophiles—microorganisms capable of thriving in conditions previously deemed inhospitable. These engineered life forms could be designed to withstand high radiation levels, low temperatures, and low moisture availability. By carefully crafting the metabolic pathways of these organisms, scientists could facilitate nutrient cycling, soil stabilization, and even atmospheric adjustments, gradually invigorating once barren landscapes.

The prospect of terraforming planets introduces the transformative potential of synthetic biology, a field of science focused on designing and engineering new biologically based parts, devices, and systems. Through advanced techniques, scientists can modify existing microorganisms or create novel organisms that serve specific functions in their environments—such as generating oxygen, facilitating nitrogen fixation, or breaking down toxins. In this sense, bioengineering becomes not only a tool for transformation but also an exercise in creative ecological artistry, where life is reshaped and repurposed to enrich planetary landscapes.

The introduction of engineered flora and fauna necessitates a carefully calibrated approach to ensure the health and viability of newly formed ecosystems. Beyond microbial introductions, the deployment of genetically modified plants that can withstand extraterrestrial climates adds complexity to the task of ecosystem establishment. For example, robust plants capable of photosynthesis in low light conditions, or those that can draw moisture from the atmosphere, could create microhabitats, facilitating the emergence of higher trophic levels and contributing to a well-rounded food web. Such life forms could mimic the layered complexity found in Earth's ecosystems, bridging the gaps between producers, consumers, and decomposers.

Nonetheless, the challenges of bioengineering on a planetary scale are not confined solely to the technical realm. Ethical considerations loom large, demanding that we confront the profound questions surrounding our role as engineers of life. What responsibilities do we bear towards existing ecosystems, even those presumed lifeless? Introducing new species into unfamiliar environments invariably risks disruption of any native life forms, irrespective of their extant status. A deep sense of accountability must guide our decision-making, calling for robust ecological assessments and an understanding of potential ramifications on known and unknown biological interactions.

As humanity explores the cosmos in search of new worlds, the use of bioengineering in forging ecosystems will inevitably intersect with questions of biological integrity and the preservation of alien environments. The potential impact of our interventions must guide the development of policies that emphasize conservation and respect for the integrity of extraterrestrial systems. These considerations prompt a collaborative approach, bringing together experts from biology, ecology, ethicists, and policymakers, ensuring that strategies prioritize sustainability and ecological harmony.

The future trajectory of bioengineering on a planetary scale embodies the dual nature of ambition and caution. As we harness advanced technologies to create novel life forms, we must concurrently embrace a mindset of humility and stewardship, recognizing that our role as potential terraformers demands respect for the intricate tapestry of life in all its forms. By acknowledging the interdependence of ecosystems and the importance of collaborative relationships between species, we can craft robust, thriving environments that resonate with diversity and resilience.

In conclusion, the exploration of bioengineering on a planetary scale holds the key to unlocking extraordinary potential and ushering in a new era of ecological innovation. Through the careful design, adaptation, and management of engineered organisms, we can reimagine the possibilities for life beyond Earth. The journey into this exciting frontier challenges us not only to push the boundaries of scientific discovery but also to reflect upon our ethical responsibilities as we shape the future of ecosystems across the cosmos. As we aspire to create new worlds filled with flourishing life, a commitment to curiosity, collaboration, and stewardship will guide our efforts toward a thriving interconnected tapestry that resonates throughout the universe.

9. Galactic Oddities: Signs Unexplained

9.1. Infrared Anomalies

The significance of infrared anomalies in the context of alien terraformation opens a window into the exploration of astronomical bodies, allowing us to glean insights into possible modifications made by extraterrestrial civilizations. Infrared observations offer unique advantages, revealing thermal signatures and atmospheric characteristics that are typically obscured in visible light. In understanding these anomalies, we can begin to form hypotheses regarding the presence of advanced life and their potential engineering activities on other planets.

First, it's essential to define what constitutes infrared anomalies. Infrared radiation is emitted by all objects with a temperature above absolute zero, which includes a variety of celestial phenomena. In many cases, unexpected thermal emissions can signify geological, atmospheric, or biological processes that deviate from what is naturally anticipated. Such emissions may suggest technological influences or terraforming efforts on planetary surfaces. When researchers detect unusual infrared signatures—such as unexpected heat distributions, elevated temperatures in specific regions, or irregular patterns of thermal radiation—the implications for understanding extraterrestrial modifications become profound.

In the context of planetary observation, infrared telescopes like the Spitzer Space Telescope have illuminated our comprehension of celestial bodies by revealing features imperceptible in the visible spectrum. For instance, observations of exoplanets have unveiled unusual temperature gradients across their surfaces. These variations implicate possible atmospheric anomalies or thermal engineering efforts aimed at creating or sustaining habitable conditions. A prime candidate for investigation could be the mid-infrared emissions from regions of these planets indicating the presence of engineered biospheres or structural constructs facilitating the stabilization of local climates.

One intriguing case study revolves around the identification of thermal pollution on regions of celestial bodies. For example, observations of the dark side of exoplanets reveal significantly higher temperatures than expected, challenging existing models of planetary behavior. Is it possible these anomalies stem from artificial structures harnessing heat? Might they reflect advanced civilizations attempting to engineer their environments to optimize for habitation or agricultural practices? The implications of such anomalies suggest that people may have employed controlled thermal dynamics as part of terraforming exercises.

Additionally, infrared anomalies can provide evidence of planetary surface changes through thermal inertia measurements—sleuthing out historical shifts that may indicate transformation efforts. Variations in heat retention suggest that alterations to a planet's surface, whether from engineered vegetation or artificial constructs, are taking place. If the thermal response of an ecosystem follows the introduction of engineered elements, these gradient variations could signal an adaptive biosphere in progress. By employing infrared observation techniques, scientists can discern patterns in energy absorption and emission, enriching our understanding of these engineered worlds.

Infrared spectroscopy also stands as an essential tool for analyzing the chemical makeup of atmospheres surrounding planets. Oftentimes, the composition of gases can divulge information about biological processes or industrial activities. Detecting synthetic gases, such as perfluorocarbons or unusual ratios of methane and oxygen, might signal advanced ecological management practices typically associated with terraformation. If such signatures appear alongside infrared emissions from suspected biospheres, scientists could infer intentional modifications tailored to support life.

However, while exploring infrared anomalies provides tantalizing possibilities and powerful avenues for investigation, it is important to ground our findings in the scientific method. The credibility of interpreting these signals rests on rigorous validation and careful evaluation of alternatives. The infrared emissions we observe may stem from natural geological processes, such as volcanic activity or climate fluctuations, necessitating comprehensive studies to isolate potential anthropogenic influences.

Furthermore, ethical considerations arise from the prospect of interpreting such anomalies as evidence of extraterrestrial terraforming. The data collected from these observations may lead down paths of speculation regarding the rights of existing or potential life forms that inhabit these spaces. If we confront the evidence of alien civilizations shaping their worlds, how do we balance scientific curiosity with respect for unknown ecosystems?

In conclusion, infrared anomalies in the context of alien terraformation provide a compelling nexus of inquiry—illuminating possible interactions between civilizations and their environments while inviting critical reflections on our role as cosmic explorers. As we enhance our capabilities to detect and analyze thermal emissions, the quest for understanding life in the universe becomes increasingly enriched by observations that straddle the line between exploration and ethics. Through these investigations, we gain not only insight into potential terraforming but also a deeper awareness of our responsibilities as stewards of the cosmos. The interpretation of these anomalies evokes a sense of wonder, challenging us to explore the intricate tapestry of life in its various forms, while embracing the ethical implications of our ambitions to shape the universe.

9.2. Mystery of the Dark Matter

In the grand narrative of cosmic exploration and understanding, the mystery of dark matter presents both a significant puzzle and a profound opportunity for future investigations. Dark matter remains one of the most enigmatic components of our universe, constituting approximately 27% of its total mass-energy content while eluding direct observation. Unlike ordinary matter—comprising stars, planets, and galaxies—dark matter does not emit, absorb, or reflect light, making it profoundly difficult to detect. Our understanding of dark matter fundamentally reshapes our perceptions of the universe and our place within it, stirring the imagination and fostering transformative theories about the nature of reality.

Primarily, the quest to understand dark matter has revealed its gravitational influence, shaped the formation and evolution of galaxies, and provided context for the large-scale structure of the cosmos. Advanced techniques, such as gravitational lensing, enable astronomers to infer the presence of dark matter by analyzing how its gravity bends light from distant objects. Through this lens, researchers discover that dark matter forms vast halos around galaxies, influencing their rotation and the movement of surrounding ordinary matter. Such observations lay the groundwork for deeper explorations into the interconnectedness of dark matter and the potential for life throughout the universe.

As humanity seeks to unravel the mystery surrounding dark matter, it raises poignant questions about the implications of its existence for terraforming and the engineering of planets. Consider the possibility that advanced extraterrestrial civilizations might harness the gravitational properties of dark matter to manipulate celestial environments. If civilizations possess the technology to control dark matter, they could theoretically influence the orbits of celestial bodies, stabilizing them to create habitable zones. The prospect of tapping into dark matter's gravitational effects could serve as a cornerstone of their terraforming efforts, enhancing their capacity to shape worlds.

Moreover, dark matter's role in the cosmic tapestry extends to the connections we draw between galaxies and their ecosystems, including any life that may exist within them. Given the sophisticated interactions between dark matter and visible matter, it becomes imperative to explore how this cosmological phenomenon may influence planetary atmospheres and climates. The gravitational effects of dark matter may impose patterns on the distribution of ordinary matter across galaxies, impacting planetary formation and the subsequent conditions for life.

As tantalizing as these prospects may seem, the enigma of dark matter remains laced with uncertainties. Theoretical physicists and cosmologists continue to explore various candidates for dark matter, ranging from weakly interacting massive particles (WIMPs) to axions, each accompanied by unanswered questions. The challenges of detecting dark matter directly through experiments—whether via particle colliders or underground detectors—add layers of complexity to our understanding. As potential signs of alien terraformation come into view, we must remain cognizant of dark matter's influence, while awaiting breakthroughs that may unlock its secrets.

Moreover, the mysteries of dark matter intertwine with discussions about the possibility of multiple universes or dimensions. Some theories posit that dark matter may originate from phenomena occurring beyond our observable universe, linking our search for extraterrestrial life with the exploration of realities yet to be understood. This intersection of ideas prompts consideration of what life might entail in those alternate realms and whether civilizations manipulating dark matter might thrive.

In terms of terraforming and its implications, dark matter represents both a source of challenge and inspiration. The potential to influence gravitational forces and celestial interactions underlines the sophistication and ambition of advanced civilizations. Furthermore, as researchers continue to study and debate the implications of dark matter, we stand on the threshold of a paradigm shift that could revolutionize our comprehension of the universe.

In summary, the mystery of dark matter is a captivating frontier that straddles the boundaries of physics, astronomy, and astrobiology. As we delve deeper into its nature and implications, its gravitational influence on cosmic structures emphasizes the interconnectedness of our universe. The prospect of harnessing dark matter to facilitate terraforming and shaping worlds invites imaginative explorations, inviting us to reflect on the nature of both existence and interstellar possibility. Dark matter serves not just as a puzzle to be solved but as a testament to our desire for understanding and innovation, ultimately guiding us toward new horizons in our quest to unearth the cosmic mystery.

9.3. Pulsars: Natural or Engineered?

In exploring the question of whether pulsars can be considered natural phenomena or engineered constructs, we navigate a fascinating intersection of astrophysics, cosmic engineering, and the search for extraterrestrial intelligence. Pulsars, rapidly rotating neutron stars emitting beams of electromagnetic radiation, have captured the imagination of scientists and the public alike since their discovery in 1967. Their characteristics and behaviors present an opportunity to examine the possible influence of advanced civilizations, heralding both intrigue and skepticism.

At the core of a pulsar's function is its precise rotation, often measured in milliseconds. As it spins, the magnetic field generates beams of radiation that sweep through space like lighthouse beams. Observations of pulsars reveal their unique attributes, such as their extreme density and rapid rotation, leading to questions about their natural origins. Theories have emerged for the mechanisms that create pulsars, predominantly linking them to the remnants of supernova explosions. However, certain characteristics, such as their precision, prompt speculation about potential engineering efforts.

One intriguing aspect in this discussion is the observation of "pulsar timing." The extreme regularity of pulsar signals—often surpassing atomic clocks in accuracy—invites questions about whether such precision could, hypothetically, be a result of intentional engineering rather than sheer natural processes. As scientists study pulsars for their potential applications—such as using them to create cosmic clocks for navigating interstellar distances—one cannot help but consider the possibility that advanced beings may have harnessed these celestial bodies for communication or navigation markers.

Just as we examine pulsar regularities, the variations in their emissions raise provocative questions. Instances of irregularities or anomalous emissions have led to debates about the influences exerted by interacting astrophysical phenomena—perhaps even suggesting potential engineering alterations. As we contrast natural stellar evolution versus purposeful manipulation, the case for analyzing pulsars as engineered constructs gains traction.

Pulsars serve as natural laboratories for testing theories on the fundamental forces of physics. Some researchers speculate that civilizations could exploit these celestial bodies as repositories of energy, directing emissions for extraction or resource synthesis. This concept transforms the narrative from purely observational science to one steeped in the search for intelligent design. Resonating with thoughts of harnessing cosmic forces, this notion stirs the imagination surrounding the intersection of astrophysics and astrobiology.

Moreover, if pulsars were conceived as cosmic beacons, they might serve not just as astronomical phenomena but as navigational aids for advanced civilizations traversing the galaxy. Speculation on the purpose and design of pulsars prompts questions about cosmic engineering on a grand scale. Take, for example, the possibility of intentional pulsing patterns serving as markers directing extraterrestrial travelers; an advanced civilization capable of modifying a pulsar's behavior could communicate encoded messages across the galaxy.

Yet, skepticism reinforces the need for scientific rigor in such inquiries. The profound accuracy of pulsar timing, while suggestive of potential engineering, must be interpreted within the broader context of astrophysical mechanisms. While it's tempting to posit intelligent design, definitive evidence must be established before jumping to conclusions. The body of evidence must distill regularity from randomness, employing tools such as statistical modeling to examine the nature of pulsar behaviors.

Consideration of pulsars also sheds light on the ethical dimensions that accompany the search for extraterrestrial intelligence. If pulsars were engineered, what would that imply about the civilizations that developed them? Should we perceive such creatures as potential galactic architects or as cosmic neighbors with whom we might one day establish contact? These inquiries bear weight as humanity treads the fine line of curiosity and responsibility in the vast cosmic tapestry.

In conclusion, while pulsars exemplify the profound wonders of the universe, the question of their origins—natural or engineered—remains a question ripe for investigation. Pulsars' intriguing precision, combined with implications of advanced civilizations utilizing them for navigation or communication, opens a Pandora's box of cosmic speculation. Yet, as we pursue answers, we must anchor our inquiries in scientific principles, engaging with the depths of astrophysics while embracing the ethical dimensions of our cosmic ambitions. The pursuit of unraveling the true nature of pulsars is but a small chapter in humanity's grand adventure across the stars—a journey where the line between the naturally occurring and the scientifically engineered remains tantalizingly blurred.

9.4. Unusual Gravitational Waves

Unusual gravitational waves represent a significant frontier in the study of the universe, providing profound insights into its structure, dynamics, and potential for the existence of advanced civilizations. These gravitational waves, ripples in the fabric of spacetime, are produced by massive celestial events, such as the merging of black holes or neutron stars. Understanding the manifestations of these waves and their atypical behaviors offers clues to the nature of the cosmos and the possible interventions of intelligent beings.

The detection of gravitational waves has transformed astrophysics, allowing scientists to observe phenomena previously hidden from sight. The first direct detection of these waves by the LIGO observatory in 2015 marked a new era in astrophysics, confirming predictions made by Einstein's general theory of relativity. This newfound capability to "hear" the cosmos amplified our understanding of colossal astronomical events, beckoning a deeper inquiry into the potential implications of unusual gravitational waves—particularly in the context of alien terraformation.

When we speak of "unusual" gravitational waves, we delve into the anomalies that deviate from standard gravitational wave signatures that typically arise from conventional astrophysical events. For example, detected wave patterns that display unexpected amplitude or frequency modulation could suggest influences beyond known stellar activities. Such anomalies prompt exploration into the possibilities of engineered gravitational systems, leading scientists to question whether advanced civilizations harness these phenomena for communication, transportation, or energy generation.

To appreciate the implications of such unusual gravitational waves, we must first understand their potential sources. While the merging of compact objects—such as black holes or neutron stars—has provided the bulk of gravitational wave detections, the sheer variety of potential astrophysical events raises intriguing questions. Could there be civilizations manipulating massive objects or employing large-scale gravitational engineering? The notion of civilizations developing technology to create gravitational waves as communication tools evokes both excitement and skepticism within the scientific community. If intelligent aliens cultivated gravitational control, it might reveal advanced technological capabilities that far exceed our current understanding.

Research into unusual gravitational signals has sparked creative theorizing within the scientific community. Some scientists propose that massive artificial constructs, perhaps reminiscent of Dyson spheres or other megastructures, could yield unexpected gravitational emissions. These celestial constructions, designed to capture or manipulate energy from stars or other cosmic sources, could produce gravitational waves that deviate from natural signatures. The exploration of how such cosmic phenomena might link back to alien civilizations offers a fascinating glimpse into the intersection of engineering and astrophysics.

While speculative in nature, the search for unusual gravitational waves also hinges on the development of advanced detection techniques. Current gravitational wave observatories use sophisticated algorithms and machine learning models to identify signals amidst a backdrop of noise, filtering out everyday cosmic events to isolate potential anomalies. Innovations in detector sensitivity and the establishment of global networks of observatories will be paramount to uncovering elusive gravitational waves associated with advanced civilizations—should they exist.

Moreover, the study of gravitational waves intersects with the larger conversation surrounding cosmic ethics. If future discoveries reveal the intentional manipulation of spacetime by distant civilizations, what ethical responsibilities do we hold? Assessing the implications of advanced technology on cosmic scales invites complex reflections on the rights of original inhabitants of those structures or celestial bodies. As humanity focuses on future explorations, grappling with ethical considerations surrounding intervention and the preservation of the integrity of unknown ecosystems becomes paramount.

Furthermore, the broader implications of unusual gravitational waves extend to our understanding of the universe's expansion and fate. Insights gleaned from an array of gravitational wave phenomena may contribute to resolving outstanding questions surrounding dark energy, cosmic inflation, and the dynamics governing the universe. The duality of studying unusual gravitational phenomena—as windows into potential advanced civilizations while also seeking to understand the universe's architecture—presents a fascinating dialogue between scientific inquiry and philosophical contemplation.

In conclusion, unusual gravitational waves serve as a plunging point into the mysteries of cosmic engineering and the quest for understanding advanced civilizations. By delicately teasing apart signals that deviate from anticipated gravitational patterns, scientists and theorists can broaden the narrative surrounding the definitions of advanced technology, communication, and exploration in the cosmos. As we endeavor to unravel the enigma of gravitational waves, we must remain mindful of the implications concerning ethics, collaboration, and the awe-inspiring possibilities that interweave our place within the grand cosmic narrative. The journey ahead invites us not only to listen but to probe deeper into the vast expanse of the universe—where the threads of existence align across the realms of astrophysics and the infinite potential of life beyond our imagination.

9.5. The Enigma of Void Spheres

The Enigma of Void Spheres delves into the unusual existence and properties of void spheres—hypothetical constructs that may present themselves in the vastness of space. These structures pose a serendipitous challenge to our understanding of astrophysics, cosmology, and potential life beyond our planet. As we venture into this intrigue of celestial phenomena, we are confronted with tantalizing questions about their origins, formations, and the roles they could play in the overarching structure of the universe.

Void spheres are posited as vast, hollow regions in the cosmos, almost resembling celestial bubbles devoid of matter. Scientific inquiry into their existence catalyzes investigations into gravitational dynamics, dark matter interactions, and the intricate architecture of galaxies. If void spheres do indeed exist, they could potentially reconfigure our perception of cosmic processes, including galaxy formation and the distribution of dark matter.

The foundations of void sphere theory hinge on the principles of cosmic inflation and the significant anisotropies observed in the cosmic microwave background radiation. Cosmic inflation—a theory positing that the universe underwent exponential expansion immediately after the Big Bang—could have given rise to voids as it drove matter distribution unevenly across the young universe. This leads to the fascinating question of whether cosmic voids might grow into these massive spheres, shaping the environments around them by retaining or repelling nearby matter through gravitational influences.

One hypothesis is that void spheres may act as cosmic filters, segregating regions of space that could harbor life from those that remain barren. By absorbing the quantifiable mass that composes neighboring galaxies, voids might create pockets conducive to enhanced galactic behaviors, thus fostering environments suitable for the emergence of life. Consequently, understanding the underlying dynamics of void spheres could enlighten our understanding of where to look for extraterrestrial civilizations and how to initiate terraforming processes.

These void structures, if real, may also reveal the delicate balance of forces within the universe. They could embody the consequences of massive cosmic events, like dark energy fluctuations, causing peculiar gravitational distortions. Should scientists unravel the enigma of void spheres, we might also uncover new avenues to manipulate gravitational influences effectively. Such discoveries may incorporate leveraging the gravitational repulsion or attraction of void spheres to modulate the motion of celestial bodies, providing innovative approaches to planetary engineering.

Interestingly, the notion of void spheres may connect with advanced civilizations capable of constructing or manipulating them—a tantalizing proposition. Could an alien civilization possess the technology to engineer these vast structures for energy harvesting, navigation, or even terraforming? If advanced beings can influence gravitational field interactions, such spheres could serve as controlled habitats or experimental domains designed for biological or technological purposes.

Moreover, exploring the enigma of void spheres necessitates rigorous scientific proof and inquiry. Current observational limitations make direct studies of cosmic voids difficult; however, next-generation telescopes and advancements in astrophysics may prove invaluable in unveiling these mysteries. Techniques such as gravitational lensing and advanced simulations could aid in characterizing the geometry and dynamics surrounding void spheres, bridging the gap between theory and observational data.

The implications surrounding void spheres extend to broader discussions about life in the universe, cosmology, and the future of extraterrestrial exploration. Should these peculiar structures exist, they can redefine how we conceptualize cosmic architecture and the fabric of life. The possibilities that arise from understanding void spheres challenge us to reassess our definitions of habitability, encouraging explorations of celestial environments previously considered inhospitable.

As we delve further into the unknown, the exploration of the enigma of void spheres invites profound reflections on our cosmic journey. Are we merely spectators in a grand cosmic play, or can we learn to manipulate these ethereal realms? The answers may reshape our perspective on existence itself, inspiring humanity to contemplate the relationship shared not just with other life forms across the universe, but also with the very structures that comprise the cosmos itself.

In closing, the pursuit of understanding the enigma of void spheres embodies the spirit of exploration that has propelled humanity through the ages. This inquiry prompts us to question the known and the unknown, challenging the paradigms through which we comprehend our celestial surroundings. As we navigate the intricacies of cosmic phenomena, the exploration of void spheres beckons us toward new horizons—an invitation to unearth the truths that lie within the vast and intricate web of the universe. By embracing curiosity and inquiry, we may one day unlock secrets that could illuminate our understanding of life's potential beyond our fragile blue planet, revealing the majesty and mystery that resides within the expanses of space.

10. Cosmic Neighborhoods: Habitable Zones

10.1. The Goldilocks Planet Paradigm

The Goldilocks Planet Paradigm is a pivotal concept in the pursuit of understanding potential extraterrestrial life and the underlying principles of terraforming. Rooted in the iconic children's tale, this paradigm plays on the notion of finding a just-right setting that is neither too hot nor too cold, but comfortable for life as we know it. In astrophysics and astrobiology, this translates to identifying celestial bodies that exist within a habitable zone—the so-called "Goldilocks Zone"—where conditions are conducive to sustaining liquid water and supporting various forms of life.

The search for Goldilocks planets is notably focused on identifying exoplanets—planets that orbit stars outside our solar system. Current discoveries through missions such as the Kepler Space Telescope and TESS (Transiting Exoplanet Survey Satellite) illuminate the complexities of finding worlds positioned at distances from their stars that allow for temperate environments. This delicate balance depends not only on the distance from the star but also on factors such as stellar type, planetary atmosphere, and geophysical characteristics.

Establishing habitability on these planets requires nuanced considerations of survivable atmospheres and temperatures. The thin margins within which biological processes can occur pose challenges for astrobiologists seeking to understand the implications of these environmental conditions. For example, atmospheric composition plays a crucial role in mediating greenhouse effects—too little carbon dioxide may lead to freezing, while too high levels could induce extreme heat. Oxygen-rich atmospheres, in turn, are critical for aerobic life forms but can present complications in maintaining equilibrium, especially if coupled with high levels of methane or other gases.

Moreover, prominent exoplanetary systems such as the TRAPPIST-1 system—home to seven Earth-sized exoplanets—offer both inspiration and challenges. The discovery of several planets situated within the habitable zones sparks excitement and encourages new studies surrounding their atmospheric properties and potential for sustaining life. However, ongoing scrutiny is essential to assess each exoplanet's atmosphere for signs of stability and habitability.

The role of moons and satellites significantly contributes to our understanding of Goldilocks planets. Many of our solar system's most intriguing potential habitats do not lie with planets directly but rather with their moons. Consider Europa, a moon of Jupiter known for its subsurface ocean, or Titan, Saturn's largest moon, which possesses a nitrogen-rich atmosphere and liquid methane lakes. These celestial bodies may present conditions necessary for life, shaping the broader context of planetary exploration.

Zones of influence and control also weave into the Goldilocks Planet Paradigm, as they articulate the gravitational and radiation dynamics that determine habitable conditions. Space weather patterns, such as cosmic rays emitted by nearby stars, could affect planetary atmospheres and ecosystems in ways yet to be fully understood. Furthermore, the gravitational interactions between planets and their moons not only affect their respective orbits but also promote stabilizing phenomena, such as moderating axial tilt and influencing seasonal changes—both critical for potential habitability.

In conclusion, the Goldilocks Planet Paradigm serves as a foundational framework in our search for life beyond Earth, spotlighting the delicate balance required to sustain habitable conditions in various extraterrestrial contexts. As we continue to probe deeper into the universe, understanding the complex interplay of stellar systems, planetary atmospheres, and ecological dynamics will be essential. Our aspiration to terraform will require not only a recognition of the science driving these efforts but also a commitment to ethical considerations surrounding our place within the vast cosmic tapestry. Ultimately, the quest for Goldilocks planets embodies humanity's inherent curiosity and desire to understand our universe, fueling the dreams of exploration that resonate throughout history.

10.2. Survivable Atmospheres and Temperatures

Survivable atmospheres and temperatures are foundational concepts in the quest for recognizing signs of alien terraformation and understanding the ecological viability of extraterrestrial environments. The significance of these factors cannot be overstated; the atmospheres and thermal conditions present on a planet dictate not only the potential for supporting life but also the methodologies by which a civilization might transform a hostile world into a nurturing habitat.

At the crux of creating a survivable atmosphere is the balance of various gases and elements critical for life as we know it. For terrestrial life, this predominantly includes oxygen, nitrogen, carbon dioxide, and trace gases that play roles in metabolic processes. The presence of these gases in suitable proportions fosters conditions under which ecosystems can develop and thrive. For example, human survival hinges on an atmosphere composed of about 21% oxygen; deviations from this norm can lead to hypoxia or other detrimental health effects. Therefore, determining the right balance of atmospheric elements is paramount for establishing any form of sustained life in environments beyond Earth.

Consider, for instance, the atmospheric composition of Mars. Currently, its atmosphere consists of approximately 95% carbon dioxide, with fractions of nitrogen and argon and minimal oxygen. To render Mars survivable for Earth-like lifeforms, a substantial alteration would be required—one that could involve releasing oxygen-producing organisms, such as specially engineered cyanobacteria, capable of converting carbon dioxide into oxygen through photosynthesis. This biomimetic approach points to the necessity of understanding the interactions among various components of the atmosphere in establishing a balanced ecological system.

The role of temperature in these dynamics cannot be overlooked. Temperature influences the state of matter and the chemical reactions crucial to biological functions. For life as we understand it, a narrow temperature range supports liquid water—the foundation for all known biological processes. The ideal temperature necessary for life

126

varies significantly depending on the environmental context and the organisms involved. For example, extremophiles can thrive in conditions that would be lethal to most life forms, yet their habitats are often defined by their specific temperature tolerances. As such, terraforming strategies must take into account the feasible temperature ranges for possible life forms, targeting climates that enable liquid water without pushing organisms beyond their limits.

Beyond merely adjusting the atmospheric composition, technological interventions must be deployed to regulate temperatures on target planets. One theoretical approach involves the introduction of greenhouse gases, such as methane or perfluorocarbons, designed to capture heat and increase overall atmospheric pressure. In controlled experiments, such gases can selectively enhance surface temperatures, prompting shifts in phases that transition solid water (ice) into liquid water—an essential catalyst in the journey toward establishing habitable conditions.

Furthermore, the location of exoplanets within their stars' habitable zones—areas where conditions might allow for liquid water—is a critical factor in assessing survivability. The concept of the "Goldilocks Zone" serves as a guide for identifying potentially habitable planets. Identifying planets orbiting stars with stable output radiation ensures that temperatures remain within the bounds necessary for supporting life. This includes consideration of different types of stars—G-type (like our Sun), K-type, or M-type stars—each influencing the orbital characteristics required for a planet's habitability and ultimately its atmospheric sustainability.

When investigating temperatures and atmospheres, the phenomenon of solar flares also requires examination. Solar activity can lead to atmospheric stripping or losses, particularly for planets with weak magnetic fields, such as Mars. Such dynamics must be understood when planning long-term terraforming efforts to bolster atmospheric resilience, employing techniques to generate protective magnetic fields or strategic emissions that might absorb solar radiation.

As we delve deeper into the possibility of survivable atmospheres and temperatures, the ethical considerations surrounding terraforming alien worlds emerge as critical dimensions that engage with these scientific inquiries. What responsibilities do we hold when engineering atmospheres for the benefit of life? As the potential for unintended consequences looms large, discussions about the rights of existing or potential life forms must inform our terraforming ambitions.

Additionally, the historical precedence on Earth reveals challenges associated with modifying environments. We must remain acutely aware of lessons learned from human-driven ecological changes, holding them as cautionary narratives that shape contemporary thoughts on extraterrestrial interventions.

In conclusion, survivable atmospheres and temperatures form the cornerstone of our understanding of alien terraformation. Balancing atmospheric composition while managing thermal conditions presents a colossal undertaking whereby technological intervention marries natural processes to promote sustainable ecosystems. As these scientific inquiries deepen, they invite not only curiosity and passion but also a reflective consideration of our responsibilities as stewards of both our planet and potentially those we aspire to terraform. The journey toward understanding atmospheres and temperatures across the cosmos is rife with discovery and ethical reflection, propelling humanity closer to the uncharted realms of life that await beyond our world.

10.3. Prominent Exoplanetary Systems

In the context of the broader discussion around alien terraformation, prominent exoplanetary systems stand as the focal points of exploration and inquiry. These systems are not simply collections of stars and planets; they embody the potential for diverse conditions that could support life. Each system presents distinct characteristics that make it unique—varying atmospheric compositions, gravitational influences, and orbital dynamics allow scientists to theorize about the habitability of their planets and the implications for intelligent civilizations possibly residing within them.

One prominent example of an exoplanetary system is the TRAPPIST-1 system, which has garnered significant attention due to its seven Earth-sized planets located within the habitable zone of a cool dwarf star. The proximity of these planets to one another raises stimulating questions regarding interplanetary interactions and the potential for cross-contamination—whether dynamically intertwined environments might foster shared or divergent evolutionary paths. Each of these planets boasts unique atmospheric pressures and compositions, showcasing the range of conditions that might be conducive to sustaining life.

Another notable system is the Proxima Centauri system, which is home to Proxima b, an Earth-sized exoplanet located within its star's habitable zone. The close proximity of Proxima Centauri to our solar system invites speculation about the potential for human exploration and the possibilities for terraforming this potentially habitable world. Its status as the nearest star to Earth ignites imaginations around interstellar travel and the ways conditions might be altered to create more favorable environments for life.

Additionally, the Kepler-186 system has captured scientific interest due to the discovery of Kepler-186f, the first Earth-sized exoplanet confirmed to orbit in its star's habitable zone. This discovery positioned it as a candidate for potential life, promoting further investigation into its atmospheric composition and geological characteristics. The implications of such findings expand our understanding of what it means for an exoplanet to be considered habitable, enriching both the scientific narrative and public enthusiasm for space exploration.

The examination of prominent exoplanetary systems extends to binary star systems, where two stars orbit a common center of mass, and how these gravitational dynamics influence planetary formation and stability. The existence of planets orbiting within binary systems poses unique challenges and opportunities for habitability, leading scientists to explore how such environments affect atmospheric retention and climatic conditions. For instance, the gravitational tug-of-war from two stars might influence the thermal and solar dynamics for planets, complicating their capacity to maintain stable atmospheres.

The role of exoplanetary atmospheres becomes increasingly significant as we explore these systems. When considering potential terraformation, the atmospheric composition serves as an essential criterion for evaluating the viability of any ecosystem. Through methodologies such as spectroscopy, scientists investigate the specific gases present in exoplanet atmospheres, looking for indications of habitability or the signatures of unnatural interference. The presence of certain gases like methane, oxygen, and even industrial pollutants can hint at biological processes or technological activity that sheds light on civilization potential.

Moreover, the interaction between moons and their parent planets introduces additional layers of complexity in exoplanetary systems. Moons can contribute to the habitable conditions of their host planets by stabilizing axial tilt, regulating climatic variations, and enhancing the likelihood of having a suitable atmosphere. The study of moon systems, particularly those around gas giants like Jupiter and Saturn, enables scientists to expand their parameters of habitability beyond traditional planetary contexts.

As we contemplate the future of exoplanetary studies, we are often driven by the possibility of discovering life as we know it—or perhaps something entirely alien. The ongoing search for Earth-like planets within the habitable zones of their stars prompts us to consider what resilience and adaptation might look like in an ever-expanding universe. If civilizations exist in these diverse systems, what technological advancements might they employ to terraform inhospitable environments into lush paradises?

In summary, prominent exoplanetary systems unravel the intricacies of cosmic exploration, extending our understanding of the conditions that allow life to thrive beyond Earth. These investigations fuel our collective imagination while presenting both challenges and prospects for understanding extraterrestrial civilizations and their potential for terraforming. As we delve deeper into the study of these systems, we not only broaden our knowledge of the universe but also reflect on our role as cosmic stewards, committed to finding harmony in the intricate balance of life across the galaxies. The journey into the realm of exoplanets ultimately serves as a testament to humanity's unending quest to explore, discover, and understand the complexities of our vast and magnificent universe.

10.4. The Role of Moons and Satellites

The exploration of moons and satellites provides a critical dimension in our understanding of alien terraformation and the intricate dynamics of planetary ecosystems throughout the cosmos. Often overlooked in discussions centered on planetary bodies, moons and natural satellites play pivotal roles in shaping their host planets and can be instrumental players in the quest for life beyond Earth. This subchapter will delve into the significance of moons, highlighting their potential for supporting life, influencing planetary climates, and facilitating the broader narrative of terraforming efforts.

At the forefront of the conversation around moons is the recognition that many of the solar system's most intriguing environments are located not on planets, but on their orbiting satellites. One of the most prominent examples is Europa, one of Jupiter's moons, known for its subsurface ocean concealed beneath an icy crust. Europa presents tantalizing prospects for potential life, as the interaction between its ocean and rocky mantle could create the chemical reactions necessary for life's sustenance, mirroring some of the processes believed to have occurred on early Earth. The exploration of Europa is increasingly positioned as a priority in astrobiological research, as the search for signs of life on alien moons may reveal rich ecosystems unfathomably diverse.

Similarly, Titan, Saturn's largest moon, offers a unique case study for potential extraterrestrial habitats. Possessing a dense atmosphere composed primarily of nitrogen, Titan features lakes and rivers of liquid methane and ethane on its surface. This unusual chemistry presents unique challenges and possibilities for life, prompting researchers to investigate whether life might thrive in environments radically different from those on Earth. In this context, Titan exemplifies the vital role moons can play in shaping our understanding of habitability across diverse environments.

The influence of moons extends to providing stability to their host planets. The gravitational pull exerted by moons can moderate the axial tilt of the planets around which they orbit, ensuring that seasonal variations remain within a range conducive to life. Earth's Moon is a prime example of this stabilizing effect; its presence plays a crucial role in maintaining the planet's axial tilt, thereby moderating climate fluctuations that significantly influence terrestrial ecosystems. The implications of this stabilizing influence become even more critical when considering planetary engineering on exoplanets—illustrating how the presence of a moon could facilitate habitability by enhancing environmental stability over time.

Moreover, as we envision terraforming efforts, the relationship between planets and their moons opens avenues for innovative approaches. For instance, gravitational interactions between a planet and its moons can facilitate atmospheric retention. If a planet possesses a thin atmosphere, the presence of an orbiting moon could exert tidal forces strong enough to maintain stability within that atmosphere, thereby allowing for the modifications required to make the planet habitable. Planning terraforming initiatives would necessitate evaluating the existing dynamics between planets and their moons, determining how they can best work together to cultivate a thriving ecosystem.

Additionally, moons and satellites could serve as hubs for terraforming activities, providing resources for engineering projects in orbit. The exploration and mining of materials, water, and volatiles from moons like Enceladus or Ganymede could facilitate atmospheric engineering programs on their corresponding planets. In this scenario, moons become launchpads for subsequent missions or sources of essential components for creating livable environments elsewhere.

The ethical implications surrounding the manipulation of moons—and, by extension, the development of their ecosystems—cannot be overlooked. The introduction of engineered organisms or the alteration of lunar environments necessitates a respect for any existing ecosystems that may dwell in these unique realms. As discussions regarding terraforming intensify, acknowledging the rights of potential life forms becomes fundamental to responsible exploration. The narratives surrounding moons should emphasize stewardship approaches that prioritize the conservation of existing environments while harnessing the potential for innovation.

Furthermore, the examination of moons within broader planetary contexts enhances our understanding of interstellar dynamics and the diversity of life that may exist in various forms across the universe. By studying the conditions in which moons might support life, researchers can refine their definitions and criteria for habitability. The study of moons as laboratories for evolution and survival highlights the boundless adaptability of life, suggesting that astrobiological studies must remain open to diverse possibilities beyond our Earth-centric models.

In conclusion, the role of moons and satellites is indispensable in the dialogue surrounding alien terraformation and the search for extraterrestrial life. Their influence on planetary climates, stability, and potential for supporting ecosystems underscores the depth of interconnections that define our universe. As we navigate the cosmic journey of exploration, recognizing the significance of moons will enable us to develop more nuanced approaches to understanding life beyond Earth. The intricate tapestry of interactions among moons, planets, and celestial bodies invites us to remain curious, vigilant, and reverent as we uncover the secrets that lie within these distant realms. Ultimately, the journey into the sphere of moons opens pathways toward the profound possibilities that exist within our cosmic neighborhood—a testament to humanity's enduring desire to explore and understand the universe we inhabit.

10.5. Zones of Influence and Control

In contemplating the interplay between zones of influence and control, we dive into a realm that intricately ties the complexities of planetary dynamics to the ambitious aspirations of terraforming efforts. As the quest to identify and potentially reshape environments beyond Earth gains traction, understanding how celestial mechanics govern the relationships between stars, planets, moons, and other celestial bodies evolves into a fundamental necessity. This subchapter elaborates upon how these interactions define potential habitats, influence conditions conducive to life, and shape the strategic approaches undertaken by advanced civilizations or future human endeavors.

Zones of influence arise from the gravitational interactions between celestial bodies, dictating the extent to which one body exerts force over another. On a planetary scale, this notion permeates various layers of the cosmos—from the gravitational pull of a planet's moon stabilizing its axial tilt to the effects of nearby stars shaping the orbits of planets within their gravitational wells. For instance, Earth's Moon has played a crucial role in moderating seasonal variations and maintaining a relatively stable climate over millions of years, conditions fundamental for the flourishing of terrestrial life.

In the context of terraforming, understanding these gravitational influences offers insight into how we might utilize or manipulate them to create optimal conditions for life. The exploration of the dynamics between planets, their moons, and the stars they orbit is critical in defining habitable zones. As we design theoretical models for terraforming, we must consider the gravitational interactions that could either favor or jeopardize our efforts. For example, in a tightly-knit system with multiple planets exhibiting complex gravitational behavior, alterations made to one planet's orbit could induce an array of changes on its neighbors, subsequently affecting their atmospheres and environmental stability.

Control over these gravitational influences is integral to successful terraforming plans. This notion leads to discussions about advanced technologies that might allow for manipulation of celestial mechanics, enabling deliberate adjustments that could alter the trajectories of planets or moons. The concept of mass drivers—mechanisms that could utilize kinetic energy to redirect celestial bodies—highlights potential strategies through which we may exert influence over nearby orbits. The ability to exert control is accompanied by substantial ethical considerations; changes made to celestial bodies must be grounded in responsible engagement with existing ecosystems, ensuring that our interventions do not inadvertently damage emerging biospheres or disturb the gravitational order of neighboring worlds.

The significance of zones of influence extends into broader discussions about ecological interdependence and the interconnectedness of celestial bodies within systems. Planets and their moons do not exist in isolation; the transformations brought about by one entity can influence the environmental conditions of others. For example, altering the atmosphere of a planet could also affect the gravitational interactions with its moons, which in turn may experience changes in temperature and atmospheric pressure—potentially sparking a chain reaction of ecological adjustments. Recognizing these interactions emphasizes the importance of multi-faceted approaches to terraforming that take into account not only the target planet but also its larger cosmic neighborhood.

As scientists and engineers explore the potential of shaping environments beyond Earth, they must remain vigilant in assessing the consequences of these manipulations. Understanding the complex web of gravitational influences allows us to minimize unintended repercussions within the intricate ecosystems we aspire to create. By employing advanced simulations and computational modeling, researchers can anticipate how various changes might reverberate through systems, informing responsible decision-making and fostering adaptive strategies.

Moreover, the exploration of zones of influence raises tantalizing questions about the role of intelligence in cosmic dynamics. If advanced civilizations are capable of manipulating gravitational systems, might they deploy technologies that allow them to shape the environments of neighboring planets to suit their needs? This line of speculation underscores an imagination rooted in both ambition and caution; the interplay between influence and control could define not only our understanding of celestial mechanics but also the ethical implications of extraterrestrial engineering.

As we expand our knowledge in this terrain, we face the dual challenge of curiosity and responsibility. The exploration of zones of influence and control offers profound insights into how we might navigate the cosmos in our pursuit of understanding and terraforming alien worlds. It beckons us to not only consider the technical aspects of these engagements but also to reflect upon our place within the grand cosmic narrative, guiding our choices as we reach for the stars. Ultimately, a deeper understanding of these dynamics will equip us to wield our influence over the cosmos with respect and foresight, fostering conditions where life can flourish in whatever forms it may take.

11. Clues in Stellar Evolution

11.1. Star Life Cycles and Planetary Adaptations

The complex relationship between stars and their life cycles fundamentally shapes the potential for extraterrestrial terraformation and planetary adaptations. Each star undergoes a series of transformative phases throughout its existence, influencing the environments of the planets within its grasp. Understanding these stellar lifecycles is essential for recognizing how they can create habitable conditions or challenge the very methodologies of terraformation.

Stars are born from the collapse of gas and dust within molecular clouds—regions rich in materials essential for planetary formation. As a protostar condenses, it enters the main sequence phase, where it spends the vast majority of its life fusing hydrogen into helium in its core. This process generates immense energy and heat, creating a stable environment for orbiting planets that could potentially support life. The duration of time a star remains in the main sequence phase directly correlates with its mass; larger stars burn brightly and rapidly, exhausting their fuel in a few million years, while smaller stars, like red dwarfs, can shine for tens of billions of years, providing extended opportunities for life to evolve.

The main sequence phase of a star can serve as a vital period for the development of terrestrial adaptations. Planets orbiting within the habitable zone—the region where temperatures allow for liquid water to exist—maximize their potential for sustaining life. For instance, Earth has benefited from its stable Sun, which has facilitated a consistent climate over millions of years, allowing life to flourish and adapt. The longevity and reliability of a star's energy output are critical when considering the feasibility of terraforming efforts—advanced civilizations must harness stellar characteristics to create conditions that support ecological diversity.

As a star exhausts its hydrogen supply, it enters the red giant phase, during which its outer layers expand significantly and its internal processes transition. This phase is crucial for understanding potential adaptations required of planets as a star evolves. Planets orbiting a red giant may experience extreme temperature fluctuations and unpredictable stellar activities, altering their atmospheric compositions and internal dynamics. The implications for terraformers working with planets in this phase must consider how such drastic changes affect existing ecosystems, requiring innovations to regulate temperatures and sustain habitable conditions.

The end of a star's life cycle introduces additional complexities. Massive stars explode in supernovae, unleashing bursts of energy and heavy elements into space, enriching surrounding celestial environments. These explosive events can catalyze the formation of new stars and planetary systems, emphasizing the intricate interplay between life and death among stars. For terraforming endeavors, understanding how supernovae redistribute materials and influence the formation of new planets becomes paramount. When materials are spread across space, they may seed new worlds with the potential for supporting life, offering fresh opportunities for future terraforming initiatives.

Consequently, the processes associated with stellar evolution present both opportunities and challenges when considering alien terraformation. The presence of a stable star remains essential for initiating and sustaining habitable conditions on orbiting planets. The radiative and gravitational forces imparted by stars play crucial roles in regulating planetary atmospheres, climates, and ecosystems, ultimately determining the potential for life to thrive or perish. The adaptability of life relies on its ability to respond to changed conditions, showcasing the delicate balance between evolutionary resilience and the unforgiving nature of cosmic transformations.

In summary, the life cycles of stars intricately intertwine with planetary adaptations and opportunities for terraformation. The evolutionary processes of stars dictate conditions for planets in habitable zones, influencing their capacity to support life. Consequently, understanding these stellar phenomena is essential for exploring the methodologies and implications of creating habitable environments beyond Earth. The synthesis of knowledge concerning stellar life cycles, planetary development, and potential adaptations reveals a complex yet harmonious connection within the broader cosmic tapestry—one that invites us to imagine the possibilities of life sustained under the light of distant stars.

11.2. The Effects of Supernovae

In the grand tapestry of the universe, the phenomenon of supernovae holds a significant place. These catastrophic explosions mark the death throes of massive stars, unleashing colossal amounts of energy and matter into the surrounding cosmos. The effects of supernovae extend far beyond their immediate impact; they also influence star formation, chemical evolution, and potentially even the conditions necessary for life on nearby planets. As we explore the intricacies of supernovae, a more profound understanding emerges regarding how these cosmic events can reshape stellar neighborhoods and catalyze the processes of terraforming or sustaining life.

At its core, a supernova is a dramatic stellar event usually resulting from one of two scenarios: the core-collapse of a massive star or the thermonuclear explosion of a white dwarf. During a core-collapse supernova, the core's inability to sustain gravitational forces leads to a catastrophic explosion, while any remaining material is expelled outward, generating shock waves that can trigger the formation of new stars and planetary systems in the surrounding gas and dust. The universe, rich in contrast, adapts and evolves in the wake of these stellar demise events, allowing for the recycling of elements that form the building blocks of life.

The release of tremendous amounts of elements such as carbon, oxygen, nitrogen, and iron occurs within supernova explosions, dispersing these vital materials into interstellar space. This chemical enrichment creates a fertile environment for star formation, as these elements combust to forge new stars and their accompanying planetary systems. The remnants of supernovae form nebulae, where new stars can be born, and thus, they play a critical role in the cosmic lifecycle, underscoring the interconnectedness of death and rebirth in the universe.

Understanding the environmental effects of supernovae extends to their influence on planetary atmospheres and potential habitability. The energetic shock waves produced by nearby supernovae can compress surrounding gas clouds, instigating gravitational collapse and star formation. However, supernovae also have destructive potential. The intense radiation and high-energy particles emitted can strip away the atmospheres of nearby planets, destabilizing any existing conditions that could support life. As such, the spatial dynamics surrounding supernovae are vital to consider when exploring habitable zones within our galaxy.

It is worth noting that the timing of a supernova in relation to stellar neighborhoods is equally fundamental. The most significant influence occurs within distances of several tens of light-years, as the energetic effects of a supernova can disrupt the orbit of nearby objects, lead to atmospheric loss, or trigger geological activity. Consequently, planets located within these zones must possess robust atmospheric protection mechanisms or be positioned optimally to withstand the effects of such cataclysmic events, preserving their potential for life.

The eventualities of supernovae on planetary systems present intriguing avenues for terraforming possibilities. In scenarios where planets escape devastating direct impacts, the deposition of heavy elements can enhance soil and atmospheric compositions over time, rendering worlds richer and potentially more suitable for future sustainability. Notably, the concept of "panspermia" emerges, proposing that life may spread through the cosmos via material ejected from supernovae. This theory emphasizes a connection between explosive cosmic events and the potential seeding of life across planetary systems.

However, amidst the potential benefits of supernovae lies the acknowledgment that they also embody risk. Within a galaxy, the distribution of life may rule out certain planets as candidates for terraforming due to the potential violent aftermath of nearby celestial explosions. A world too close to a supernova may face existential threats that outweigh the prospects of fostering life.

In conclusion, the effects of supernovae underscore a dynamic interplay of creation and destruction central to the cosmos. Recognizing how these stellar explosions impact planetary environments and star formation patterns enables deeper insights into processes governing habitability and the potential for terraforming efforts. While they may act as agents of chaos within the universe, supernovae simultaneously serve as catalysts for rebirth, fueling the ongoing saga of life across galaxies. As we explore these phenomena, we embrace the profound interconnectedness of all things, uncovering the tantalizing possibilities that arise in the aftermath of cosmic events. Each supernova becomes a reminder of our place in the dark majesty of the universe —a testament to the forces shaping existence in its many forms.

11.3. Stellar Energy Harvesting

In the grand narrative of galactic exploration and planetary transformation, the concept of stellar energy harvesting emerges as a crucial mechanism through which advanced civilizations might manipulate their substrates to enable habitability and sustain life. This chapter delves into the intricacies of this practice, examining the theoretical frameworks, technological implications, and ethical considerations surrounding the harvesting of energy from stars. As we explore this uncharted territory, we are compelled to reflect on how stellar energy production can not only enlighten our understanding of the universe but serve as a resource for terraforming efforts on celestial bodies.

The concept of stellar energy harvesting hinges on the observation that stars emit enormous quantities of energy in the form of light and heat, with our Sun alone radiating approximately 386 billion billion watts of energy every second. This vast potential can be harnessed using advanced technologies—transforming the astronomical output of a star into usable energy forms that facilitate ecosystem development on distant worlds. Whether through focused solar collectors or massive energy-harnessing satellites, the utilization of stellar energy forms the backbone of extraterrestrial engineering, promoting environmental stability and enabling life-sustaining systems.

By focusing on solar energy as a primary resource, advanced civilizations may build vast solar farms, potentially resembling Dyson spheres or Dyson swarms—hypothetical constructs designed to capture stellar energy at incomprehensible scales. A Dyson Sphere would encompass a star entirely, capturing its energy output for use across planetary systems. Dyson Swarms, which feature a network of orbiting satellites, could allow for more modular and scalable approaches to energy capture while reducing the risks associated with large structures.

The utilization of stellar energy extends beyond mere power generation; it encompasses fundamental strategies for planetary climate control. Advanced civilizations might employ reflective materials to manage the energy balance of celestial bodies through orbital shades or gigantic mirrors. These devices could counteract excessive heat, provide light in shadowed regions, and regulate temperature variances across engineered environments—facilitating the establishment of supportive conditions for complex life forms.

As we contemplate the implications of stellar energy harvesting, it is crucial to recognize the emerging technologies integral to such endeavors. Advances in materials science, photovoltaics, and energy storage offer promising avenues for harnessing solar energy more efficiently on both planetary and interstellar scales. Research into highly efficient solar cells, composed of advanced materials that can capture and convert a broader spectrum of sunlight into energy, aligns closely with the ambitions of harvesting stellar radiation. The exploration of supercapacitors and next-generation batteries is equally essential, as they will enable effective storage and distribution of this harvested energy for use in terraforming efforts and sustaining ecosystems.

However, while the potential for energy harvesting is exciting, ethical considerations loom large. The quest to harness stellar energy may inadvertently lead to the depletion of natural resources in a target ecosystem, posing questions about the rights of pre-existing life forms and the responsibilities of advanced civilizations. As we consider the ramifications of energy extraction on alien worlds, we must tread with caution, ensuring that our ambitions to harvest stellar energy do not come at the expense of untouched ecosystems.

Furthermore, understanding the long-term consequences of harvesting energy from stars is crucial. The Sun, for example, has a finite lifespan, transitioning through phases such as red giant expansion before ultimately evolving into a white dwarf. As advanced civilizations embark upon stellar energy harvesting, strategies must be developed to account for the lifecycle of stars and the ramifications of energy depletion on planetary systems dependent on that energy source. Planning for the eventual transitions of these stars—whether it be redirecting energy harvesting efforts to younger stars or managing its dwindling outputs—becomes essential in maintaining habitability over extended timescales.

The exploration of stellar energy harvesting offers profound insights into our understanding of cosmic civilizations. If advanced societies indeed employ these energy resources to terraform planets, it elevates the conversation about potential interactions with alien life and our shared responsibilities within cosmic ecosystems. Identifying and interpreting energy signatures stemming from such civilizations could yield tantalizing clues regarding their activities and intentions.

In conclusion, stellar energy harvesting emerges as a significant concept in the dialogue surrounding alien terraformation. It speaks to the boundless creativity and technological prowess that advanced civilizations might possess while underscoring the delicate balance of exploitation and stewardship of cosmic resources. As we aspire to understand the cosmos and our place within it, the complexities of stellar energy harvesting invite reflection on the broader implications of our quest—to explore, harness, and coexist with life beyond our home planet. The journey into the realms of stellar engineering and cosmic construction beckons, revealing both the vast potentials and profound responsibilities we must embrace amid the stars.

11.4. Binary Star Systems

In the vast tapestry of existence, binary star systems emerge as intriguing arenas of exploration and speculation, holding profound implications for our understanding of cosmic evolution, planetary formation, and the potential for life beyond Earth. Unlike solitary stars, binary systems consist of two stars orbiting a common center of mass, intricately influencing one another through their gravitational interactions. The dual nature of these celestial pairings not only enriches the dynamics of astrophysical processes but also offers unique opportunities and challenges for the development of planetary systems that might harbor life.

To understand the significance of binary star systems, we must first unravel their formation. Many stars are born within molecular clouds, where gravitational instabilities can lead to the formation of multiple stellar objects. In these scenarios, binary star systems can form, where two stellar masses emerge from a shared progenitor cloud. The resulting gravitational interactions between these stars can lead to complex orbital configurations, including wide binaries that orbit at large distances or those that orbit closely, exerting significantly stronger gravitational effects on one another.

The dual nature of binary systems has far-reaching implications for the planets that may form within these configurations. The habitable zones of planets in binary systems can vary dramatically compared to planets orbiting single stars. The stability of orbits is a vital consideration, especially for Earth-like planets positioned in the habitable zones. In close binary systems, the gravitational pull of each star can result in eccentric orbits that might expose planets to extreme temperature fluctuations and variations in radiation. Consequently, planets within these environments face unique challenges as they adapt to varying energies and climate fluctuations.

However, binary systems also present tantalizing opportunities for the genesis of life. If conditions are right, planets within the habitable zones of binary stars can benefit from influences that promote stability and encourage the development of biospheres—an interesting prospect considering that the energy dynamics from multiple stellar sources can lead to enriched atmospheres. For example, some planets in wide binary systems may enjoy favorable conditions from a stable primary star while receiving supplementary energy from a secondary star, creating a dual-source of light that could enhance solar warmth and facilitate diverse ecological adaptations.

Furthermore, interactions among binary stars often lead to phenomena such as mass transfer, wherein one star strips gas and matter from its companion. This transfer can significantly impact the lifespan and characteristics of both stars and any surrounding planetary bodies. In systems where one star evolves into a red giant, it may shed outer layers that affect neighboring planets' atmospheres—creating environments that may either hinder or facilitate the conditions necessary for life.

Significantly, the dynamics in binary systems may influence the trajectory of life in our search for extraterrestrial intelligence. The potential for diverse planetary environments within binary systems suggests that contact and communication could extend beyond simple, isolated stellar systems. The variability inherent in binary configurations presents the possibility of advanced civilizations developing adaptive technologies that harness the unique characteristics of their celestial systems, amplifying echoes of ingenuity across cosmic distances.

Furthermore, binary systems may compel us to reconsider the traditional models we apply to our understanding of planetary habitability. The richness and complexity of these systems may illuminate the pathways to life that seem unattainable under conventional expectations. This enhancement of our definitions of habitable zones emphasizes the importance of ongoing research into the intricate relationships shaping these systems.

The exploration of binary star systems resonates with broader questions regarding our place within the cosmos and the potential for life that pervades its reaches. As we advance our search for exoplanets and engage in observations and simulations, the duality of these stellar systems serves as a reminder to embrace curiosity and open-mindedness about the diverse manifestations of life. Our evolving comprehension of the cosmic environment will serve to guide future terraforming aspirations and exploration initiatives as we probe deeper into the intricate celestial web connecting us all.

In summary, binary star systems stand as pivotal players in the cosmic dance of creation and evolution, highlighting the complex interdependencies that govern the behavior of stars and their planets. The exploration of these unique configurations enriches our understanding of how life might emerge and adapt, inviting us to redefine our perspectives on habitability and intelligence. As we venture forth into the cosmic unknown, the dual nature of binary systems breaks conventional boundaries, ushering in a renewed sense of wonder for the possibilities awaiting us among the stars.

11.5. Healing Stars: Myths and Facts

In this section, we will systematically unravel the myths and facts surrounding the concept of "Healing Stars," a term that encapsulates the interplay between astronomical phenomena and their potential implications for life and civilization in the cosmos. As humanity endeavors to explore extraterrestrial realms and comprehend the origins of life, our understanding of stars—and their dual roles as both celestial powerhouses and harbingers of change—grows increasingly poignant.

The first myth to address is the notion that stars, as life-giving forces in the universe, are immutable and unyielding in their capacity to support life. While it is true that stars serve as the primary source of energy for planets in their proximity, the life cycle of stars is anything but static. Stars are born, evolve, and eventually die, with each phase offering opportunities for cosmic rejuvenation. The process of stellar evolution allows for the dissemination of essential elements, such as carbon, nitrogen, and oxygen, into interstellar space. These elements, enriched by ancient stars, form the building blocks of life on planets orbiting those stars or newly created celestial bodies. Thus, rather than merely acting as celestial providers, stars embody a dynamic cycle, fostering an environment where life may blossom and adapt.

Another prevalent myth is the belief that the energy emitted by stars is uniformly beneficial and static over their life spans. In reality, as stars evolve, they undergo fluctuations that can dramatically change the environment of surrounding planets. For instance, a star entering the red giant phase drastically increases its luminosity and can violently shed layers, impacting the atmospheres of any orbiting planets. Such profound transformations highlight the need to continuously assess the habitability of the cosmos; the once stable conditions may become inhospitable, requiring adaptive measures or advanced technologies to ensure survival.

Turning to the facts, it is essential to recognize the implications of supernovae—catastrophic stellar explosions that herald the end of a star's life cycle. Supernovae eject vast quantities of energy and materials into surrounding space, profoundly affecting both the fabric of their local cosmic neighborhoods and the potential for planetary births. These events not only spread essential elements but also influence the formation of new stars and planetary systems, ultimately contributing to the cycle of life across the galaxies. Understanding the role of supernovae is crucial in the context of healing stars, as it reinforces the interconnectedness between stellar evolution and the genesis of life.

Moreover, the study of pulsars—rapidly rotating neutron stars known for their precise emissions—illustrates not only the characteristics of stellar remnants but also the potential for communication and connectivity across the cosmos. While originally viewed simply as stellar remnants, pulsars may indeed represent communication beacons or markers for advanced civilizations navigating the vast expanse of space. As scientists continue to investigate the unique emissions from these celestial objects, they raise questions that evoke broader discussions about the existence of intelligent life and the technology that may exist within the framework of the universe.

It is imperative to consider technological developments that may arise alongside the scientific understanding of healing stars and their role in supporting life. The concept of stellar engineering—which includes the hypothetical manipulation of stellar output through advanced technologies—invites speculation about the capabilities of future civilizations. If we possess an understanding of how to harness stellar energy, can we then engineer stars to sustain life in surrounding environments? Engaging in this dialogue creates pathways for envisioning coexistence with advanced life forms that may operate on scales beyond our current comprehension.

Furthermore, as we reflect on the mystical qualities attributed to stars, they remain the subject of mythology and inspiration across cultures. Throughout history, humanity has sought to extract meaning from the cosmos, often attributing healing properties to the energy emanating from the stars. In contemporary scientific discourse, this intertwines with a recognition that, while we may not have harnessed the full potential of stars, the healing influence they exert—through their light, energy, and influence in formation processes—cannot be understated.

In closing, disentangling the myths and facts surrounding healing stars invites us to appreciate the intricacies of celestial phenomena in light of life formation. Understanding that stars are dynamic entities reshapes our perception of existence and fuels our curiosity about the potentials woven through cosmic narratives. As we continue to explore the universe, we must remain vigilant, reflexive, and ethical regarding our ambitions to navigate these realms—ensuring that we foster environments where life may flourish amid the majestic backdrop of stars that guide our inquiry. The enigma of healing stars thus serves as both an invitation to embrace exploration and a reminder of our interconnectedness with the cosmos that envelops us.

12. Communication Across the Cosmic Divide

12.1. The Language of Signals

The quest to interpret and understand extraterrestrial signals represents a monumental facet of our interstellar aspirations and scientific endeavors. In the vast expanse of the cosmos, where the potential for life beyond Earth remains tantalizingly elusive, the notion of communication establishes a profound bridge between humanity and the unknown. Signals—or the absence thereof—embody the complexity of this search, compelling scientists to grapple with the intricacies of detecting, decoding, and responding to potential messages from advanced civilizations. This exploration of the language of signals invites us to delve deep into the mechanisms of cosmic communication, the technologies that facilitate these dialogues, and the profound implications of engaging with those who may inhabit the stars.

At the core of the discussion surrounding the language of signals is the recognition that the universe is rich with a cacophony of electromagnetic waves—radiating from stars, pulsars, and galaxies—each contributing to the ambient cosmic soundtrack. In searching for extraterrestrial signals, researchers largely focus on electromagnetic signals within radio wavelengths, as they can traverse vast distances with relative clarity and minimal cosmic interference. However, distinguishing between what may be natural astrophysical phenomena and intentional signals from intelligent life forms poses a significant challenge.

The discipline known as the Search for Extraterrestrial Intelligence (SETI) has emerged as a dedicated effort to monitor and analyze these signals. SETI employs a diverse array of telescopes and antennas that listen actively for narrow-bandwidth radio signals—characteristics often thought to indicate intelligent design. Within this context, the signal-to-noise ratio emerges as a crucial factor. The method involves filtering out background noise from cosmic sources to identify unusual patterns or frequencies that deviate significantly from the anticipated norms.

One notable signal that has captivated imaginations and discussions in the scientific community is the sheer mystery surrounding the WOW! signal, detected by the Big Ear radio telescope in 1977. This brief burst of radio waves remains unexplained to this day, inciting speculative inquiries about its origin—prompting scientists and enthusiasts to evaluate whether it could represent evidence of an extraterrestrial civilization. Such tantalizing echoes across the cosmos reveal the intricacies inherent in discerning the intentional messages found within the noise of the universe.

In parallel with direct signal detection, the interception of potential alien communications calls for advanced technologies and strategies. The innovations in signal processing, machine learning, and artificial intelligence have transformed the ways we search for and categorize radio emissions, expediting the identification of potential extraterrestrial signals. Employing patterns of anomaly recognition enables researchers to sift through the data influx efficiently, pinpointing possible orchestrated messages amid the vast cosmic tapestry of noise.

However, the challenge remains to decode these signals once they are identified. The act of deciphering cosmic messages involves not only recognizing the signals but also attempting to make sense of the content. This beckons intriguing considerations of communication methods and languages that might be employed by extraterrestrial civilizations—a potential confluence of mathematics, physics, and linguistics. As humanity contemplates a response or even a proactive outreach effort, the complexity of understanding the universal languages comes to the forefront of these discussions.

The exploration of the future prospects for cosmic dialogues brings us to the realization that the technological age is inextricably tied to our quest for interstellar understanding. The development of next-generation observatories, enhanced signal detection mechanisms, and persistent monitoring systems places humanity on an increasingly promising trajectory toward uncovering the potential echoes of other civilizations. With advancements in radio astronomy and detection technologies, our endeavors to communicate with potential extraterrestrial intelligences evolve, allowing us to envision a future where we may not only receive signals but engage meaningfully in a cosmic dialogue.

Nevertheless, it is crucial to confront the ethical dimensions tied to these pursuits. What are the implications of making contact or responding to potential signals? How do we grapple with the responsibilities that arise from engaging with life forms, should they exist? As we explore these cosmic connections, the necessity for balanced considerations becomes paramount—serving as a reminder that our endeavors towards discovery must be accompanied by a commitment to respect for the unknown.

In summary, the language of signals serves as a bridge that connects humanity to the enigmatic cosmos beyond our grasp. All the efforts we undertake in seeking, interpreting, and potentially engaging with extraterrestrial communications promise to reshape our understanding of existence across the universe. As we advance our capabilities in detecting and decoding signals, we embark on a journey rich with possibility—one that invites us to ponder our responsibilities, ambitions, and the very fabric of communication amid the stars. The quest for understanding these cosmic narratives transcends mere scientific inquiry; it stands as a testament to humanity's essential drive to explore the unknown and connect with the tapestry of existence woven throughout the vastness of space.

12.2. SETI and the Quest for Contact

In the expansive pursuit of understanding our cosmos and the potential for life beyond Earth, the Search for Extraterrestrial Intelligence (SETI) represents a crucial initiative aimed at answering humanity's most profound question: Are we alone? The quest for contact with intelligent life forms—those beings that may have made their mark on distant worlds—spans decades, uniting the efforts of astronomers, astrophysicists, and the field of astrobiology. The technological advancements that accompany these endeavors enhance our chances of detecting signals indicative of extraterrestrial life, while simultaneously illuminating the intricacies of the universe's broader narrative.

SETI's approach engages in the analysis of radio waves and other electromagnetic signals emanating from outer space. By scanning vast sections of the sky and employing advanced computational methods to filter through noise, researchers aim to identify patterns or anomalies amidst the cacophony of cosmic sounds. The foundation of SETI rests on the belief that communicating civilizations may transmit messages—deliberate signals aimed at making contact —leaving behind trails that researchers can interpret. This makes the identification of such signals an art as much as a science, infusing the search with creativity and speculative enthusiasm.

One of the most notable emphasis points of SETI is the search for narrow-bandwidth radio signals, which are of particular interest due to their association with artificial sources. Such signals—characterized by small ranges of frequencies—are suggestive of intentional transmissions, potentially engineered by advanced civilizations as a means of communication. The ambitious efforts within this field have yielded marginal successes and ongoing challenges, as the vastness of the universe means that even the smallest fractions of light-years can distance us from potential signs of life.

While SETI largely depends on the technological capabilities available in the present, its search has often been tempered by skepticism within the scientific community. This skepticism serves as a critical framework for validating findings and ensuring that claims surrounding potential signals warrant cautious scrutiny. As previously encountered signals, like the WOW! signal, illustrate, the reality of interpreting cosmic observations involves complex layers of uncertainty and challenge. Researchers must navigate the fine line between hope and realism, often facing the dilemma of verifying a signal's origin against possible natural astrophysical sources.

In refining these methodologies, collaboration becomes instrumental. SETI's influence extends beyond single-entity research; it has sparked collective endeavors among international observatories, enhancing the reach and breadth of the search for extraterrestrial signals. This spirit of collaboration not only promotes the sharing of findings and resources but also amplifies public interest and engagement, fueling a growing field that captures humanity's curiosity to the stars.

As we gaze into the cosmic abyss, pondering the existence of other life forms, the question of how to communicate with such civilizations becomes paramount. Should signals be detected, considerations surrounding potential contact raise profound ethical and philosophical dilemmas. These questions extend to the implications of engaging with intelligent life, weighing the responsibilities that accompany the understanding of new forms of existence and consciousness.

Looking ahead, the prospects for future cosmic dialogues remain both tantalizing and complex. The evolution of technology—including advanced telescopes and signal-processing capabilities—will likely enhance the capacity to discern potential signals more effectively. Quantum computing, for instance, may revolutionize our ability to analyze massive datasets efficiently, while algorithms informed by artificial intelligence may identify anomalous patterns that hint at extraterrestrial sources. The quest for contact continues, urging researchers to push boundaries, adapt methodologies, and engage with evolving questions about existence.

In conclusion, SETI epitomizes the convergence of human curiosity, scientific innovation, and the profound yearning to connect with other forms of consciousness within the cosmos. The endeavor to seek extraterrestrial signals compels us to reflect on the profound implications of understanding life beyond our planet. As we tirelessly pursue knowledge, each step taken toward seeking contact brings us closer to unveiling the mysteries of the universe, echoing the oldest human aspirations to explore, discover, and connect with the myriad forms of life that may exist among the stars. The search continues —an eternal dialogue that signifies our place in the intricate web of cosmic existence, linking us to the great unknown that beckons from the depths of space.

12.3. Interception of Alien Communications

In the pursuit of understanding extraterrestrial life and potential terraformation, the interception of alien communications presents one of the most compelling avenues of inquiry. This complex endeavor addresses not just the technological and scientific challenges involved, but also philosophical, ethical, and societal implications. As we delve into this subchapter, we explore the mechanisms through which humans seek to identify, decode, and interpret signals from beyond our planet, aiming to engage with possible intelligent life forms residing in the vast reaches of space.

Fundamentally, the interception of alien communications relies on the assumption that advanced civilizations may deploy technologies capable of generating signals that can traverse the distances of the cosmos. The Search for Extraterrestrial Intelligence (SETI) has been at the forefront of this pursuit, employing radio telescopes to survey the sky for narrow-bandwidth radio signals that could indicate the presence of intelligent sources. The methodology hinges on the premise that such signals, by virtue of their specific frequencies, would stand out amidst the cosmic background noise of natural phenomena.

To initiate this search, researchers utilize a range of strategies, experimenting with numerous frequencies and signal patterns. As instruments and technologies advance, the capacity to detect signals has improved significantly, allowing scientists to sift through enormous data sets with greater efficiency and precision. The introduction of machine learning algorithms has revolutionized the analysis process, enabling researchers to identify distinct patterns within the noise, a task that would be unfeasible through manual analysis alone.

However, the quest for intercepting alien communications is not merely a technical challenge; it also raises profound philosophical inquiries. How do we define communication? Signals sent from distant worlds may embody concepts and languages vastly different from what we understand. As scientists strive to decode potential extraterrestrial messages, they grapple with the complexities of deciphering meanings that arise from alien contexts. The possibility of linguistic barriers and cultural differences introduces multiple layers of complexity—acknowledging that the very constructs of language may be inherently tied to the form of life that produces it.

Moreover, the ethical implications of intercepting and responding to alien communications emerge as a significant concern. Should humanity initiate contact, we must consider the consequences of engaging with potential extraterrestrial societies. What responsibilities do we hold as representatives of life on Earth? The potential reactions of advanced civilizations to our attempts at communication carry profound implications for our understanding of interstellar relations. This ethical dimension urges a candid reflection on the policies guiding such interactions, advocating for a respectful approach that acknowledges the complexities inherent in any form of contact.

As researchers explore the depths of the universe looking for potential signals, they also remain cognizant of the possibility that we are not alone in our search; various organizations and projects around the world collaborate to identify and analyze signals from distant stars. The collaborative nature of these efforts fosters a sense of unity in the scientific community, reinforcing a collective commitment to unraveling one of humanity's most profound questions—the existence of life beyond Earth.

The potential ramifications of intercepting alien communications extend into the societal sphere as public interest and curiosity about extraterrestrial life intensify. As announcements of potential signals or discoveries circulate through media channels, they spark imagination and dialogue within society. These discussions often mirror humanity's historical pursuit of understanding our place within the universe, driving cultural narratives around contact with alien civilizations.

While the search for extraterrestrial signals and the interception of alien communications remain paramount scientific endeavors, it is crucial to ground these efforts in transparency and public engagement. Clear communication regarding the methodologies, goals, and findings of SETI activities can enhance public understanding while managing expectations regarding the possibilities of encountering extraterrestrial intelligence.

In conclusion, the interception of alien communications encapsulates a complex interplay of scientific inquiry, philosophical exploration, and ethical consideration as humanity reaches beyond its planetary confines. The potential signals from distant civilizations hold the promise of unlocking cosmic secrets, but they simultaneously challenge us to reflect on our responsibilities in an interconnected universe. As we continue to explore this frontier, the journey to decode the language of signals beckons with the promise of discovery, reflection, and the ever-elusive hope of connection among the stars. Through these endeavors, humanity boldly ponders the profound question—what might we learn from the voices echoing across the cosmic void?

12.4. Decoding Cosmic Messages

Decoding cosmic messages allows humanity to delve into the enigmatic realm of extraterrestrial communication, revealing a tapestry of potential dialogues between civilizations and cosmic intelligences. As we advance in our understanding of the universe and harness the technology to make meaningful contact, this undertaking will shape our engagement with life beyond Earth and redefine our existence among the stars.

At the heart of decoding cosmic messages lies the quest for understanding signals transmitted across the vast expanses of space. Radio waves, visible light, and other forms of electromagnetic radiation traverse interstellar distances, serving as potential conduits for communication between intelligent beings. The foundational work set forth by the Search for Extraterrestrial Intelligence (SETI) symbolizes humanity's endeavor to sift through the cosmic background noise to identify signals indicative of intelligent design. This multifaceted approach encompasses the use of established telescopes as well as innovative methodologies, employing computational algorithms capable of discerning patterns in vast datasets.

As researchers convert these signals into discernible messages, the complexities inherent in communication become evident. Human linguistics, shaped by cultural and biological foundations, cannot be assumed to apply universally to all intelligent beings. The challenge lies in interpreting any received communication within a framework that transcends human-centric paradigms. Theoretically, an extraterrestrial message could utilize mathematical constructs, universal constants, or geometric principles as the basis for communication —entities not bound to specific languages or contexts. It becomes imperative for scientists to remain open to myriad forms of expression that may arise from the unknown.

When a potential extraterrestrial message is identified, decoding it requires a deep understanding of the fundamental principles of science and mathematics. Prime numbers, frequencies, and patterns often resonate as likely candidates for an intelligent signal, embedding meaning in a universal language of order and structure. In this context, the deciphering of such communication can serve as a bridge between civilizations, laying the groundwork for interstellar dialogues that might transcend time and space.

The very act of interpreting these signals also prompts thoughtful engagement with ethical considerations. The implications of contact with extraterrestrial civilizations invoke questions of responsibility, and humanity must grapple with the consequences of reaching out. What ethical obligations arise from establishing communication with another intelligent species? How do we navigate potential disparities in technology, culture, and understanding? These reflections offer valuable opportunities for discourse within the scientific community and beyond, shaping our approach to cosmic engagement.

Furthermore, the pursuit of decoding cosmic messages extends beyond mere reception; it embodies humanity's existential questions about our place in the universe. Each potential signal holds the promise of knowledge and connection, invoking thoughts of shared experiences and aspirations among intelligent beings. Engaging with these profound questions compels us to contemplate our interconnectedness, ultimately expanding our sense of identity as we explore new realms of consciousness and understanding.

As we stand on the precipice of cosmic exploration, potent advancements in technology catalyze our efforts in decoding cosmic messages. The integration of artificial intelligence, advanced signal processing, and interdisciplinary collaboration facilitates the analytical methods necessary to sift through the outputs from various cosmic observatories. As scientific investigations unfold and methodologies continue to evolve, we inch closer to the realization that the universe might echo with vibrant discussions waiting to be heard.

Ultimately, decoding cosmic messages signifies humanity's relentless pursuit of understanding and connection with the cosmos. Each endeavor reveals our potential to foster relationships with life forms that transcend the limitations of our Earth-bound experiences. This journey is not simply about receiving messages; it embodies the potential for dialogue, exploration, and the deepening of our understanding of existence. The intricate dance of communication invites us to engage with curiosity, inspiration, and responsibility as we seek to unravel the majestic mysteries of the universe. The task ahead is as monumental as it is thrilling, reminding us of our collective aspiration to explore the various pathways of life spread across the stars.

12.5. Future Prospects for Cosmic Dialogues

In the realm of speculative science and astronomical endeavors, the future prospects for cosmic dialogues are characterized by layered complexities and profound aspirations. As humanity pushes the boundaries of exploration, the possibility of establishing communication with extraterrestrial beings awakens a deeply rooted curiosity within our species. The evolving technologies, scientific advancements, and philosophical reflections surrounding these interactions shape not only our understanding of the cosmos but also our vision of existence itself.

The foundation of these future prospects lies in the relentless pursuit of knowledge. As observational technologies continue to evolve, the threshold for detecting potential signals from distant civilizations broadens. Enhanced telescopes, sophisticated signal-processing algorithms, and collaborative networks among global scientific institutions coalesce to elevate our search for extraterrestrial life. With advancements such as the James Webb Space Telescope and radio observatories like the Square Kilometer Array, the window through which we view the cosmos expands, offering tantalizing opportunities to decipher the myriad signals that may traverse the void.

As we refine our methodologies, the ethical implications of establishing contact come into sharper focus. The philosophical dilemmas regarding communication with alien civilizations anchor our discourse in moral responsibilities. Should we reach out, the potential consequences—both positive and negative—must be carefully weighed. The engagement with intelligent life not only carries the promise of shared knowledge and cultural exchange but also poses significant risks, necessitating a framework that prioritizes respectful dialogue and accountability.

The languages of signals become central to cosmological dialogues, inviting us to explore communication paradigms that transcend human-centric frameworks. As we theorize about the forms these communications might take—be they mathematical constructs, symbols, or unique patterns—our understanding of language itself expands toward a more inclusive definition. The very essence of communication underscores the interconnectedness that can exist between civilizations, urging us to embrace curiosity about the nature of life, intelligence, and shared existence across dimensions.

Additionally, the inquiry into the nature of alien civilizations shapes our understanding of interstellar interactions. The question of how we might respond to messages or signals becomes a defining theme in our exploration. As we navigate through advancements in artificial intelligence and quantum computing, our ability to process vast amounts of data grows, facilitating attempts to decode and interpret potential extraterrestrial communication. Each wave of discovery aligns intricately with the hopes, fears, and aspirations tied to connecting with other intelligent beings.

Furthermore, ongoing dialogue within the scientific community emphasizes the importance of transparency and public engagement. Maintaining an informed and curious society fosters interest in both the scientific processes and the cosmic narrative that underpins our understanding of existence. As knowledge expands, so too does the clarity with which we frame the conversation surrounding the ethical and societal implications of our search for extraterrestrial life.

Exploring the implications of cosmic dialogues also fosters a deeper understanding of our place in the universe. In reaching out, we not only seek others but also reflect upon our shared humanity. As potential signals pierce through the cosmic expanse, they beckon us to consider not only the content of the messages we hope to receive but the interconnections and responsibilities that arise from engaging with life outside our planet.

In conclusion, the future prospects for cosmic dialogues stand as an invitation to explore the richness of existence, treading paths that intertwine curiosity, ethics, and innovation. As humanity continues its quest to traverse the stars and connect with other intelligences, the exploration of these dialogues will illuminate profound truths: truths about ourselves, the universe, and the myriad possibilities of life that may thrive among the stars. Through our engagement in these cosmic conversations, we acknowledge our roles not merely as observers but as active participants in the larger narrative of the universe—a narrative that unites us all in our shared pursuit of understanding and connection.

13. Terraformed Landscapes: Artistic Visions

13.1. Depictions in Media and Art

The impact of media and art on the understanding of alien terraformation and the cosmos is multifaceted, enriching our cultural narrative with imaginative depictions and interpretations that inspire inquiry and fascination. As humanity grapples with profound questions about life beyond Earth, artistic visions serve as essential conduits for expressing our aspirations, fears, and ethical considerations related to extraterrestrial encounters. This subchapter will explore how depictions in various forms of media and art shape public perception, drive scientific curiosity, and reveal the interconnectedness of creative expression and cosmic exploration.

Artistic representations of alien worlds and terraformation have a storied history, dating back to early science fiction literature and evolving with the advent of film, television, and digital media. Literature, in particular, has illuminated the possibility of life on other planets, playing a pivotal role in shaping societal imagination around space travel and the intricacies of planetary engineering. Classic works such as H.G. Wells' "The War of the Worlds" and Arthur C. Clarke's "Childhood's End" have thoughtfully explored themes of contact, adaptation, and the ethical dilemmas that arise from terraforming endeavors. These narratives provide a foundation for audiences to ponder the profound realities surrounding existence in the cosmos, forging dialogues about the implications of human actions on distant worlds.

Cinema has played an equally crucial role in delving into the realms of alien worlds and terraformation. Iconic films such as "Interstellar" and "The Martian" have captivated generations with their compelling characters and vivid depictions of the efforts needed to survive on inhospitable planets. These films not only engage audiences but also foster discussions about the science underpinning these imaginative narratives, bridging the gap between fiction and scientific inquiry.

In the artistic interpretation of alien landscapes, visual effects enable filmmakers to showcase the beauty and diversity of planetary environments, igniting public interest and curiosity in the scientific endeavors that underpin these creative visions.

Moreover, popular culture has embraced the theme of terraforming, reflecting societal aspirations for expansion beyond Earth. Video games, graphic novels, and illustrations have imagined worlds shaped by technologies and the interplay between life forms. These portrayals invite players and readers to engage deeply with the concept of terraformation, exploring theoretical models and strategies for transforming environments across the cosmos. The dynamic interplay between gaming, visual art, and storytelling creates a unique opportunity for individuals to reflect on the ethical implications of altering alien worlds—a dialogue echoed through many cultural expressions.

Famous artistic interpretations, ranging from traditional paintings to contemporary digital art, have further influenced public perception of alien worlds and terraforming through imaginative depictions of planetary landscapes. As artists conceptualize environments informed by scientific knowledge and speculation, they evoke a sense of wonder, merging elements of reality with fantastical visions. Artists like Chesley Bonestell and contemporary digital creators capture the possibilities of terraforming through their imaginative landscapes, providing visual representations that stimulate scientific curiosity and invigorate discussions about the viability of creating habitable environments on distant worlds.

Symbolic representations in culture also play a significant role in framing our understanding of cosmic possibilities and challenges. These artistic expressions often convey deeper philosophical questions about humanity's relationship with nature, technology, and the unknown. The symbolism found in artworks can prompt individuals to reflect on their role in shaping not just Earth but the wider celestial realm. As we grapple with the ethical dilemmas inherent in terraforming, these representations serve as critical touchstones, encouraging thoughtful dialogue and fostering awareness surrounding our responsibilities toward the cosmos.

Furthermore, the intersection of science, art, and public engagement extends into the realm of educational initiatives. Art serves as a medium for facilitating learning about complex scientific concepts related to exoplanets, atmospheric engineering, and ecological dynamics. Programs that marry scientific inquiry with artistic expression —such as workshops, exhibitions, and collaborative projects—can catalyze newfound interest in science and inspire future generations to explore the possibilities of life beyond Earth.

In conclusion, depictions in media and art shape our understanding of alien terraformation and the cosmos, weaving together imagination, inquiry, and ethics. Through literature, film, and artistic expression, the narratives surrounding extraterrestrial encounters invite us to ponder what lies beyond our planet while reflecting on our role within the greater universe. As humanity embarks on its quest for exploration and discovery, creativity becomes a vital ingredient, illuminating paths toward understanding the complexities of life across the cosmos. Ultimately, these artistic visions challenge us to explore not only the potential for terraforming distant worlds but also the implications for existence and the responsibilities we carry into the vast unknown that awaits.

13.2. Imagined Planets: Creativity in Film

Imagined planets have long served as a fertile ground for creativity in film, inviting audiences to explore the possibilities of alien worlds and the impact of terraforming on those environments. The vast expanse of the cosmos, dotted with unexplored planets and hidden civilizations, captures the human imagination and provides a rich backdrop for exploring existential and philosophical questions about life beyond Earth. As filmmakers and storytellers craft their narratives, they lend artistic expression to scientific theories, enhancing our understanding of the universe and the ethical dilemmas that come with cosmic exploration.

From the classics of science fiction literature to the visually stunning adaptations on screen, imagined planets serve as key characters in narratives of adventure, conflict, and discovery. Films such as "Interstellar" and "The Martian" have brought attention to the challenges and triumphs associated with extraterrestrial colonization and terraforming, while also addressing the resilience of human spirit against the backdrop of alien landscapes. The portrayal of planets as complex, living ecosystems pricked with intricacies often reflects real scientific theories, encouraging audiences to reflect on the tangible aspects of these fictional environments and their relevance to our understanding of alien life.

Visual representations play a significant role in shaping our perception of imagined planets. The aesthetic choices made by filmmakers —ranging from lush green landscapes teeming with alien flora to desolate and barren terrains—inform how audiences engage with the ideas presented. These artistic visions ignite curiosity while fostering a deeper appreciation for the scientific foundations that underline these environments. Digital effects and animation allow creators to envision worlds beyond our own with vivid detail, transporting viewers into realms of possibility that stretch the boundaries of human experience.

Moreover, the themes explored in imagined planets often resonate with pressing concerns about our own planet. Many narratives tackle the consequences of environmental degradation and climate change, reflecting a growing awareness of humanity's impact on Earth. Such storytelling encourages audiences to consider the responsibilities that accompany the exploration of other worlds, urging us to reflect on the potential consequences of terraforming endeavors. Entertainment becomes a vessel for raising awareness about ethical considerations, encouraging the audience to engage with ideas surrounding stewardship, respect for existing ecosystems, and the preservation of unique planetary environments.

One particularly notable aspect of imagined planets is their ability to serve as reflections of societal values and aspirations. Filmmakers often employ world-building to explore notions of utopia and dystopia, crafting societies that embody either the potential for harmony or the pitfalls of excess. These narratives compel audiences to grapple with the implications of humanity's reach into the unknown, prompting questions about our role in shaping the futures of both Earth and distant planets. In engaging with these stories, audiences cultivate a broader understanding of the delicate balance between ambition and responsibility.

As audiences immerse themselves in these films, a dialogue emerges between science, art, and culture that transcends mere entertainment. The exploration of imagined planets encourages viewers to embrace the curiosity that drives scientific inquiry while simultaneously reflecting on the ethical considerations surrounding terraforming and cosmic exploration.

In conclusion, the role of imagined planets as vehicles for creativity in film profoundly influences our understanding of extraterrestrial life and terraforming. These artistic expressions navigate the intricate web of human curiosity, scientific inquiry, and ethical responsibility, inviting audiences to ponder their place in the cosmos. Through visual storytelling and imaginative narratives, films encourage us to dream of distant worlds while holding that sense of wonder in balance with respect for existing life. As we seek to understand the universe's mysteries, the creativity woven into these imagined planets fuels our aspirations of exploration and nurtures our innate desire for connection among the stars.

13.3. Literary Inspirations from Alien Worlds

In the narrative of humanity's quest to understand the universe, the concept of literary inspirations from alien worlds stands as a powerful testament to the profound interplay between science fiction and scientific inquiry. This exploration captures the imaginative spirit that has long driven our fascination with extraterrestrial life and the prospects of terraforming distant planets. As we traverse through the pages of literature, art, cinema, and cultural expressions, we uncover profound insights that resonate with our seeking nature, fueling aspiration and inquiry about what lies beyond our own planet.

The literary roots of our fascination with alien worlds can be traced back to seminal works of science fiction, where writers like H.G. Wells, Arthur C. Clarke, and Philip K. Dick championed narratives that pushed the boundaries of imagination and examinations of technological possibilities. These authors crafted fantastical visions of extraterrestrial civilizations, technologically advanced societies, and the transformative impacts of contact with other beings. Such representations carved out a space where readers could grapple with speculative concepts winding through themes of alien diplomacy, terraforming aspirations, and the ethical nuances of humanity's role in the cosmos.

In the 20th century, science fiction further blossomed, entering a phase characterized by the exploration of alien landscapes with vivid narratives. The works of Isaac Asimov and Ursula K. Le Guin echoed sentiments about adaptation and survival, evoking questions about interstellar collaboration and understanding. Asimov's Galactic Empire, for instance, presented a universe steeped in complexity, where life and evolution intertwined across different planets, showcasing the potential for diverse ecosystems shaped by civilizations both ambitious and fraught with peril.

The artistic interpretations that emerged from these literary inspirations found a mesmerizing place in film and visual media. Directors like Ridley Scott, with "Blade Runner," and Steven Spielberg, with "Close Encounters of the Third Kind," breathed life into imaginative representations of alien worlds, stimulating visuals that celebrated the allure of the unknown. These cinematic interpretations not only brought forth questions around the nature of intelligence and existence but also showcased the visceral beauty of the stars, reminding audiences of the potential diversity of life in the universe.

Furthermore, adaptations in graphic novels and art exhibitions have reinforced the artistic journeys across alien landscapes, capturing the interplay of light and shadow, color and form—each visual serving as a canvas for exploring extraterrestrial life forms and their potential interactions with humanity. Artists have long interpreted what alien landscapes might embody, whether lush, verdant worlds ripe for exploration or barren, desolate terrains inviting curiosity and adventure from human explorers. Such artistic representations invite viewers to bridge the gap between fantasy and the scientific discourse around what terraforming could entail.

Central to these literary inspirations is the exploration of philosophical questions. The themes prevalent in science fiction often reflect humanity's own desires and fears regarding exploration, colonization, and the responsibilities we carry as custodians of life. In contemplating how we might manipulate alien worlds, authors spark conversations about ecological ethics, the implications of interference, and the moral dilemmas posed by engaging with beings far different from ourselves. As humanity moves toward a future characterized by potential interactions with extraterrestrial life, these discussions within literature become more pressing, reminding us of the rich legacies we carry as we reach for the stars.

Moreover, contemporary science fiction continues to thrive as a medium for exploring the implications of future technologies and how they might influence society. Today's authors include diverse voices, each contributing to the overarching narrative surrounding alien worlds and terraforming. Works of N.K. Jemisin and Ann Leckie probe societal structures, detailed environments, and the potential of technology to reshape life in unexpected ways, reflecting contemporary realities as they consider the complexities of interactions that could occur in the broader universe.

In conclusion, literary inspirations from alien worlds play an essential role in shaping our collective understanding of extraterrestrial life and terraformation. Through the narratives crafted by luminaries of science fiction, the portrayals of imagined landscapes in films and art, and the philosophical questions posed by these works, we forge a connection with the cosmos that transcends mere observation.

These inspirations invite us to reflect upon not only our curiosity and wonder but also our responsibilities as humanity seeks to unlock the mysteries embedded within the universe. The relationship between literature, art, and science forms a rich tapestry of exploration inviting us to dream, discover, and dare—to envision futures where the stars beckon and possibilities abound.

13.4. Famous Artistic Interpretations

Famous Artistic Interpretations serve as a compelling lens through which humanity explores its fascination with extraterrestrial forms of life, environments, and the possibilities of terraforming. In art and literature, these imaginative representations not only transcend boundaries of science and fiction, but also evoke profound questions surrounding existence, identity, and our role in the universe. This subchapter investigates the myriad ways that creative expressions have influenced our understanding of alien worlds, the ethical considerations of cosmological engagement, and the aspirational narratives tethered to the notion of life beyond Earth.

Art has long been a medium for interpreting the unknown, allowing artists to visualize concepts that science is only beginning to understand. The portrayal of alien landscapes has captured hearts and minds, inviting deep engagement from audiences. Iconic representations—whether in science fiction literature, cinematic masterpieces, or visual art—offer imaginative frameworks in which we navigate the complexities of extraterrestrial exploration and colonization. Works by visionary authors like H.G. Wells and Arthur Clarke set foundational narratives in the early 20th century, exploring the implications of contact and the human condition within the context of interstellar existence.

Films, notably, have elevated these creative interpretations to new heights. The imagery of iconic movies such as "2001: A Space Odyssey," "Blade Runner," and "Avatar" showcase visually stunning depictions of alien worlds, each crafted within their own ecological contexts. By traversing otherworldly environments, audiences are invited to ponder the potential for life, the impact of technology, and themes of coexistence and dominance. These portrayals transform what may seem like speculative fantasies into rich cultural reflections that resonate with inquisitive minds.

Furthermore, artistic interpretations play a significant role in shaping public perception. By residing at the intersection of science and imagination, various media forms engage society in dialogues surrounding the ethics of extraterrestrial exploration and the implications of terraforming other worlds. Presenting narratives that warrant reflective questioning helps shape the cultural discourse on interstellar ethics, guiding humanity's pursuit of understanding in a universe as rich as it is mysterious.

Prominent artistic interpretations also serve to amplify our collective vision, propelling discussions surrounding potential terraforming initiatives. The ability to visualize environments made hospitable through human ingenuity offers an optimistic view that juxtaposes the stark reality of our ecological challenges on Earth. Artistic representations can instill hope and curiosity, inviting audiences to visualize worlds transformed into lush, dynamic ecosystems, where life can blossom against all odds.

Equally important is the acknowledgment of symbolic representation in culture, where art intersects with humanity's experiences of exploration and discovery. Humanity's historical narrative of reaching beyond its terrestrial confines has fostered a sense of ambition and curiosity. Each artistic symbol—from ancient mythologies and folklore to modern adaptations—serves to reflect our values, ambitions, and the inherent desire to connect with the unknown. In many respects, these representations challenge us to consider our responsibilities toward any life forms that we might encounter.

As we explore famous artistic interpretations, we must also consider how they align with the scientific principles that govern astrobiology and terraforming. Artistic works have the potential to serve as educational tools, fostering a deeper understanding of scientific realities while inspiring future generations of explorers. This relationship between art and science nurtures a culture of curiosity that propels innovation, as artists and scientists alike collaborate to envision futures that integrate discovery and creativity.

In conclusion, famous artistic interpretations play an essential role in shaping humanity's understanding of extraterrestrial life and the possibilities of terraforming. They act as bridges between science, imagination, and cultural reflections, compelling us to engage deeply with the questions that arise from our explorations. As we journey into the cosmos, these artistic visions challenge us to consider the implications of our actions, the relationships we forge with alien worlds, and the stories we tell about our identities as explorers of the majestic universe. Through these creative expressions, we are reminded of our shared aspirations and responsibilities as we endeavor to understand the nature of life beyond our own home planet.

13.5. Symbolic Representation in Culture

In exploring symbolic representation in culture, we delve into an intricate realm where art, mythology, literature, and existential inquiry intersect to echo humanity's deep desire to understand the cosmos and ourselves. Symbolism has long served as a vehicle for conveying profound ideas and themes relating to alien life, terraforming, and our connection to the universe. Through various forms of artistic expression, symbols shape our perceptions, inspire exploration, and evoke contemplation about the potential existence of intelligent life beyond Earth.

Throughout history, cultures have turned to the stars, crafting myths and stories that articulate our relationship with celestial phenomena. The symbols created within these narratives often reflect humanity's aspirations, fears, and ethical considerations in the context of cosmic exploration. From ancient civilizations that likened celestial bodies to gods and deities, to modern science fiction that imagines interstellar travel and terraformed worlds, symbols permit fluid expressions of our inherent curiosity and interconnectedness with the cosmos.

The representation of extraterrestrial landscapes and civilizations in literature serves as a foundation for this discussion. Renowned science fiction writers, like Arthur C. Clarke and H.G. Wells, have fueled imaginations throughout generations, presenting thought-provoking portrayals of life beyond Earth. Their rich symbolism encapsulates the existential questions posed by contact with alien beings. The imagery of stars as gateways to the unknown and planets as battlegrounds of potential conflict or collaboration embodies the dual nature of human encounters with the cosmos.

Artistic interpretations of alien worlds further enrich the narrative of symbolic representation. Artists across different mediums, from painters and sculptors to digital creators, conjure imaginative landscapes that visually embody the prospects of life beyond our planet. The vibrant, swirling colors of a distant exoplanet or the haunting stillness of a barren moon invoke a sense of wonder and exploration. The symbols imbued within these creations speak to a collective yearning—an aspiration to transcend earthly limitations and connect with the vastness of the universe.

Science fiction films, prominently featuring imaginative planets and extraterrestrial species, contribute significantly to the conversation surrounding terraforming and cosmic exploration. Iconic films like "Contact," "Arrival," and "Interstellar" explore themes of communication, the ethics of encountering alien life, and the paradox of humanity's place within an expansive universe. These cinematic depictions often utilize symbols of light, darkness, and the unknown to forge emotional connections with audiences, guiding them through philosophical quandaries while simultaneously igniting curiosity about the realities of life beyond Earth.

Symbols also weave their way into scientific discourse and public perception. The language that scientists use to discuss concepts such as terraforming, astrobiology, and interstellar travel is often laden with metaphorical meaning. Describing the search for extraterrestrial life as an "ocean of possibilities" encapsulates the vast and profound implications of this inquiry, bridging the gap between complex scientific ideas and the cultural narratives that shape our understanding of them.

Moreover, the emergence of public engagement through social media and interactive platforms has enabled the visual symbols of the cosmic narrative to permeate public consciousness, fostering interest and dialogue surrounding scientific discoveries and discussions about life in the universe. As audiences share art, literature, and media interpretations, the symbols of cosmic exploration coalesce into a shared cultural identity—a testament to humanity's collective journey toward uncovering the mysteries nestled among the stars.

While symbolism provides a rich terrain for exploration, it's essential to approach these symbols with critical awareness. The narratives surrounding alien life and terraforming often carry inherent biases and reflect societal values, impacting how we interpret the unknown. Engaging in reflective conversations about the implications of these representations allows us to recognize that the symbols we create also shape our actions and values as we delve deeper into the cosmos.

In conclusion, the symbolic representation in culture serves as a powerful lens through which we navigate the complexities of alien worlds and the prospect of terraforming. By examining the intricate interconnections between art, mythology, literature, and scientific inquiry, we recognize how these symbols influence our understanding of the universe and our place within it. As humanity continues its quest for knowledge, the blend of imagination and inquiry becomes an essential tool for exploring the plurality of life's expressions across the cosmos—a reminder that our stories, aspirations, and symbols intertwine with the rich mysteries that await us among the stars.

14. Planetary Protections: Avoiding Contamination

14.1. Understanding the Cosmic Frontier

Understanding the Cosmic Frontier is a journey that extends beyond the mere observation of celestial bodies; it is an exploration of the vast, dynamic nature of the universe and the potential for life beyond Earth. As we stand on the brink of significant scientific advancements, the quest to decode the cosmic framework becomes intertwined with the search for extraterrestrial influences in terraforming efforts. This subchapter seeks to unravel the cosmic expanse as a frontier of possibilities, illuminating the unseen forces and intricate relationships that govern the life and death of stars, planets, and possibly, civilizations.

At the forefront of our understanding lies the recognition that the universe is an expansive tapestry, governed by the laws of physics and the delicate balance of forces. The cosmic frontier encompasses a multitude of interstellar phenomena—from the birth of stars in gaseous nebulae to the violent aftermath of supernovae that enrich the cosmos with the elements necessary for life. It poses fundamental questions about existence, pushing the boundaries of our comprehension and inspiring a cultural narrative that embraces exploration and curiosity.

The processes that shape the cosmic frontier are not random; they are deeply interconnected. The lifecycle of stars—those brilliant beacons in the night sky—provides a reliable framework for understanding the origin of elements foundational to life. The journey of a star, from its initial fusion of hydrogen in the main sequence to its explosive death as a supernova, creates a series of events that enable the evolution of planets and their potential habitats. The materials expelled by these dying stars sequentially coalesce, forming new celestial objects, and hence, nurturing the conditions necessary for life elsewhere.

As we navigate this cosmic landscape, we must consider how factors such as gravity and radiation dictate the conditions of habitable zones —regions within star systems where temperatures allow for liquid water to exist. The Goldilocks principle captures this idea, emphasizing the need for specific environmental thresholds that support the delicate balance required for life to flourish. The exploration of exoplanets, particularly those residing within their stars' habitable zones, continues to captivate scientific inquiry, opening avenues for discovering innovative ways to manipulate environments through terraforming practices.

Furthermore, the cosmic frontier invites speculation about the existence of extraterrestrial civilizations that might wield the knowledge and technology to engineer their worlds. These advanced societies could potentially modify atmospheres, create energy sources harnessing stellar radiation, and facilitate the ecosystems necessary for sustaining life. As we aspire to decode the signs of alien terraforming, we must consider how understanding the cosmic frontier may provoke our imaginations to envision what life might look like among the stars—and what ethical implications accompany such vast ambitions.

The knowledge derived from our exploration of the cosmic frontier also informs our scientific practices and policies. Global initiatives to study the universe encourage collaboration among nations, fostering dialogue that transcends political and cultural boundaries. The quest for cosmic knowledge can unite humanity, prompting collective efforts to explore the unknown and understand our place within the larger cosmic narrative.

Ultimately, understanding the cosmic frontier provokes a deeper reflection on existence itself. It beckons humanity to engage with its curiosities and fears, urging us to recognize our responsibilities as stewards of both our planet and any other potential worlds we may encounter. As we gaze into the abyss of the cosmos, we realize that our journey to comprehend the cosmic frontier is more than a scientific endeavor; it is an odyssey of the human spirit in pursuit of connection, understanding, and exploration.

In summary, navigating the cosmic frontier is a multifaceted exploration that intertwines science, philosophy, and creativity. It challenges us to decode the mysteries of the universe, expanding our perceptions of life and igniting our imaginations with the boundless possibilities that lie beyond our current understanding. As we continue our ambitious search for extraterrestrial life and the potential for terraforming, we stand poised at the threshold of discovery—a testament to the enduring human spirit that yearns to chart its path among the stars.

14.2. Isolation Protocols

In the vast tapestry of the cosmos, human curiosity stands as one of our most defining traits. From the time we gazed up at the night sky and imagined constellations to today, sending probes to the farthest reaches of our solar system, our desire to understand the universe has propelled civilization forward. At the heart of that quest lies a singular question: Are we alone? With recent technological advancements, what was once limited to the realm of science fiction is now a serious field of study.

To truly appreciate the potential for extraterrestrial terraformation, we must examine the systematic intricacies of what lies within the cosmic neighborhood surrounding our planet. Isolation protocols emerge as paramount in the context of practical scientific exploration, guiding our ethical considerations as we venture into the unknown. When the possibility of encountering alien life forms lurks at the fringes of our cosmic outreach, it becomes essential to manage and mitigate any risks that might arise during our interactions with these environments.

Isolation protocols offer structured guidelines designed to safeguard both human explorers and the extraterrestrial ecosystems we may encounter. Whether through the principles of planetary protection or the meticulous containment strategies utilized for sample returns from other celestial bodies, the underpinning ethos emphasizes reverence for the unknown and its inherent complexities. By adhering to these protocols, researchers ensure that potential biological contamination does not compromise unique alien life forms or disrupt indigenous ecosystems.

Furthermore, microbial dangers loom large as an ever-present consideration in the development of isolation strategies. The possibility of inadvertently transporting terrestrial microbes to other planets—or vice versa—poses severe repercussions for both environments. Understanding the resilience of Earth-based microbes in alien conditions and their potential to proliferate highlights the necessity for careful preventative measures. Rigorous sterilization protocols and quarantine practices are integral to uphold integrity within alien ecosystems as we probe for knowledge.

The regulatory frameworks governing space exploration continues evolving, responding to emerging scientific findings and ethical imperatives surrounding potential cosmic interactions. International treaties, including the Outer Space Treaty and the Biological and Toxin Weapons Convention, provide essential guidelines on how humanity engages with extraterrestrial environments, articulating responsibilities to preserve existing biospheres and ensure protection against harmful microbes.

Alongside these regulations, precautionary measures in space exploration serve as proactive strategies to prevent contamination and ecological disruption. Education and rigorous training for astronauts, mission planners, and researchers become paramount; emphasizing a comprehensive understanding of the complexities of life on Earth and beyond fosters an awareness of the ethical responsibilities tied to our cosmic endeavors. This awareness will shape not only how we conduct scientific missions but also how we approach potential terraforming projects as we navigate the responsibilities of cosmic stewardship.

Ultimately, isolation protocols, microbial danger considerations, and ongoing regulatory developments coalesce to form a complex framework that guides us in our pursuit of understanding the universe. These elements compel us to reflect on our role within this cosmos and the responsibilities that accompany any exploration of celestial environments. As we journey forward, grounded in curiosity and ethical awareness, we seek to embark on an inclusive venture into the vast unknown—one that honors the delicate complexities of all forms of life while embodying the enduring spirit of exploration that has defined humanity's quest for understanding.

In conclusion, isolation protocols encapsulate the delicate balance between curiosity and caution as we step beyond the boundaries of our world. They ultimately prompt us to consider the significance of preserving the wonders of the universe while exploring the possibilities of life beyond our planet, laying the groundwork for a future where exploration serves as both an aspiration and a moral imperative in our ever-expanding understanding of the galaxy.

14.3. Microbial Dangers

In the vast tapestry of the cosmos, microbial dangers represent a significant yet often overlooked element in the quest for extraterrestrial life and the possibilities of terraforming. As humanity strides into the unknown realms of space exploration, the implications of encountering alien microbes, whether within our solar system or on exoplanets, must be carefully scrutinized. The potential risks posed by microorganisms—whether from Earth contaminating other worlds or vice versa—necessitate a comprehensive understanding of microbial interactions and ecosystems.

The sheer resilience and adaptability of microbes cannot be understated. On Earth, extremophiles thrive in extreme environments, from the scorching depths of hydrothermal vents to the icy realms of Antarctica. This resilience hints at the possibility that extraterrestrial ecosystems could also harbor microorganisms capable of surviving harsh conditions, effectively reshaping our understanding of habitability. As we consider terraforming initiatives, the introduction of Earth-based organisms must be approached with caution, as existing alien microbial life may interact unpredictably with introduced species, potentially leading to ecological disruption or catastrophe.

When exploring the microbial dangers associated with terraforming, the inherent risks of contamination become paramount. If we were to introduce engineered organisms into an alien environment, even well-meaning interventions could have dire consequences—such as the extinction of indigenous life forms or the alteration of existing ecosystems. Historical precedents on Earth, where invasive species have wreaked havoc upon native populations, serve as cautionary tales that remind us of the fragility of ecosystems.

To mitigate these risks, isolation protocols and contamination controls must be foundational in any space exploration endeavor. The planetary protection guidelines formulated by organizations such as NASA and the European Space Agency delineate strict protocols designed to prevent biological cross-contamination during exploration missions. These guidelines include sterilization processes for spacecraft, monitoring of sample return protocols, and stringent quarantine measures for any materials returned from extraterrestrial environments.

Furthermore, the research community must engage in vigilant studies of microbial behavior in varying extraterrestrial conditions, allowing scientists to anticipate potential interactions with introduced Earth life forms. Understanding how Earth microbes adapt to and thrive in alien environments is crucial for shaping policies that govern space exploration and terraforming. This research can also inform the selection of microbial strains that may exhibit desirable traits for ecological interventions, leading to harmonious interactions with existing ecosystems.

The public trust in the scientific processes guiding exploration efforts also comes into play. As interest in the discovery of microbial life beyond Earth heightens, transparency regarding practices and potential risks becomes essential. Engaging the public in conversations surrounding microbial dangers fosters awareness and encourages a broader dialogue about our responsibilities as explorers. By building this understanding, we can effectively manage expectations while preparing society for the complexities that interstellar engagements may entail.

Moreover, as we consider the ethical dimensions of microbial dangers, we must grapple with the moral implications of our actions in the cosmic landscape. The protection of potential indigenous microbial life must trump our inherent curiosity to explore and exploit. Should contact occur with extraterrestrial microorganisms, how do we balance scientific inquiry with the preservation of ecosystems? The questions proponents of astrobiology face today compel us to pursue answers not only through scientific investigation but also through reflection on our ethical roles in the cosmos.

In conclusion, microbial dangers present challenges and opportunities as humanity prepares for the exploration of alien worlds and the pursuit of terraforming. With proper precautions, awareness, and reflection, we can navigate this intricate landscape while maintaining a commitment to respect existing ecosystems—both terrestrial and extraterrestrial. As we venture forth into the unknown, the task ahead is not one of conquest; it transcends that ambition, aiming to understand and build relationships with all forms of life we may encounter. Ultimately, grounding our exploration in ethical stewardship will shape our future as cosmic custodians and expand our understanding of the myriad possibilities that lie beyond our planet.

14.4. Regulations and Treaties

The intricate tapestry of cosmic exploration is interwoven with a range of regulations and treaties that emerge as essential frameworks guiding humanity's engagement with the universe. As we increase our understanding of the potential for alien life, terraforming efforts, and planetary protection, these regulations ensure that scientific endeavors are conducted with responsibility and respect for the delicate ecosystems we may encounter. This subchapter seeks to explore how international agreements shape the legal landscape for space exploration and the ethical responsibilities that accompany cosmic discovery.

At the outset, it is essential to acknowledge the foundation laid by key treaties, such as the Outer Space Treaty of 1967, which established fundamental principles governing the activities of states in outer space. This treaty emphasizes that space exploration is to be conducted for the benefit of all humankind, prompting nations to recognize their shared responsibility in safeguarding the rights and interests of future generations. This fundamental premise shapes the ongoing discussions surrounding the regulations and protocols guiding potential terraforming efforts and interactions with extraterrestrial entities.

One of the critical elements of these regulations is the delineation of planetary protection protocols. These guidelines aim to prevent biological contamination during exploration missions, ensuring that Earth microorganisms do not inadvertently invade other celestial bodies—a concern that could result in irreversible consequences for unknown ecosystems. Furthermore, they highlight the importance of protecting Earth from potential extraterrestrial microorganisms, emphasizing the dual imperatives of planetary stewardship.

As the exploration of Mars and other celestial bodies progresses, the regulatory frameworks governing the activities undertaken in these environments continue to evolve. The science of astrobiology, requiring insights from various disciplines, must interlace with policy discussions as international stakeholders solidify their positions on ecological preservation and sustainable practices. This dialogue becomes crucial as advanced technology introduces novel possibilities for terraforming, which may pose both ethical and practical dilemmas centered around the alteration of alien worlds.

The ongoing discourse surrounding regulations and treaties also invites reflection on the ethical considerations associated with terraforming. Questions arise regarding humanity's right to manipulate cosmic landscapes, especially in light of the uncertainties surrounding indigenous life forms and ecosystems. Acknowledging these complexities allows for a broader understanding that transcends simple scientific inquiry—prompting us to confront our moral obligations to respect and preserve all forms of life we may encounter.

Engaging with regulations also positions nations favorably for collaboration in shared cosmic endeavors. As the pursuit of knowledge about the universe transcends geopolitical boundaries, international cooperation fosters a sense of unity in common goals: exploring, understanding, and preserving the cosmos while respecting diverse perspectives surrounding space ethics. Collaborative frameworks will enable global scientific communities to pool resources, share findings, and actively contribute to developing comprehensive action plans that address the complexities of space exploration.

Furthermore, as we consider the technological advancements shaping our engagement with the cosmos, the regulation and committee discussions surrounding their implementation must remain balanced with ethical considerations. The rapid pace at which robotic exploration and human-led endeavors unfold necessitates foresight in assessing the potential ramifications of such activities on celestial environments. Novel technologies, such as autonomous systems and AI, must align with ethical guidelines that prioritize the protection of any life forms or ecosystems we may encounter.

In conclusion, the landscape of regulations and treaties governing space exploration is vital in promoting responsible engagement with the cosmos. As humanity prepares for an adventurous voyage into the unknown, these frameworks serve as guardians, guiding our interactions and fortifying our commitment to stewardship and preservation. By elaborating on the need to balance exploration with ethical responsibilities, we pave the way for informed and conscientious approaches to cosmic discovery—a journey that reflects not only our insatiable curiosity but also our overarching duty to protect and cherish the mysteries of the universe we seek to unravel.

14.5. Precautionary Measures in Space Exploration

In the annals of human exploration, the significance of precautionary measures in space exploration cannot be overstated. As we expand our reach into the cosmos, the motivations surrounding our quest for knowledge must be coupled with an acute awareness of the potential risks involved. These precautionary measures are a blend of rigorous scientific approach, ethical considerations, and protective strategies designed to safeguard both the originality of alien worlds and our own ecological integrity.

At the forefront of precautionary measures is the foundational concept of planetary protection. This guiding principle is anchored in the understanding that the introduction of Earth-based life to other celestial bodies may lead to unforeseen consequences, potentially disrupting or destroying existing ecosystems that may harbor their own unique forms of life. As we embark on our exploration of Mars, Europa, and beyond, the necessity for stringent sterilization protocols becomes apparent, compelling mission designers to consider everything from spacecraft materials to the potential for contamination through human activities.

The risk of microbial contamination is of particular concern, as microbes on Earth are tenacious and exhibit incredible adaptability. Studies have shown that certain terrestrial microbes can survive in extreme environments—harsh, airless vacuums, blinding radiation, and, in some cases, even the chill of space itself. Understanding these biological realities forms the crux of our protective measures, forcing scientists to adopt strict containment practices during experimentation, transportation, and in the fieldwork for missions exploring other planets.

A noteworthy example of such measures is the sterilization protocols that have guided past planetary missions, including those to Mars. These protocols ensure that spacecraft are meticulously cleaned and free from biological contamination before launch. Additionally, once a mission is on course, the collection, quarantine, and analysis of samples must occur within controlled environments to prevent potential cross-contamination—ensuring that any organisms we may find remain unaffected and undisturbed.

Equally vital is the consideration of incoming risks to Earth from extraterrestrial microbial life. The burgeoning interest in planetary exploration and the potential discovery of alien microbes raises moral and ethical questions—what responsibilities do we carry as stewards of life on Earth? The introduction of extraterrestrial organisms back to our planet must be approached with caution, driven by concern for any unforeseen ecological consequences that may arise from such interactions.

These precautionary measures also encapsulate the importance of international cooperation and collaboration in the realm of space exploration. As we traverse the cosmos, no single nation can claim ownership of the celestial bodies we encounter, nor can any solely dictate the terms under which we engage with them. Establishing frameworks for planetary protection that incorporate diverse perspectives—from scientific experts to ethicists and policymakers —promotes a collaborative approach, ensuring that our explorative endeavors honor the integrity of alien worlds while prioritizing the well-being of our own environment.

Public engagement is another layer of the precautionary discourse, as the involvement of diverse societal perspectives fortifies our collective understanding and approach to exploration. Education initiatives designed to raise awareness about planetary protection can cultivate a more informed citizenry, fostering curiosity, understanding, and support for responsible engagement with the cosmos.

The focus on precautionary measures in space exploration begs the question: what future responsibilities accompany our search for life and our ambitions of terraforming? As we contemplate altering any planetary environments, these precautionary measures will serve not only as guidelines but also as ethical compasses that guide our actions toward cosmic stewardship.

In summary, precautionary measures in space exploration embody the ethos of responsible scientific inquiry as humanity reaches toward the stars. They weave the threads of planetary protection, risk management, public engagement, and international collaboration into a comprehensive approach grounded in ethical considerations. As we journey into the expansive unknown, these precautionary strategies will guide our efforts, ensuring that we advance in a manner that honors both the celestial environments we explore and the rich tapestry of life that exists on our own planet. Through careful stewardship, curiosity, and accountability, we can forge paths not only toward discovery but toward lasting harmony in the cosmos.

15. Ethics of Cosmic Discovery

15.1. Moral Implications of Contact

As we navigate the intricacies of potential alien contact and the implications of terraforming, the moral implications become increasingly significant. The prospect of encountering another civilization—intelligent and advanced—raises profound ethical questions that extend beyond mere curiosity.

One of the primary moral dilemmas is the responsibility humanity bears in contacting alien worlds. Should we actively send signals into space, attempting to reach out to extraterrestrial beings? The ethical implications become evident; the very act of making contact could catalyze a series of unforeseen consequences. Engaging with civilizations at different technological and cultural extremes raises concerns about power dynamics, potential exploitation, and the preservation of those civilizations' autonomy. This invites the larger question: what right do we have to impose our presence upon others, irrespective of their stage of development or worldview?

If we were to encounter an advanced civilization, the ethical framework surrounding that contact becomes critical. The notion of "space colonialism" arises, echoing epochs in human history where the interactions with less advanced societies led to domination and exploitation. An ethical paradigm must prioritize respect for alien civilizations, seeking mutual understanding and dialogue rather than unilateral influence. The reluctance to create an imbalance of knowledge and power between established humans and emerging alien civilizations is essential in maintaining a just and collaborative approach.

In addition to the ethical considerations surrounding contact, a significant moral question looms regarding the alteration of alien worlds. As aspirations of terraforming take center stage, the question arises: should we alter worlds that may harbor life, or those that, while barren, may have ecosystems we do not yet comprehend? The act of terraforming could irrevocably change environments, possibly even extinguishing unknown life forms before we possess the knowledge to identify them. The moral implications of prioritizing human habitation over potential ecosystems present a stark ethical dilemma that invites reflection on our responsibilities as stewards of life in all its forms.

The protection of alien civilizations becomes paramount in discussions surrounding the ethics of cosmic discovery. If we have the means to reshape environments, introducing Earth organisms or technological processes, we must consider the rights of any indigenous species that might exist—encasing them in the sanctity of their natural ecosystems. This acceptance of our responsibilities sharpens our focus on preserving the integrity of alien life forms before we engage in transformative actions.

Finally, the question emerges concerning what role humanity plays in the universe. As we strive for connection and understanding among the stars, do we perceive ourselves as explorers, conquerors, or guardians? The narrative thread binds back to our fundamental ethics around exploration, dictating how we shape our strategies for engaging with the unknown. Aligning the values of compassion, respect, and responsibility with our cosmic ambitions enables us to navigate the expansive universe while fostering relationships that uplift and honor the complexity of life—whether terrestrial or extraterrestrial.

In addition to these moral implications, garnering international consensus on space ethics becomes essential as humanity charts its course into the cosmos. The diverse perspectives surrounding ethical norms and responsibilities demand dialogue and collaboration among global entities, ensuring that our ventures into the unknown reflect the collective will of society. Engaging various cultural narratives in developing a comprehensive ethical framework establishes a pathway for responsible exploration that champions inclusivity and foresight.

Addressing these ethical nuances within the broader discussion surrounding terraforming, potential contact with alien civilizations, and the roles we can — and should — play in shaping ecological futures allows us to reflect upon our shared humanity and responsibility as cosmic custodians. As we prepare to reach out into the depths of space while considering the moral complexities of our endeavors, our reflections will undoubtedly shape the future contours of humanity's interactions across the vast cosmic expanse.

15.2. Should We Alter Alien Worlds?

Should We Alter Alien Worlds?

As humanity stands on the precipice of interstellar exploration and the potential for terraforming distant planets, the question of whether we should alter alien worlds is one that evokes complex ethical considerations. The drive to expand our horizons is fueled not only by an insatiable curiosity about the universe but also by pressing concerns regarding our own planet's sustainability and capacity to support burgeoning populations. Yet, the implications of such ambitious endeavors compel us to reflect deeply on our responsibilities as stewards of life and the potential consequences of our actions on environments we may know little about.

At the center of this debate lies the concept of consent—do we have the right to reshape environments that might harbor indigenous life forms, or ecosystems that have evolved independently over eons? The ethical considerations surrounding the alteration of alien worlds resonate with historical narratives of colonialism and the often devastating impacts of human interference in local ecosystems on Earth. As we contemplate terraforming efforts on planets like Mars or moons like Europa, we must grapple with the question of whether the potential benefits justify the risks posed to existing natural systems.

As we consider the implications of altering alien terrains, we are drawn to the promise of creating habitable environments that could support human life or other forms of existence. The potential to terraform planets may seem like a hopeful solution to the challenges we face on Earth—climate change, resource depletion, and overpopulation—but such action requires careful calibration. The fine balance of ecological and atmospheric conditions necessary for life is complex, and we risk irreversibly harming unique alien ecosystems if we fail to fully understand the interconnectedness of those systems before enacting change.

The act of terraforming is never a single initiative; it involves a multitude of ongoing processes that must be continuously monitored and adjusted. For instance, introducing Earth life forms into alien worlds may lead to unintended consequences such as ecological competition, disease spread, or the extinction of indigenous life forms. In many respects, our ignorance represents a ticking clock, and as we push the boundaries of exploration, the imperative for comprehensive studies and multifaceted approaches to terraforming becomes paramount.

Furthermore, as we ponder the rights of any existing life that may inhabit distant worlds, the principles of conservation and respect for existing ecosystems must guide our choices. Viewing alien worlds as potential homes for humanity should not eclipse the appreciation for their intrinsic value as unique environments, regardless of their current forms of life. Engaging in compassionate ecological stewardship, analogous to the methods of conservation employed on Earth, enables us to embrace a more responsible approach to cosmic exploration.

In addition, the concept of terraforming raises profound questions regarding the limits of human innovation. Should we engineer entire ecosystems to meet our needs, or should we prioritize discovering how life might already adapt within those environments? By placing value on both scientific inquiry and ethical explorations, humanity has the opportunity to learn from other worlds while nurturing a respect for the cosmic tapestry of life.

If we envision collaborative efforts encompassing multiple species or intelligent beings, then the imperative for ethical frameworks surrounding terraforming becomes even more critical. Our discussions should reflect a commitment to cooperation rather than domination—promoting dialogue that values perspectives beyond our own, united in a desire for understanding and mutual flourishing.

Ultimately, the question of whether we should alter alien worlds symbolizes the profound interplay between scientific ambition, curiosity, and ethical stewardship. As we reach for the stars, the responsibility to engage with other planets and potential life forms must be accompanied by deep reflection on our actions and their consequences. Moving forward, the principles of respect, ecological understanding, and collaboration will serve as guiding tenets in our quest to comprehend the universe and our place within it.

By embracing these principles, humanity may forge pathways toward a future where exploration and terraforming are pursued with care and consideration. As we navigate the challenges and opportunities ahead, our journey into the cosmos can illuminate not only the potential for thriving alien worlds but also the possibilities for learning and growth that enrich our humanity. In the end, to search for and possibly alter life beyond Earth may reveal deeply interconnected stories—inspiring a quest that transcends the boundaries of space and time, and ultimately connects us all.

15.3. Protection of Alien Civilizations

The exploration of alien civilizations and the many possibilities that exist within the vast expanse of space stimulates profound scientific, ethical, and philosophical discussions. As humanity continues to advance its technological and exploratory capabilities, the question of how to engage with other civilizations—should they exist—becomes a central theme in our cosmic journey.

Protection of Alien Civilizations is paramount in any discussion surrounding the potential for terraforming or interaction with extraterrestrial life. If we hold the prospect of encountering advanced civilizations, the ethical implications of such encounters cannot be overstated. The responsibility to preserve existing life forms and ecosystems on other planets challenges our existing frameworks for exploration and inquiry. Just as the historical narratives of colonialism on Earth illuminate the consequences of premature contact, we must carry these lessons forward, ensuring that our cosmic engagements reflect respect and stewardship for all forms of existence.

Within this context, the exploration of the Role of Humanity in the Universe invites significant reflection. What rights do we possess as intelligent beings to impose our will upon other worlds? The pursuit of knowledge must be harmonized with humility; an acknowledgment that we are but one among many potential expressions of intelligence and life. As we venture into the unknown, the essence of our interactions must resonate with compassion, fostering understanding rather than subjugation.

In recent years, the importance of International Consensus on Space Ethics has become increasingly apparent. Establishing a unified framework for navigating the ethical dimensions of space exploration serves as a crucial step toward fostering responsible cosmic stewardship. The Outer Space Treaty, coupled with subsequent international discussions, provides a foundation upon which to build global cooperation in the search for extraterrestrial life. Engaging a diverse array of cultures and philosophical perspectives in crafting these treaties reinforces our commitment to ethical exploration and respect for other forms of existence.

A key component of the narrative surrounding Human Innovation and Societal Impact lies in the concept of Influences on Technology and Design. Advancements in fields such as robotics, artificial intelligence, and biotechnology continue to reshape our strategies for cosmic exploration and terraforming. These technologies not only influence our approaches to inhabiting alien worlds but also impact societal perspectives regarding our responsibilities as explorers. As these innovations unfold, a conscious alignment with societal needs and ethical considerations will ensure that our efforts remain grounded in a vision of sustainability and respect.

The Cultural Changes and Adaptations that arise from ongoing exploration are equally noteworthy. As public interest in extraterrestrial life intensifies, we see cultural representations evolve, spurring imaginations while driving scientific inquiry. The intersection of art, literature, and media invites audiences to contemplate the many possibilities of life beyond our planet, fostering a collective narrative that reflects humanity's innate curiosity and yearning for connection.

Moreover, Potential Economic Shifts prompted by advancements in space exploration cannot be overlooked. The burgeoning fields of astrobiology and terraforming create new economic opportunities, influencing industries ranging from technology and engineering to manufacturing and tourism. As societies invest in these futuristic ventures, they must also remain attuned to the ethical responsibilities tied to the exploration of new environments, ensuring that commerce does not overshadow the imperative of ecological preservation.

Aligning Science with Society's Needs is crucial in navigating the complex interplay between innovation and ethical responsibility. Public engagement, education, and interdisciplinary collaboration serve to empower citizens in their understanding of cosmic exploration while nurturing a sense of accountability toward other forms of life. By fostering an inclusive dialogue, we embolden communities to participate actively in the scientific process, shaping the trajectory of exploration in ways that resonate with our shared values.

As humanity contemplates Future Developments in Human Exploration, we stand at a pivotal juncture. With each discovery—be it the detection of exoplanets, the unveiling of new technologies, or our understanding of the universe's complexities—we approach the cosmic frontier equipped with knowledge, curiosity, and responsibility. The journey ahead beckons, with countless opportunities awaiting those who dare to reach for the stars.

In summary, the exploration of alien civilizations, the ethical considerations surrounding cosmic engagements, and the potential for terraforming are interwoven narratives that call upon us to embrace our responsibilities as stewards of life and knowledge. As we venture forth in our search for understanding, we solidify our roles as explorers of existence—reflecting on the profound complexities that define our place in the universe. Together, we must navigate the future with care, compassion, and consciousness as we embark on the path toward the unknown.

15.4. The Role of Humanity in the Universe

The exploration of cosmic phenomena has ignited humanity's imagination, leading us to ponder the grand mysteries of the universe. Our innate curiosity about the existence of life beyond Earth intertwines with our drive to understand the delicate balance of the cosmos. At the very heart of this inquiry is the role of humanity in the universe, a theme that permeates through our scientific ambitions, our philosophical reflections, and our ethical considerations as we reach out into the unknown.

As we consider our position in the cosmic tapestry, we recognize that humanity bears a unique responsibility. This responsibility extends to ensuring that our explorations are guided by principles of respect, stewardship, and curiosity. The vastness of space invites us to contemplate not just the wonders that lie beyond our planet, but also the ethical implications of our potential encounters with extraterrestrial life. The balance between exploration and preservation must frame our dialogues about terraforming and transforming worlds.

Integral to this pursuit is our ability to innovate. Human ingenuity has propelled us to develop advanced technologies that allow us to explore planets, analyze atmospheres, and monitor signals from stars. As we delve into the mechanisms of cosmic exploration, it becomes evident that our innovations are not simply tools; they represent our aspirations to connect with something greater than ourselves. This intertwining of technology and human impact illustrates the transformative power of curiosity: how it drives scientific advancements and invites us to engage with the cosmos.

The cultural changes and adaptations triggered by our endeavors resonate deeply with societal values. As tales of potential alien life captivate public imagination—spurring interest in the scientific community—these narratives reflect humanity's broader existential questions. What does it mean to be part of a universe that may harbor diverse forms of life? The exploration of these themes in literature, film, and art speaks to our enduring desire for understanding and connection.

Additionally, the potential economic shifts that accompany advancements in space exploration must be woven into our discussions. As we envision a future enriched by the opportunities that space presents —ranging from resource utilization on asteroids to advancements in technology—we must also consider how these economic pursuits align with our ethical principles and responsibilities to protect both our home planet and any newly discovered realms.

Importantly, aligning science with society's needs shapes our journey into the universe. As we navigate the ethical complexities surrounding terraforming, we must invite diverse perspectives into the dialogue, ensuring that our exploration remains grounded in ethical considerations that prioritize respect for alien ecosystems and cultures. Engaging communities in discussions about our shared cosmic future fosters a sense of ownership and collaboration among humanity, as we collectively explore the beauty and challenges of existence across the cosmos.

As we look to the future of human exploration, the promise of discovery resides in the questions that remain. What wonders await us as we venture into distant star systems and uncharted territories? Will we identify signals from intelligent life or unveil the beauty of habitable worlds? The unknown beckons us to remain steadfast in our quest for knowledge, cultivating an ethos of curiosity and ethical stewardship as we chart our course among the stars.

In essence, the role of humanity in the universe is not merely defined by our technological advancements or scientific inquiries; it captures the essence of our quest for connection, understanding, and respect for the intricate web of life that may flourish beyond our planet. As we navigate this cosmic journey, we must do so with a sense of purpose and responsibility—honoring the past, embracing the present, and fostering hope for a future where all beings may thrive in harmony across the tapestry of existence. In recognizing the vast potential of the universe, we become not only explorers but stewards tasked with weaving our narratives into the grand story of life that unfolds among the stars.

15.5. International Consensus on Space Ethics

International consensus on space ethics has become a pivotal discussion as humanity stands on the brink of significant cosmic exploration and the possibility of encountering extraterrestrial life. The ethical considerations that arise from these endeavors shape not only our approach to discovering life beyond Earth but also our responsibilities toward protecting other celestial environments from human contamination or exploitation. This growing discourse within the scientific, policy-making, and public arenas is crucial as we venture into a universe filled with potential for both discovery and missteps.

At the heart of achieving international consensus on space ethics is the notion of stewardship—one that emphasizes responsibility toward the ecosystems we may encounter. The Outer Space Treaty of 1967 serves as the cornerstone for discussions surrounding the exploration and use of outer space. This foundational document asserts that space exploration should be conducted for the benefit of all humankind, advocating for cooperation among nations as they engage in cosmic endeavors. As interest in extraterrestrial exploration and the search for signs of life intensifies, the principles articulated within the treaty have become increasingly relevant, with a focus on how we engage with worlds that may harbor unique ecosystems.

The ethical responsibilities we carry become magnified when considering the potential for terraforming alien planets. The prospect of altering extraterrestrial environments prompts critical questions about the rights of any existing life forms that may inhabit those worlds. What are the ethical implications of introducing Earth organisms to alien landscapes? Should we prioritize the potential benefits of human expansion over the preservation of unique ecosystems? These inquiries compel scientists, ethicists, and policymakers to engage in rigorous discussions that foster informed and nuanced approaches to cosmic exploration.

Moreover, as we venture further into the cosmos, the diversity of perspectives around space ethics highlights the interplay between culture and science. Different societies may hold varying beliefs about the value of extraterrestrial life and the ethics of engagement. Establishing international dialogue and collaboration across cultures opens up pathways for understanding and addressing the ethical dilemmas surrounding space exploration. This cultural integration is vital for creating a more comprehensive approach to regulations and frameworks that guide cosmic activities, emphasizing respect for diverse viewpoints in discussions about planetary protection and the preservation of alien ecosystems.

Additionally, concrete frameworks for planetary protection are necessary to mitigate the risks of contamination—both of extraterrestrial environments and the return of materials to Earth. The planetary protection protocols established by space agencies like NASA and ESA seek to prevent biological cross-contamination during exploration missions. By following stringent sterilization and quarantine processes, we can minimize the impact of human activities on other worlds while safeguarding Earth from potential extraterrestrial organisms. This interplay between prevention and exploration underscores the importance of transparent communication regarding these protocols, ensuring that the public understands the necessity of responsible engagement as we seek to unlock the mysteries of the cosmos.

The implications of international consensus on space ethics extend beyond the immediate scientific community; they reach into public discourse, societal engagement, and the development of policies that govern human activity in space. As interest in extraterrestrial life grows, the need to educate and involve the public in discussions about cosmic stewardship becomes essential. This involvement cultivates a sense of shared responsibility, igniting curiosity while reinforcing ethical considerations central to exploration and discovery.

Lastly, as we set our sights on future cosmic endeavors, the quest for international consensus on space ethics remains a journey marked by collaboration, dialogue, and reflection on our role as custodians of the universe. The delicate balance between ambition and responsibility reminds us that exploring uncharted territories must evolve with consideration for the cosmic tapestry of life that intertwines our existence. Learning from our past experiences on Earth, where missteps led to ecological degradation, positions us to approach our future in space with humility and reverence.

In conclusion, the pursuit of international consensus on space ethics serves as both a guiding principle and a foundational framework for the exploration of extraterrestrial environments. As humanity strikes forth into the cosmos, the ethical considerations that arise underscore our responsibilities to protect the delicate complexities of alien ecosystems while fostering curiosity and understanding. Achieving a comprehensive and inclusive dialogue around these issues will ultimately shape our legacy as cosmic explorers, allowing us to engage with the universe in ways that honor the interconnections of all life. The future beckons with promise, inviting us to imagine new possibilities amid the stars while navigating the profound ethical landscapes that accompany such aspirations.

16. Human Innovation and Societal Impact

16.1. Influences on Technology and Design

In the ever-evolving exploration of technology and design, various influences play a pivotal role in shaping the methodologies and ideas behind terraforming and our understanding of alien life. As humanity reaches out to the cosmos, its innovations draw from an intricate tapestry woven from historical, scientific, cultural, and ethical threads. Engaging with these influences enables us to effectively navigate the profound complexities of creating and manipulating environments that may one day support life beyond Earth.

One of the fundamental influences on technology and design lies in humanity's historical interaction with the natural world. As we gaze into the cosmos, we draw on millennia of accumulated knowledge about engineering structures, adapting agricultural practices, and understanding the delicate balance of ecosystems. These historical precedents guide our contemporary efforts to create environments that are sustainable and can support complex life forms. Understanding how societies have thrived or faltered due to their interactions with their environments fosters insight into how we might successfully implement terraforming initiatives.

The scientific advances of the 21st century further reshape the landscape of technology and design, offering breakthroughs in various fields that enhance our capacity to genetically engineer organisms, construct habitats, and manipulate planetary systems. Recent innovations in biotechnology, materials science, and artificial intelligence come together to support ambitious endeavors that once resided solely in the realm of science fiction. For example, adaptive organisms designed to thrive in specific extraterrestrial environments are informed by research on extremophiles, our understanding of DNA manipulation, and the genetic engineering techniques that allow for tailored responses to harsh conditions.

Cultural influences also significantly affect how we conceptualize technology and design for terraforming efforts. The narratives and mythology surrounding space exploration and the existence of life beyond Earth fuel both public fascination and scientific inquiry. Popular culture—through literature, film, and media—shapes societal perceptions of aliens, terraforming, and the moral implications of our cosmic outreach. As stories of interstellar travel and engineered worlds captivate the collective imagination, they inspire scientists and engineers alike to consider both the wonders and ethical dilemmas embedded in their pursuits. For instance, when films portray advanced alien cultures responsibly engaging with their ecosystems, they lend credence to the broader ethical discourse surrounding our interactions with potential extraterrestrial life.

Economic shifts are another noteworthy influence that intersects with technological development and design. The increasing interest in extraterrestrial colonization, resource extraction, and terraforming catalyzes investment in space exploration industries, prompting governments and private entities to allocate resources toward developing new technologies. These economic phenomena prompt a reconsideration of how scientific research is conducted and funded, encouraging interdisciplinary collaboration among experts and fostering innovation necessary for ambitious terraforming initiatives.

As society progresses, aligning science with public needs remains an essential element in shaping technology and design. Perceptions about terraforming, its feasibility, and the ethical ramifications must be grounded in clear communication between the scientific community and the public sphere. Diligent engagement with communities fosters an environment where science thrives, cultivating interest and support for cosmological initiatives. This alignment may also inspire future generations to engage with science, particularly in fields related to astrobiology and planetary engineering, by offering frameworks to facilitate responsible action and promote public health.

The future of human exploration holds immense promise as we harness the influences of technology and design to forge ahead into the unknown. The lessons learned from past scientific endeavors, historical legacies, cultural narratives, and economic frameworks collectively provide fertile ground for continued investigation and innovation. The emerging potentials for humanity to terraform worlds and explore alien environments challenge our understanding of limits, adaptability, and resilience.

In summary, the influences on technology and design in the exploration of extraterrestrial life and terraforming weave together a complex interplay of historical, scientific, cultural, and economic threads. Understanding these influences allows us to approach the vast challenges posed by cosmic exploration with vision, responsibility, and creativity. As humanity reaches out into the cosmos, the desire to create habitable environments reflects our unyielding curiosity and determination to foster connections and possibilities within the grand tapestry of the universe. The journey ahead beckons us to blend exploration with ethical consideration, ensuring we tread carefully as we engage with the wonders awaiting us among the stars.

16.2. Cultural Changes and Adaptations

The pursuit of understanding the cosmos, particularly the concept of terraforming and the implications of extraterrestrial life, has led to significant cultural changes and adaptations in society. As humanity develops the technological capabilities to explore the stars and even alter the environments of distant worlds, our collective imagination has been ignited, fostering a rich dialogue regarding what life beyond Earth may entail and how we might relate to it. This subchapter investigates the ways in which the quest for alien terraformation has influenced cultural perspectives, ethical frameworks, and societal behaviors, reflecting an ever-evolving relationship with cosmic matters.

At the heart of these cultural changes is the rise of interest in space exploration and the conceptualization of alien life forms. As scientific advancements have brought us closer to discovering potentially habitable exoplanets, narratives surrounding extraterrestrial life have proliferated across various media channels, inspiring excitement and curiosity. Television shows, films, and literature have expanded audiences' awareness of what life might look like beyond our planet, often intertwining scientific realism with speculative elements that challenge conventional understandings of existence. These narratives have prompted audiences to reflect on fundamental questions about their own humanity, the impact of technology, and the ethical dilemmas we may face if we were to encounter intelligent civilizations.

An essential aspect of these cultural shifts is the evolving perception of our own planet and its ecological challenges. The discourse surrounding terraforming and the potential to create habitable environments on alien worlds is inextricably linked to the urgent need for environmental stewardship on Earth. As discussions about resource depletion, climate change, and sustainability have gained momentum over recent decades, the desire to explore the cosmos has fueled the push for accountability regarding our planetary ecosystems. Thus, terraforming as a topic not only inspires futuristic aspirations but compels us to cultivate a sense of responsibility and ethical consideration toward our own home—highlighting the interconnectedness of local and universal ecological principles.

Moreover, advancements in technology have facilitated enthusiastic discussions surrounding the ethics of terraforming and interaction with other worlds. Widespread awareness of the potential implications raises crucial questions regarding the preservation of alien ecosystems, the impact of introduced life forms, and the moral dilemmas surrounding colonization efforts. The juxtaposition of scientific ambition and ethical responsibility invites a broader dialogue that engages various cultural perspectives, leading to the emergence of initiatives aimed at promoting ethical standards in cosmic exploration.

Institutional responses to these cultural changes have also become increasingly salient. The roles of organizations responsible for overseeing space exploration, such as NASA or the European Space Agency, must be recalibrated to reflect the values of stewardship and ethical exploration. As public interest swells, these organizations face mounting pressure to implement rigorous planetary protection protocols to prevent contamination of alien environments while reinforcing the idea that space exploration should benefit all humankind.

From a societal perspective, adaptations regarding education and outreach have become imperative. As fascination with extraterrestrial life and terraforming grows, educational programs that promote scientific literacy and curiosity about space are essential. Through initiatives designed to introduce students and the public to astrobiology, planetary science, and ethical exploration, society can cultivate informed citizens who actively participate in discussions surrounding humanity's role in the cosmos.

In addition, the economic dimensions of terraforming and alien exploration present new paradigms for societal adaptation. The potential for commercial interests—ranging from resource extraction on asteroids to developing technologies that aid terraforming efforts—fuels both investment and entrepreneurial initiatives. Society must consider how these economic pursuits align with ethical principles concerning ecological preservation and the exploration of new horizons in a responsible manner.

Ultimately, the cultural changes and adaptations associated with the pursuit of terraforming and understanding life beyond Earth culminate in a profound understanding of our place in the cosmos. As we engage with the possibilities presented through science and imagination, we reflect on the responsibilities that accompany our reach toward the stars. In this converging journey, we embrace a commitment to explore not only the depths of space, but also the ethical complexities of existence in all its forms. Through this lens, the quest for alien terraformation becomes not only an exploration of worlds unseen, but a deepening inquiry into what it means to be part of the larger cosmic narrative. As we tread this path, we do so with respect and anticipation for that which lies beyond our understanding, united by the shared pursuit of knowledge and interconnectedness that defines the human experience.

16.3. Potential Economic Shifts

In examining potential economic shifts in the context of alien terraformation, we uncover a nuanced landscape that intertwines science, technology, and society with far-reaching implications for humanity's future as cosmic explorers. As conditions and technologies evolve, the economic dynamics surrounding space exploration and terraformation will naturally undergo transformation, prompting changes in industry, investment, labor markets, and societal engagement.

The push toward terraforming, whether on planets like Mars or moons like Europa, reflects a burgeoning space economy that offers prospects for innovation and investment in a diverse array of sectors. Industries dedicated to aerospace engineering, longevity of life in hostile environments, and biological sciences will emerge as key players in this new economy, driving advancements essential for human survival in extraterrestrial habitats. Enterprises focused on developing technologies that support sustainable ecosystems—such as closed-loop systems for recycling resources and bio-engineered crops that thrive in alien conditions—will pave the way for sustainable ventures in space.

As this new economic landscape unfolds, a shift in investment patterns will be inevitable. Governments and private entities are increasingly recognizing the potential benefits of engaging with extraterrestrial environments. The commercial space sector, emerging as a major player, stands to capitalize on the technological advancements spawned by the drive to terraform. Companies engaged in launching payloads to Mars or mining asteroids for resources can create new financial ecosystems that generate jobs and economic growth. Furthermore, investments in satellite technology and orbital infrastructure will enhance communication, research, and resource management—creating interconnected networks that bolster both terrestrial and extraterrestrial economics.

In tandem with emergent industries, the trajectory of human exploration will necessitate an adaptive labor market capable of responding to the evolving demands of the space economy. Specialized training in fields such as astrobiology, planetary science, robotics, and environmental engineering will inform educational programs designed to equip individuals with the necessary skills to engage with extraterrestrial challenges. Societal interest in space exploration will inspire generational shifts in career aspirations, encouraging young minds to pursue careers aligned with the prospects of terraforming and interstellar travel.

Yet amid these economic possibilities is the need for critical examination of ethical implications surrounding terraforming initiatives. The notion of transforming alien worlds prompts reflection on our responsibilities as stewards of life, igniting pertinent debates regarding the potential impact on existing alien ecosystems. The economic pursuits associated with terraforming must balance ambition with reverence for the delicate interplay of life—fostering an economy that respects ecological integrity while driving advancements that could enhance environmental sustainability.

Moreover, the public discourse surrounding terraforming will play a substantial role in shaping perceptions of these economic shifts. Advocacy for responsible exploration and conservation will impact funding decisions, policy-making, and public engagement. As scientific discoveries ignite public interest, societal conversations about the ethical responsibilities accompanying interstellar expansion will shape the trajectory of economic initiatives. Educational outreach and transparent discussions regarding the implications of terraforming will empower communities to engage actively with evolving economic landscapes and assert their values in the face of scientific advancement.

In conclusion, the potential economic shifts arising from the pursuit of alien terraformation herald a transformative future for humanity, intertwining innovation with ethical stewardship. As our reach extends toward distant worlds, we stand poised at the intersection of aspiration and accountability—reflecting on the responsibilities that accompany exploration. While the pursuit of knowledge and progress fuels our endeavors, we must remain aware of our commitments to preserving ecological integrity, ensuring that as we venture into the cosmos, we do so with respect and reverence for all forms of life that inhabit it. The journey ahead invites us to balance ambition with responsibility, harnessing the promise of economic transformation as we chart our path among the stars.

16.4. Aligning Science with Society's Needs

In the ever-expanding narrative of our understanding of alien terraformation, the idea of aligning science with society's needs emerges as a key concept that not only facilitates progress but also ensures that our ventures into the cosmos reflect collective values and ethical responsibilities. As we seek to uncover the mysteries of life beyond Earth and consider the potential for transforming extraterrestrial environments, it is crucial to cultivate a harmonious relationship between scientific inquiry and societal aspirations.

At the forefront of this alignment is the recognition that scientific exploration is not an isolated undertaking but one deeply rooted in the fabric of human experience. The motivations behind terraforming initiatives—whether driven by the desire to secure a future for humanity or to explore the unknown—underscore the necessity of public engagement. As discoveries unfold and technologies advance, the public's perception and understanding of these endeavors will play a significant role in shaping the trajectory of scientific endeavors. The questions of whether we should alter alien worlds or how we can responsibly engineer ecosystems require input from diverse voices and perspectives, fostering a dialogue that echoes the aspirations of humanity as a whole.

Educational initiatives serve as critical pathways for aligning science with societal needs. As we build cultural narratives around space exploration and terraforming, we must empower communities with knowledge and understanding. Programs that promote scientific literacy create a foundation for informed discussions regarding the ethical implications of terraforming. By encouraging curiosity and engagement, we can ensure that society remains active participants in the discourse surrounding extraterrestrial exploration, inspiring future generations to shape the narrative of humanity in the cosmos.

Furthermore, the collaborative nature of scientific inquiry emphasizes the importance of diverse disciplinary perspectives. Successfully understanding and implementing terraforming processes involves knowledge drawn from fields as varied as biology, engineering, and ethics. Interdisciplinary collaboration, bringing together experts from multiple arenas, is essential for developing innovative solutions that respect the complexity of ecosystems while considering technological advancements. This multifaceted approach underscores the notion that science must engage with the values and needs of society, positioning itself as an avenue for positive change and growth.

The ethical frameworks guiding our explorations into the cosmos also warrant careful consideration. As discussions surrounding terraforming and the potential for contact with extraterrestrial life stimulate excitement, they also demand a reflection on the responsibilities we bear in shaping environments on distant worlds. The principle of stewardship—a commitment to protect and care for the ecosystems we encounter—must resonate through proposed initiatives. Our engagement with the cosmos should be informed by a commitment to sustainability, prioritizing the preservation of both existing and engineered life forms in our pursuits.

Moreover, as we explore the future of human exploration, the potential for economic shifts growing from these scientific endeavors invites reflection on how society funds and supports such initiatives. The burgeoning space industry presents a unique opportunity to foster a sense of shared investment in our celestial aspirations. Encouraging collaborations among governmental entities, private enterprises, and community stakeholders can lead to economically viable paths toward exploration, creating a sense of ownership and collaboration that enhances our cosmic narrative.

As we continue to stride toward a future enriched by exploration, the alignment of science with society's needs embodies a collective journey into the unknown. This endeavor invites us to consider the intricacies of the cosmos while ensuring that our actions echo with compassion, responsibility, and respect for life's myriad forms.

Recognizing that every step we take into the vastness of space carries the potential for discovery and connection, we lean into a holistic dialogue surrounding cosmic exploration and terraforming, one that encompasses not only scientific progress but also the vital ethical considerations that shape our shared human experience.

In summary, as we align science with society's needs in the realms of terraforming and cosmic exploration, we embark on a path enriched with understanding, responsibility, and compassion. The journey ahead—one that holds the promise of exploring alien worlds and unlocking the mysteries of the universe—demands that we engage collectively, fostering a sense of unity as we traverse the stars. Through a balanced approach that integrates scientific inquiry, ethical reflection, and public engagement, we can ensure that our quests into the cosmos resonate not only with discovery but with a commitment to nurturing and honoring life in all its forms across the universe.

16.5. Future Developments in Human Exploration

In the boundless expanse of the cosmos, human curiosity stands as one of our most defining traits. From the time we first gazed at the night sky and wondered about the stars, to today, as we send probes to the furthest reaches of our solar system, our insatiable desire to explore and understand the universe propels civilization forward. As we reflect on our journey, the potential developments in human exploration and the future of extraterrestrial terraformation take center stage, promising not only to reshape our understanding of life beyond Earth but also to challenge our long-held beliefs about existence itself.

Recent advancements in technology and the fusion of interdisciplinary knowledge have transformed exploration into a multifaceted endeavor, allowing for speculative frameworks that reconsider what it means to inhabit and terraform other worlds. Progress in fields such as astrobiology, planetary science, and robotics has paved the way for ambitious cosmic outreach efforts—the ongoing search for exoplanets within habitable zones has galvanized interest in potential worlds that could sustain life.

At the crux of future developments lies the exploration of Mars, often hailed as the most promising candidate for terraforming efforts. Mars presents a unique opportunity, with its historical evidence of liquid water, polar ice caps, and varied geography, providing potential blueprints for cultivating Earth-like environments. Arbeiten on concepts such as atmospheric manipulation or increasing greenhouse gas concentrations via engineered microorganisms underscore humanity's push toward making the red planet hospitable for human life. The potential realization of such ambitions would fundamentally redefine our place in the universe, bridging the gap between science fiction and scientific fact.

The past decade has witnessed a surge in interest in the moons of other planets, where the possibilities for life may lie hidden beneath icy crusts. The exploration of Europa and Enceladus, fueled by missions like the Europa Clipper, drives home the point that the potential for life may not be limited to planets alone. These icy moons harbor subsurface oceans, rich in organic materials and energy sources, suggesting their capacity to sustain life or potentially become sites for human exploration and engineered habitats. The quest for understanding these realms highlights the need for innovation in technology and sustainable methods of exploration.

As we forge ahead, the dialogue surrounding the ethics of extraterrestrial exploration and terraformation increasingly comes into sharp focus. The moral implications of altering alien worlds and potentially disrupting existing ecosystems must guide our approaches to cosmic discovery. Advocating for responsible stewardship becomes paramount, ensuring that any initiatives we undertake are grounded in respect for the integrity of alien environments and the possibility of indigenous life.

The collaboration of nations and space agencies becomes integral in shaping future initiatives, cultivating a sense of shared responsibility toward cosmic stewardship. The ongoing international discourse surrounding space regulations—particularly in light of new discoveries —affirms that humanity must navigate its cosmic pursuits with a commitment to safeguard the unknown. By preparing policies that prioritize preservation and thoughtful engagement, we can successfully align scientific aspirations with ethical imperatives.

Moreover, the potential to encounter extraterrestrial signals prompts further speculation about the future of human exploration. As technologies for detecting and decoding these signals advance, the prospects for establishing contact with intelligent civilizations emerge as tantalizing possibilities. The quest for contact ignites the collective imagination and compels us to reflect on our ethical responsibilities should we establish communication with alien life forms.

As we look further into the cosmic landscape, the horizon of our exploration becomes imbued with hope and possibility. The continuous development of innovative technologies—such as next-generation telescopes and space probes—enhances our capacity to search for signs of life and alter environments, propelling humanity toward a new era of discovery.

In summary, the future developments in human exploration encapsulate a rich tapestry of scientific inquiry, ethical considerations, and technological advancements, all woven together in our ambitious quest to understand and interact with the cosmos. As we navigate this uncharted territory, it becomes increasingly clear that our journey is not merely about discovery; it is also about being responsible custodians of the worlds we may one day inhabit. The path ahead invites reflection on our place in the universe and, ultimately, the aspirations we hold for cultivating life across the stars. As we stride into the future, we embrace the mysteries that await us, unravelling the threads of cosmic potential as we reach for the unknown.

17. Extraterrestrial Signals: The Hunt Continues

17.1. Studying Fast Radio Bursts

Studying Fast Radio Bursts reveals a fascinating intersection of astrophysics and the search for extraterrestrial intelligence, inviting exploration into the enigmatic origins and implications of these brief, intense bursts of radio waves that have mystified scientists since their discovery in 2007. Fast radio bursts (FRBs) are noted for their millisecond-duration emissions, which seem to emanate from distant galaxies and have captured the attention of researchers eager to uncover their nature, origins, and potential connections to advanced civilizations.

The study of FRBs provides insights into the underlying mechanisms of cosmic events and their relationship with structures in the universe. Each FRB event possesses unique attributes—a specific pattern of energy, polarization, and modulation—that can reveal essential information about its source. Researchers aim to dissect these signals to ascertain whether they arise from astrophysical phenomena, such as merging neutron stars or interactions within magnetars, or if they could potentially be engineered signals from advanced extraterrestrial civilizations.

The vast distances involved in detecting FRBs serve as both a compelling challenge and an opportunity. As scientists analyze the characteristics of these signals, they must rely on advanced observational techniques and large-scale data analysis to isolate the sources of these brief bursts in the cosmic noise. Observatories armed with state-of-the-art radio telescopes are crucial in this hunt, as they capture vast amounts of information across the electromagnetic spectrum.

In addition to general observations, researchers strive to locate repeating FRBs—those that emit numerous bursts over time. The discovery of repeating signals raises questions about the underlying mechanisms responsible for their recurrence and whether they point toward a specific source. Should such repeating signals manifest predictably, they present intriguing possibilities for structured communication, echoing the aspirations of SETI researchers seeking to establish contact with extraterrestrial life.

While the detection and analysis of FRBs hold the promise of uncovering new phenomena or even potential signals from advanced civilizations, the challenge remains to differentiate between natural astrophysical processes and engineered signals. Rigorous testing and analysis are essential to ensure that any interpretations of FRBs are based on sound scientific principles. The potential for misinterpreting cosmic noise as structured signals underscores the necessity of maintaining skepticism and celebrating the scientific method throughout this exploratory journey.

Furthermore, the implications of FRBs extend into the broader discussions surrounding astrobiology and the potential for life across the universe. If some FRBs are ultimately traced to artificial sources, they could represent a new paradigm in our search for extraterrestrial intelligence. The prospect of uncovering evidence that life can generate signals, echoes hope and wonder about our place in the cosmos and the nature of intelligent existence.

In summary, studying Fast Radio Bursts serves as a captivating gateway into the exploration of the universe and the potential for communication with extraterrestrial life. As we deepen our understanding of these enigmatic signals, we position ourselves to unlock the mysteries of cosmic events and their implications for existence across the galaxies. This inquiry emphasizes the need for continued research, collaboration, and curiosity as we venture into the vast unknown, actively seeking answers and nurturing the hope of connection with life beyond our own planet. The journey into deciphering FRBs beckons with the promise of discovery, reflecting humanity's enduring desire to understand the cosmos and its many possible inhabitants.

17.2. Seeking the Wow! Signal

In the pursuit of uncovering the mysteries of the universe, the section on "Seeking the Wow! Signal" provides a compelling exploration of one of the most intriguing phenomena associated with the search for extraterrestrial intelligence. The "Wow! Signal," detected in 1977 by the Big Ear telescope, stands as a landmark moment in SETI history—a brief yet powerful radio signal that sparked imaginations and fueled inquiries about the existence of intelligent life beyond Earth. This subchapter delves into the significance of this enigmatic signal, the scientific efforts surrounding its analysis, and the broader implications for our ongoing quest to connect with extraterrestrial civilizations.

The Wow! Signal was characterized by its unusual frequency, lasting for a duration of 72 seconds, and its intensity, which far exceeded the background noise typically observed in the cosmos. Its origins, much like its nature, remain shrouded in mystery. The signal was detected in the direction of the constellation Sagittarius, resulting in considerable excitement among scientists. Given that it originated from a region of space that had been studied extensively, the signal's abrupt appearance and subsequent disappearance led to a flurry of speculation—could it be evidence of an alien civilization reaching out across the vast expanses of interstellar space?

In seeking to understand the implications of the Wow! Signal, researchers have employed various methods of analysis to investigate its potential origins. One crucial step is the examination of its frequency—a range of radio waves that might hold clues regarding its source. The fact that the signal was transmitted at a frequency of 1420 MHz, commonly associated with hydrogen, led scientists to consider the idea that it could signify an intentional message, as hydrogen is the most abundant element in the universe and its frequency is universally recognizable.

Despite extensive follow-up observations by various telescopes, attempts to detect the Wow! Signal again have been unsuccessful. This mystery raises critical questions about the nature of cosmic communication and the potential existence of technologically advanced civilizations. The fact that the signal has yet to be recaptured suggests that either the source is highly localized, transient, or perfecting the techniques necessary to communicate at interstellar scales remains a challenge.

The enduring enigma of the Wow! Signal reflects the broader discourse of search strategies in the quest for extraterrestrial life. As researchers develop and refine methods of signal analysis, they continuously evaluate the language of signals that might emerge from intelligent sources. Theories developed in response to the Wow! Signal prompt scientists to consider what characteristics a civilization's communication might embody. This inquiry leads to the exploration of possible technological advancements that could allow these civilizations to send consistent signals, manage power consumption, or utilize unique frequencies that convey meaning.

While the Wow! Signal remains a tantalizing puzzle, it underscores the importance of ongoing engagement in the search for extraterrestrial intelligence. The dialogue surrounding this singular event inspires researchers to remain vigilant in monitoring the skies, employing innovative technologies to capture potential signals from the cosmos. Consequently, the pursuit of understanding the Wow! Signal contributes to the growth of the scientific community, fostering collaboration and interdisciplinary approaches aimed at decoding the language of the universe.

Finally, the allure of the Wow! Signal extends beyond merely seeking extraterrestrial contact. It evokes introspection about humanity's place in the cosmos, urging us to consider the significance and implications of our endeavors in understanding alien worlds. As we navigate the journey toward possible communication with civilizations among the stars, we must remain responsible stewards of our own planet, acknowledging the ethical considerations that accompany attempts to contact or interact with other forms of life.

In summary, "Seeking the Wow! Signal" serves as a critical chapter in the ongoing quest for knowledge about extraterrestrial intelligence and the intricacies of cosmic communication. What was once a fleeting detection of radio waves now stands as a symbol of humanity's ambition to engage with the unknown. The unanswered questions it raises continue to inspire researchers in their pursuit of deciphering the mysteries of the universe while guiding responsible engagement with the profound possibilities that lie beyond our planet. As we venture forth, the legacy of the Wow! Signal challenges us to embrace both curiosity and ethical considerations, reminding us that the search for understanding is not just about finding answers; it is about recognizing our connection to the broader tapestry of existence woven throughout the cosmos.

17.3. New Techniques in Signal Analysis

In recent years, advancements in the field of signal analysis have significantly contributed to the quest for extraterrestrial life and the implications of terraforming planets. The intricacies of analyzing signals within the electromagnetic spectrum have opened new doors for researchers seeking to decipher potential communications from intelligent civilizations. The fusion of cutting-edge technologies, data processing algorithms, and interdisciplinary approaches continues to shape the landscape of astrobiology and exploration.

Techniques in signal analysis utilize the vast array of electromagnetic radiation emitted by celestial phenomena, allowing scientists to detect and analyze signals potentially originating from advanced civilizations. One of the most prominent strategies involves using radio telescopes equipped with advanced software that can parse through the vast amount of data collected from the cosmos. These systems are designed to filter out cosmic noise and isolate signals that deviate from what is naturally expected. Researchers can then focus their efforts on identifying narrowband signals—those that contain distinctive frequencies associated with intelligent sources.

Machine learning algorithms have further enhanced the capabilities of signal analysis by enabling researchers to recognize and categorize patterns across massive datasets. The power of artificial intelligence allows for more effective identification of anomalous signals that may serve as potential indicators of extraterrestrial activity. As scientists continue to develop comprehensive databases of known astronomical phenomena, the integration of machine learning will aid in honing the processes used to differentiate between natural signals and those that could point to intelligent life.

An essential aspect of this ongoing endeavor involves collaboration among international observatories. In order to create a global framework for the search for extraterrestrial intelligence (SETI), researchers from various institutions work together to share data, resources, and insights. This collaborative approach is critical given the vastness of space, as well as the technological challenges of detecting faint signals from distant sources. By pooling their expertise, observatories contribute to a more holistic understanding of the signals observed, pushing the boundaries of detection capabilities.

As we analyze signals from the cosmos, it is vital to remain vigilant against errors and misinterpretations that could lead to premature conclusions. Vigilance in scientific inquiry must accompany the enthusiasm that surrounds the detection of potential extraterrestrial messages; rigorous validation is required to confirm any findings before leaping to speculative conclusions. The exploration of the unknown demands both skepticism and imagination, ensuring that interpretations are grounded in empirical evidence and theoretical insights.

The hopes surrounding the possibility of decoding messages from advanced civilizations are tempered by the recognition of the complexities involved. The very nature of communication across the cosmos raises poignant questions about the ethical responsibilities accompanying contact. If signals are detected, should humanity respond? What frameworks ought to guide our interactions with unknown life forms? The potential for transformative dialogue with extraterrestrial civilizations ignites dreams of shared knowledge and collaboration, but equally calls for the creation of ethical protocols to navigate these uncharted territories.

Ultimately, the journey into the world of signal analysis and the search for extraterrestrial communication is not simply about uncovering messages from the stars; it intertwines with our own evolving narrative as a species. As we ambitiously engage with the cosmos, the technology and methodologies developed through the search for signals serve to deepen our understanding of existence itself. Navigating the complexities of the universe beckons reflection on humanity's place within it—a cosmic odyssey that transcends boundaries and resonates with our unwavering curiosity.

In summary, the new techniques in signal analysis represent a vital aspect of humanity's quest to connect with potential extraterrestrial life. The confluence of advanced technologies, collaborative research, and ethical deliberations underscores the exciting possibilities before us. As we stand at the forefront of exploration, these explorations serve as a testament to our relentless pursuits and aspirations, illuminating paths toward understanding the intricate cosmic tapestry that binds us all. The future beckons with the promise of discovery and connection, encouraging us to seek understanding where once there was only silence.

17.4. Collaboration in International Observatories

Collaboration in International Observatories is crucial in the contemporary pursuit of understanding the cosmos and identifying potential signs of extraterrestrial terraformation. As humanity's reach extends beyond Earth, fostering cooperative relationships between observatories across borders becomes paramount. These partnerships can enhance our collective ability to detect, analyze, and interpret the signals that echo across the universe, as well as offer innovative solutions to the challenges posed by extraterrestrial exploration.

International collaboration in astronomical research facilitates the sharing of resources and expertise. By pooling telescopes, data, and technological advancements, astronomers can create expansive networks capable of monitoring a wider array of celestial phenomena. Projects such as the Event Horizon Telescope, which combined observations from multiple ground-based telescopes worldwide to produce the first-ever image of a black hole, exemplify the power of collaborative efforts in advancing our scientific understanding. Such initiatives inspire similar partnerships in the search for extraterrestrial signals and the study of potential planets for terraforming.

The detection and analysis of exoplanets and their atmospheres benefit significantly from international observatories' collaborative nature. Instruments such as the Kepler Space Telescope and TESS engage a global audience of researchers, contributing to the shared knowledge of planetary systems beyond our own. The data collected from these missions are invaluable for identifying potential habitable zones within stars' Goldilocks zones where conditions might allow for life. A collaborative framework enables researchers to share findings and insights, enriching the broader discourse around potential life-sustaining planets.

The role of diverse perspectives in enhancing scientific inquiry cannot be overstated. Collaboration also invites the inclusion of various cultural viewpoints, ethical considerations, and philosophical insights, creating a holistic approach to cosmic exploration. Engaging experts from multiple disciplines—such as astrobiology, environmental science, philosophy, and engineering—fosters innovative approaches to understanding potential challenges associated with terraforming efforts. These cross-pollinations encourage the creation of ethical frameworks that guide our exploration of other celestial bodies, ensuring that the principles governing cosmic stewardship are established and adhered to.

Moreover, international collaboration lays the foundation for joint missions and research expeditions aimed at exploring planetary surfaces, analyzing atmospheres, and understanding the implications for habitability. For instance, the collaboration between space agencies, such as ESA and NASA, in joint missions like the Mars Sample Return mission reflects the recognition that cosmic exploration is a collective endeavor. By uniting forces, space agencies not only maximize resources but also strengthen the scientific community's voice —creating a unified front in the search for understanding.

Educating and engaging the public around the initiatives undertaken by international observatories is equally crucial. By fostering outreach programs and shared educational resources, these collaborations ensure that society remains informed and engaged with the strides being made in cosmic exploration. An informed public is more likely to support and contribute to initiatives aimed at exploring the universe and understanding the implications of potential extraterrestrial signals and terraformation efforts.

In conclusion, collaboration in international observatories is a vital aspect of the quest for knowledge about the universe and the signs of alien terraformation. By fostering cooperative relationships among countries and scientific disciplines, humanity enhances its capabilities to detect, analyze, and discuss potential signs of extraterrestrial life. As we navigate the complexities of cosmic exploration, these partnerships will shape our understanding of existence, inspire public engagement, and guide our ethical responsibilities as we journey into the uncharted realms of the universe. The collective pursuit of knowledge extends far beyond individual ambitions, embodying a shared responsibility to explore, understand, and cherish the interconnected web of life that spans the cosmos.

17.5. Hopes and Realities of Decoding Messages

Hopes and Realities of Decoding Messages

The endeavor to decode messages from the cosmos grants humanity a glimpse into the potential existence of extraterrestrial intelligence, inviting profound reflections about our place in the universe. As we strive to unlock the secrets hidden within the vast expanse of space, the hopes and realities of this pursuit become inextricably linked. They encapsulate our collective aspirations for connection, understanding, and exploration, while also highlighting the complexities, challenges, and ethical dimensions that accompany the search for cosmic communication.

At the onset of decoding messages from space lies the great hope: that we may one day establish contact with intelligent beings inhabiting distant worlds. This aspiration fuels our scientific inquiries and significance in both the search for extraterrestrial intelligence (SETI) and the wider discourse surrounding astrobiological exploration. Each potential signal that is detected stirs excitement and ignites imaginations, offering tantalizing possibilities for mutual discovery, cultural exchange, and collaboration among civilizations separated by light-years. This longing for connection resonates deeply, manifesting an innate curiosity about the nature of sentient life beyond our planet.

Decoding messages involves a multifaceted approach that incorporates advanced technologies, astrophysical principles, and linguistic curiosities. The process hinges on identifying signals that exhibit characteristics suggestive of artificial origins, often focusing on narrow-bandwidth radio emissions and periodic patterns. The integration of machine learning and artificial intelligence in analyzing vast datasets aids researchers in discerning anomalies amidst the cosmic noise, enhancing our capacity to detect potential extraterrestrial signals.

However, the realities of decoding messages starkly contrast with the dreams that accompany these endeavors. The path to understanding is fraught with uncertainty, challenges, and skepticism. While terrestrial scientists tirelessly analyze cosmic signals, they are ever-aware of the complexities that arise from distinguishing naturally occurring signals from those crafted by intelligent hands. The experience of detecting a promising signal only to have it reveal itself as a natural phenomenon serves to temper enthusiasm with a measured skepticism, reinforcing the need for scientific rigor.

As we navigate the landscape of decoding cosmic messages, we become acutely aware of the ethical implications attached to potential contact. Should signals from advanced civilizations be detected, questions surrounding how we should engage with them come to the forefront. What responsibilities accompany such encounters? Are we to initiate contact, and if so, how? The implications of communicating with intelligences that may possess vastly different technologies, cultures, and worldviews prompt urgent discussions about the ethical frameworks guiding our cosmic interactions.

Additionally, the engagement with cosmic messages reflects back on our own humanity. As we interpret signals from the stars, the very act of deciphering these communications invites philosophical inquiries about identity, connections, and the nature of life itself. Are we alone? What does it mean to exist in a universe teeming with possibilities? These questions resonate throughout our explorations, challenging us to reflect on the broader dimensions of existence and limiting our perception of life within a singular framework.

As the possibilities for decoding cosmic messages press onward, the future beckons with the promise of discovery and understanding. Evolving technologies and interdisciplinary collaborations continue to enhance our capabilities, enabling us to probe deeper into the fabric of the universe. Yet it is critical to ground these efforts in transparency, ensuring that the public remains engaged with the unfolding narrative of cosmic exploration.

In summary, the hopes and realities of decoding messages from the cosmos intertwine to illuminate the intricate tapestry of our quest for understanding. The drive to connect with potential extraterrestrial lives encapsulates the human spirit's longing for belonging, knowledge, and inquiry. As we navigate this complex landscape, it becomes imperative to approach our exploration with humility, responsibility, and respect for the cosmic possibilities that await us. The journey toward deciphering the messages of the universe remains a testament to our indomitable curiosity while guiding us through the corridors of existence that stretch across the infinite expanse of space.

18. Mysteries of the Cosmic Microwave Background

18.1. The CMB Puzzle

The quest to comprehend the mysteries surrounding the cosmic microwave background (CMB) is an extraordinary journey that delves into the fabric of our universe, revealing both its origins and compositions. At the heart of this exploration lies what is known as 'The CMB Puzzle', where astronomers, physicists, and cosmologists endeavor to unravel the implications of this primordial radiation, mapping the evolution of the universe itself, and examining the signals that might indicate the presence of extraterrestrial life.

The cosmic microwave background represents the afterglow of the Big Bang, a faint remnant radiation that fills the universe, visible in every direction. As humanity continues to investigate the CMB, understanding its characteristics becomes essential for delving into the early moments of the universe and probing into the fundamental forces that govern cosmic structures.

Initially, the significance of the CMB emerged from its discovery in 1965 by Arno Penzias and Robert Wilson, leading to the realization that this radiation offered crucial evidence for the Big Bang theory. The detection of this background radiation, characterized by its near-uniform temperature and blackbody spectrum, presented a distinct marker pointing to a hot and dense universe that began to expand. As we have progressed in our observational capabilities—propelled by satellites such as COBE, WMAP, and Planck—we have gathered detailed information about the fluctuations and anisotropies present in the CMB, providing a wealth of data that assists in reconstructing the timeline of universal evolution.

As scientists examine the patterns within the CMB, they uncover perturbations that hint at the distribution of matter and energy in the early universe. By mapping these fluctuations, researchers glean insights into formative processes that contributed to the large-scale structure of galaxies and clusters, constructing a more profound understanding of cosmic evolution. However, these analyses also present a series of puzzles; the measured temperature variations sometimes deviate from theoretical predictions, affording compelling inquiries into the nature of dark matter and dark energy, both of which underpin the universe's dynamic processes.

The CMB ignites curiosity in the context of identifying signs of terraforming or cosmic manipulation. If advanced civilizations exist within the universe, might they utilize their understanding of cosmic waves and signals to modify their environments? The prospect of such technological prowess stirs the imagination, leading scientists to consider the potential effects of an extraterrestrial presence on the CMB. Disconnects or anomalies within the patterns could spark intriguing discussions surrounding the possible influences that advanced civilizations might exert on the fabric of space-time.

While the allure of the CMB captures the imagination, current challenges continue to hinder our endeavors in deeply understanding its phenomena. The precision of measurements required to decipher the signals must contend with competing sources of noise—interstellar dust, cosmic rays, and other astrophysical emissions that cloud the clarity of the CMB data. Moreover, the complexity of cosmic inflation, the behavior of dark energy, and the mechanisms governing galaxy formation complicate efforts to construct coherent models that unify our understanding of cosmic history.

Future advancements and collaborations promise hope as we strive to decode the depths of the CMB and the secrets it harbors. Innovative technologies and observational projects, such as the upcoming generation of CMB experiments and advanced analytical techniques, herald a new era of understanding. By synthesizing knowledge from various disciplines, including particle physics, cosmology, and engineering, we inch closer to unraveling the enigma of cosmic origins and the expansive narratives interwoven throughout the universe.

In essence, the CMB Puzzle invites us to traverse through the mysteries of the cosmos, revealing the undeniable intricacies that define our existence. As we grapple with the profound implications surrounding the CMB, we must remain committed to curiosity, exploration, and ethical considerations in our quest to understand the universe and the potential life that may inhabit it. Ultimately, the pursuit of understanding the cosmic microwave background offers valuable insights not only into the origins of our universe but also into the connections that bind us to the broader cosmic narrative.

18.2. Tracing the Universe's Birth

Tracing the birth of the universe is an endeavor that intertwines cosmic events with the very essence of existence as we explore questions about our origins, identity, and the potential for alien life nestled within the farthest reaches of space. The journey through time and space that leads us to the birth of the universe forms a dazzling narrative, illuminating the interconnectedness of celestial phenomena and setting the stage for discussions surrounding terraforming and the possibilities of life beyond Earth.

The cosmological model of the universe's birth begins with the Big Bang, a monumental event that marks the inception of time and space approximately 13.8 billion years ago. This initial explosion yielded matter, energy, and fundamental forces that would lay the groundwork for the formation of galaxies, stars, and planets—building blocks for the diverse tapestry of life. As humanity attempts to trace its origins, the implications of the Big Bang extend beyond mere temporal markers; they offer insight into how the universe has evolved into a complex system characterized by both order and chaos.

Key to understanding this transformation is the role of cosmic inflation, a rapid expansion that occurred shortly after the Big Bang. This phenomenon smoothed out irregularities in the universe, facilitating the formation of structures that would eventually cradle planets and life. The properties associated with inflation, including the distribution of matter, give rise to the possibility of multiple habitable zones existing in various cosmic neighborhoods, thereby expanding our aspirations of discovering life beyond our own planet.

As we journey into the cosmic narrative, the birth of stars and their eventual death through supernovae plays an equally vital part in shaping the possibility of life. It is through these explosive events that heavy elements—those essential for life—are dispersed into interstellar space. Transformer processes catalyze the creation of new stars and planetary systems, transforming the cosmic palette into an environment where life has the potential to emerge and flourish.

The subsequent processes governing planetary formation entwine with our understanding of the birth of habitable worlds. Conditions on newly formed planets can dictate the likelihood of life emerging. For instance, the energetic influences from nearby stars along with the extant presence of water and essential chemicals provide a confluence of factors that can lead to successful biological evolution. When combined with the advancements in astrobiology and planetary science, our understanding deepens, illuminating the potential routes through which life may flourish on distant planets.

As we reflect on the birth of the universe and its intricate dynamics, the question of whether advanced civilizations have influenced cosmic events must also be considered. If intelligent life has evolved, what role might they play in shaping their environments, and how do they connect to the origin stories of the cosmos? The narratives surrounding the cosmos compel us to reconcile scientific endeavours with philosophical reflections, prompting inquiries about the possibilities of life existing not just on Earth, but throughout the universe.

Toward this end, the convergence of cosmology, astrophysics, and a growing understanding of exoplanets opens exciting avenues for exploration. The birth of the universe propels humanity into the future as we—equipped with knowledge and technology—endeavor to explore, discover, and engage with the possibilities that lie before us. The echoes of the universe's birth resonate through time, compelling us to reflect on our place within the grand narrative and our responsibilities as guardians of life.

In conclusion, tracing the universe's birth illuminates the intricate connections between cosmic evolution and the conditions conducive to life. As we delve deeper into the mysteries that underpin our origins, we collectively ponder the implications of our pursuits in understanding terraforming and the existence of civilizations beyond Earth. The journey through the cosmos invites us to embrace a sense of wonder and curiosity, reminding us that the story of existence is unfolding across an expanse that transcends our imagination. As we embark on this exploration, we discover that tracing the universe's birth ignites not only our aspirations for adventure but also our sense of responsibility to protect and nurture the life that emerges amid the celestial realms.

18.3. Detecting Patterns with Anomalies

Detecting patterns within the cosmos, especially when framed through the lens of anomalies, serves as a nexus of scientific exploration and imaginative inquiry in the search for alien terraformation. As humanity casts its gaze beyond Earth, the quest to uncover patterns in cosmic data becomes not only central to understanding the universe's mechanics but is also critical in identifying signs that may indicate the presence of advanced civilizations reshaping their environments. This exploration involves analyzing deviations from the expected, positing that the universe may harbor civilizations whose influence is subtly intertwined with cosmic phenomena.

Patterns in astronomical data often emerge as characteristically rhythmic or periodic signals, allowing researchers to identify anomalies in the broader context of cosmic behavior. Whether examining the frequencies of light emitted by stars or the gravitational waves created by colliding celestial bodies, the detection of patterns may lead to revelations about the forces at play or potential technological interventions being enacted by intelligent species. For instance, the discovery of fast radio bursts (FRBs) and their unpredictable yet consistent emissions provides scientists an avenue through which to explore whether these signals originate from natural astrophysical events or are a result of advanced engineering efforts.

The significance of detecting anomalies extends into the realm of planetary systems. Notable observations of atmospheric compositions or thermal emissions that do not align with existing models can offer insight into the potential for terraforming initiatives. For example, unexpected temperature variations on an exoplanet could signify artificial heating methods or engineered ecosystems designed to sustain life. The relationship between anomalous behavior and potential habitability necessitates a comprehensive understanding of how extraterrestrial societies may adapt their environments to enhance survival.

Additionally, engaging with the anomalies of cosmic behavior prompts the reconsideration of existing scientific paradigms, allowing researchers to expand their frameworks for understanding life across the universe. Not only do these discrepancies challenge current interpretations of data, but they also inspire imaginative theorizing about how life could evolve and communicate in environments entirely different from our own. Each discovery of anomaly serves as a reminder that the universe is filled with unexpected complexities, inviting curiosity and innovative thinking.

Through the lens of cosmic exploration, the notion of pattern recognition offers profound implications for the terraforming narrative. The prospect of finding consistent signals or patterns stemming from extraterrestrial engineering activities would fundamentally alter our understanding of life beyond Earth. In this sense, detecting deviations from the norm elevates discussions surrounding the ethics of intervention, recognition of existing ecosystems, and the aspirations tied to creating sustainable environments for future generations.

Yet, the study of anomalies in cosmic data also brought forth challenges and uncertainties. As the vastness of space introduces noise and variability, distinguishing genuine signals from the backdrop of natural phenomena requires scientific rigor and a commitment to empirical validation. Furthermore, adopting a scientific skeptic approach allows researchers to cultivate a steadfast methodology, ensuring that conclusions drawn from observed anomalies are grounded in sound principles rather than speculation.

In conclusion, detecting patterns through anomalies in the cosmic realm stands as a critical aspect of uncovering truths about the universe and the potential existence of advanced civilizations. The ability to recognize these deviations encourages scientific inquiry and fosters imaginative thinking, revealing how life might adapt in disparate environments. As we embark on our cosmic journey, the mysteries of the universe call us to cultivate curiosity, engage with ethical considerations, and seek connections that transcend the boundaries of our own understanding—inviting us to explore the profound possibilities inherent within the celestial tapestry that envelops us all.

18.4. Contributions to Cosmic Understanding

In the ongoing exploration of the cosmos, humanity's efforts to understand the universe through scientific inquiry and artistic expression are vital components in shaping our perception of potential alien life and the prospect of terraforming distant worlds. Contributions to cosmic understanding reflect a mosaic of knowledge that unites disciplines ranging from astrophysics and biology to culture and ethics, fostering a holistic approach to the questions that arise during our cosmic journey.

As we strive to decipher the mysteries of our universe, scientific advancements provide the foundation upon which we build our understanding of alien worlds and the conditions that might allow for life. The recent discoveries of exoplanets—many residing in the habitable zones of their stars—have reinvigorated our quest for answers about the delicate balance necessary to support life. Detailed studies of atmospheric compositions, surface temperatures, and potential resources paves the way for innovative terraforming strategies, suggesting that life could, given the right conditions, flourish far beyond Earth.

However, as exciting as these possibilities may seem, the realities of cosmic exploration are fraught with challenges. The complexities of ecological systems must be respected and understood; the act of terraforming involves more than merely engineering environments to suit our expectations. We must consider historical examples from Earth that highlight the intricacies of ecology, ensuring that our ambitions do not inadvertently disrupt the delicate balance of life, even in environments that seem barren or inhospitable.

Furthermore, as we uncover clues embedded in cosmic phenomena, the responsibilities that arise from our discoveries must also be acknowledged. The ethical implications surrounding potential alterations of alien ecosystems compel us to engage thoughtfully with the realities of cosmic interactions. This realization leads us to understand that as stewards of both Earth and the broader cosmos, our role is not solely to explore but to nurture the environments we discover—honoring the life forms that may inhabit them.

In parallel, public engagement that translates scientific inquiries into relatable narratives is fundamental to fostering a collective responsibility toward cosmic exploration. As stories of potential life beyond Earth permeate popular culture, fostering an informed public consciousness allows individuals to participate in discussions surrounding the ethical implications of terraforming and cosmic engagement. Artistic representations across literature, film, and visual arts provide ways for humanity to grapple with the intricacies of alien existence, bridging the gap between scientific exploration and cultural understanding.

Moreover, interdisciplinary collaboration plays a crucial role in advancing cosmic understanding. Scientists from diverse fields—such as astronomy, biology, engineering, and social sciences—must come together to foster a comprehensive approach toward unraveling the enigma of extraterrestrial life and terraforming. By weaving their knowledge and insights together, researchers can develop innovative techniques and ethical frameworks that honor the complexities of cosmic life.

As we continue our journey into the cosmos, we find that contributions to our understanding of the universe come from both scientific inquiry and cultural narratives. Each discovery provides fragments of knowledge that enrich our perceptions while simultaneously inviting contemplation of the ethical dimensions that accompany our exploration. Collectively, we endeavor to foster a culture that not only embraces discovery but also kindles the responsibility to protect and preserve the environments we encounter.

Ultimately, the contributions to cosmic understanding extend beyond mere exploration; they encourage humanity to reflect on our interconnectedness with the universe and our role as custodians of life. As we connect the dots of knowledge, we bolster our aspirations to uncover the mysteries of existence while manifesting a profound respect for the myriad forms of life that may share this vast and intricate tapestry we call the cosmos.

18.5. Current Challenges in CMB Studies

Current challenges in CMB studies represent an intricate web of scientific inquiry that intersects astrophysics, cosmology, and the quest for understanding the universe's origins and structures. The cosmic microwave background (CMB), a vital remnant from the Big Bang, provides not only a snapshot of the early universe but also insight into the intricate processes that govern cosmic evolution. Recent advancements in observational techniques have propelled researchers into an exciting era of CMB studies, yet numerous challenges remain that complicate the interpretation of this fundamental data.

One of the primary hurdles confronting scientists studying the CMB is the need for increasingly sophisticated observational technologies. Major efforts, such as the Planck satellite mission, have refined measurements of the CMB with unprecedented precision. However, future studies require even more advanced instruments capable of isolating the faint signals amidst increasingly complex noise. The challenge lies not only in capturing these weak signals effectively but also in ensuring that systematic errors and foreground contamination from other astrophysical sources do not skew interpretations.

The cosmological implications of CMB observations necessitate that researchers possess a deep understanding of the universe's structure over vast scales. Debates surrounding the precise measurements of the CMB's temperature fluctuations and polarization patterns are key to deciphering phenomena such as dark matter and dark energy. These debates invite researchers to revisit existing models and explore alternative interpretations, which can hinder consensus on foundational aspects of cosmology. As the quest for understanding the CMB's mysteries unfolds, a plethora of competing hypotheses emerges, illustrating the complexities of astrophysical inquiry and the difficulties associated with resolving these intricacies experimentally.

Another challenge lies in the calibration of existing and future CMB instruments. Achieving a level of accuracy in measurements that can withstand scrutiny, while accounting for potential biases, becomes increasingly complicated. Researchers are tasked with developing methodologies to validate these observations against theoretical predictions and to enhance collaboration among international efforts that contribute data and insights to the CMB studies. As these efforts progress, the collective goal remains: to ensure that the analyses conducted on the CMB yield astronomical interpretations that expand our knowledge of the universe's architecture.

Compounding these observational challenges is the need for theoretical frameworks capable of explaining the wealth of data being generated. Discrepancies between measured CMB properties and predictions derived from current cosmological models—including dark energy influences and cosmic inflation—have sparked widespread debate. For instance, tensions surrounding the measurements of the Hubble constant, which describes the universe's expansion rate, suggest that our understanding of dark energy may require a reevaluation. As researchers confront these fractures in established theories, the importance of accommodating new scientific insights becomes increasingly apparent.

Furthermore, the implications of CMB measurements extend far beyond the study of the early universe; they interlace with our ongoing discussions regarding the potential for alien life and the future of terraforming. As scientists assess the structural dynamics that arise from CMB data, the insights gleaned about galaxy formation and cosmic evolution could inform predictions about the conditions necessary for life. This exploration moves beyond mere academic inquiry, intimately linking CMB studies to the very fabric of human ambitions to inhabit and adapt worlds beyond our own.

As advancements in technology and observational systems continue to propel CMB research, ongoing scholarly dialogue encourages collaborative frameworks that enhance our understanding of cosmic phenomena. These exchanges spur a collective intellectual effort that involves astrobiologists, cosmologists, and astrophysicists alike. The challenges inherent in deciphering the CMB signal compel us not only to refine our observational strategies but also to approach cosmic questions with an appreciation for their interconnectedness.

In conclusion, the current challenges in CMB studies represent a multifaceted landscape of exploration that spans theoretical models, observational techniques, and the intertwining implications for understanding life in the universe. As humanity endeavors to decode the secrets of the cosmos, these inquiries remind us that the path to knowledge is not a linear journey; it is a labyrinth filled with dynamic complexities and profound mysteries. Engaging with these challenges ensures that our exploration is grounded in scientific rigor, ethical considerations, and a constant curiosity about the universe— all fundamental to our pursuit of cosmic understanding.

19. Dark Matter Conundrum: Terraforming's Hidden Ally?

19.1. What is Dark Matter?

In the vast expanse of the cosmos, the question, "What is Dark Matter?" stands as a crucial inquiry that affects our understanding of the universe and the potential for alien terraformation. Dark matter, which makes up approximately 27% of the universe's mass-energy content, is categorized as a non-luminous form of matter that does not interact with electromagnetic forces. This invisibility complicates our ability to observe it directly; however, its presence is inferred from its gravitational effects on visible matter.

The historical pursuit of identifying dark matter began in the early 20th century when astronomers uncovered discrepancies in the motion of galaxies that could not be accounted for by the mass visible to us. The pioneering work of scientists such as Fritz Zwicky, who observed the Coma galaxy cluster, laid the groundwork for this discovery. Zwicky noted that the visible mass, including stars and gas, was insufficient to explain the gravitational binding of the cluster, leading him to postulate the presence of unseen matter. This concept has since evolved into what we now define as dark matter.

The potential connections between dark matter and terraforming arise from hypothesizing about advanced civilizations. Should intelligent life exist, it may possess the capacity to manipulate or utilize dark matter in ways that could impact planetary conditions. Theoretical physics posits that if advanced beings were capable of direct manipulation of gravitational forces, they could leverage dark matter to influence the orbits of planets, adjust their atmospheres, or control environmental conditions to render inhospitable planets more suitable for life.

Moreover, dark matter's influence extends into the formation of galaxies and stellar structures, shaping the environments where planets may emerge. Understanding the distribution and properties of dark matter becomes a focal point for researchers aiming to connect the dots between cosmic events and the scenarios pertinent to terraforming efforts. The gravitational effects of dark matter can help define the regions where habitable planets may form, illuminating our search for potentially terraformable worlds.

Theories of dark energy manipulation also present exciting prospects in broader discussions surrounding terraforming. While dark matter is responsible for the mass and gravitational binding of cosmic structures, dark energy—an enigmatic force driving the universe's accelerated expansion—poses additional questions. If advanced civilizations possess the means to harness dark energy, the implications for controlling cosmic parameters become paramount. These technologies could enable scenario modeling for terraforming—allowing civilizations to adjust energy dynamics, stabilize environments, and foster conditions conducive to life.

The link between dark matter and natural phenomena becomes evident as researchers delve into the cosmic web that connects galaxies. The structure of the universe is characterized by vast filaments of dark matter, forming an intricate network that shapes gravitational dynamics and influences the movement of galaxies. These cosmic structures unravel further possibilities for terraforming initiatives, informing the potential locations for interstellar colonies and guiding our understanding of how to cultivate environments that can sustain life.

Additionally, dark matter may play a role in enhancing our models of terraforming. As we explore gravitational influences on planets, accounting for the hidden mass of dark matter may yield insights into how we can alter conditions for sustainable ecosystems. Understanding how dark matter interacts within a planetary context will enable researchers to develop more robust models that incorporate both visible and non-visible factors, helping to shape future terraforming strategies.

The speculation about advanced civilizations and their relationship with dark matter invites us to contemplate our own future. If intelligent life is capable of leveraging dark matter to effectuate profound transformations in their environments, this flexibility may reflect the possibilities we, as a species, may explore as we reach for the stars. Such visions of cosmic engineering extend beyond optimism; they urge us toward responsible stewardship and ethical interaction with the environments we aim to explore.

In conclusion, the question, "What is Dark Matter?" transcends a mere definition; it encapsulates the mysteries and potentialities that shape our understanding of the universe and inform our exploration of alien worlds. The interplay between dark matter, advanced civilizations, and potential terraforming initiatives underscores a multi-dimensional narrative that invites us to gaze into the extraordinary possibilities that lie beyond our terrestrial confines. As we work to decipher the cosmic enigma of dark matter, we are reminded of our aspirations, responsibilities, and the ongoing quest for understanding the infinite tapestry of existence that stretches across the galaxy.

19.2. Theories of Dark Energy Manipulation

Theories of Dark Energy Manipulation

The exploration of dark energy manipulation opens a window into the profound and often perplexing interplay of cosmic forces that govern the universe. Dark energy, which constitutes about 68% of the universe's total energy density, remains one of the most enigmatic components of our cosmological understanding. Its mysterious nature presents compelling questions regarding the role it might play in terraforming or altering planetary conditions across the cosmos. Understanding the potential for manipulation of this elusive force could redefine our approach to cosmic exploration and the very fabric of existence.

At its core, dark energy is theorized to be responsible for the accelerated expansion of the universe, pushing galaxies away from each other. Its presence raises critical inquiries into the underlying principles of cosmic dynamics; the acceleration indicates that conventional gravitational attraction may not be the only force at play in shaping the universe. Some theorists postulate that if advanced civilizations exist, they might develop the capabilities to manipulate dark energy, using it as a tool for cosmic engineering.

The possibilities around dark energy manipulation might seem speculative, but they are indeed grounded in the burgeoning field of theoretical physics. Academics have explored concepts from quantum field theory, where fluctuations in energy fields give rise to dark energy phenomena. The premise is that if such fluctuations can be harnessed, they might provide the basis for technologies capable of influencing the fundamental properties of not just galaxies, but individual planetary systems as well.

For instance, if dark energy could be controlled, civilizations might create stable orbits for planets, adjusting their trajectories to situate them within optimal habitable zones. Imagine a civilization capable of redirecting rogue planets or establishing new colonies on previously inhospitable worlds by manipulating their energetic properties through dark energy. Terraforming efforts could integrate such manipulations, using dark energy to modulate atmospheric pressure, temperature, or even climate events.

Furthermore, dark energy may offer insights into the fabric of space-time itself. By understanding its properties, advancements in manipulating gravitational fields could lead to technologies that facilitate interstellar travel, energy generation, and perhaps even time dilation —theoretical concepts that ripple through both science fiction and physicists' dreams alike. The exploration of dark energy manipulation invites us to consider not just the future of human exploration but the very essence of reality itself.

While these prospects are exciting, significant challenges remain in our understanding of dark energy and its manipulation. Theoretical frameworks may qualify as plausible avenues, yet empirical evidence remains elusive. Researchers must grapple with the complexities of experimental design and observational validation to explore dark energy's effects in meaningful ways. Current observational tools, such as large scale surveys of supernovae and the distributions of galaxies, provide some insights, but holistic models incorporating dark energy into the broader understanding of cosmic phenomena are still in development.

Consequently, the ethical implications surrounding dark energy manipulation also demand serious consideration. Should advanced civilizations exist that possess the ability to harness dark energy, the motivations guiding their applications carry weighty consequences for the cosmic landscape. Humanity's own responsibilities regarding the use of such powerful forces must be grounded in ethical frameworks and principles of stewardship—ensuring that we do not disrupt existing ecosystems or compromise the integrity of alien worlds.

Thus, as we engage with the theories surrounding dark energy manipulation, we are beckoned to open our minds to the myriad possibilities and responsibilities that accompany such a pursuit. The exploration of this enigmatic force connects us to broader questions of existence, emphasizing our intrinsic connection to the cosmos and the need for ethical reflection as we traverse the unknown.

In summary, theories of dark energy manipulation highlight the complexities and promises of cosmic exploration, inviting humanity to embrace its role within the intricate narrative of the universe. By considering the implications of dark energy on terraforming and the potential for advanced civilizations to utilize such forces, we unlock new dimensions of inquiry and possibility. The journey ahead promises to be filled with profound discoveries, compelling ethical discussions, and the exhilarating pursuit of knowledge that transcends our terrestrial experience as we reach for the stars.

19.3. Linking Dark Matter to Natural Phenomena

Linking dark matter to natural phenomena presents a captivating aspect of understanding the cosmos and the potential influence of advanced civilizations on their surroundings. Dark matter, that elusive substance which comprises a significant portion of the universe's mass, exerts gravitational effects on visible matter without emitting detectable radiation. This enigmatic nature opens intriguing pathways for linking dark matter to various cosmic events and terrestrial phenomena that may indicate efforts to manipulate or terraform environments for habitability.

One of the main connections between dark matter and natural phenomena lies in its influence on galaxy formation and the overall structure of the universe. The presence of dark matter haloes around galaxies dictates how these galaxies cluster and evolve over time. Since dark matter does not interact electromagnetically, it can only be inferred from its gravitational effects. Consequently, the observed behaviors of galaxies are often linked to the underlying mass distribution shaped by dark matter. The interplay between dark matter and stellar dynamics could lead to vital clues about whether intelligent civilizations utilize their environment for terraforming purposes, as the gravitational influences of dark matter could provide stability for engineered ecosystems on planets.

Moreover, one must consider the role of dark matter in shaping cosmic events such as supernovae, gravitational lensing, and galaxy mergers. These phenomena create unique environments that may be influenced by dark matter dynamics, prompting scientists to investigate the effects on potential life-sustaining conditions. For example, the distribution of dark matter could affect the occurrence of supernovae in star-forming regions, thereby impacting the elemental composition and energy dynamics within those regions. This relationship speaks to the potential for terraforming in the wake of cosmic events —an intriguing area for speculating how civilizations might integrate dark matter's properties into their ecological designs.

The investigation of dark matter also encourages a broader understanding of the fundamental forces within the universe that dictate life's potential. As scientists continue to unravel the intricate relationships between dark matter, visible matter, and cosmic phenomena, they hone the models used to assess stability and habitability within planetary systems. It remains critical to assess how dark matter can potentially contribute to sustaining life and what implications might arise from modifying its gravitational interactions.

Intriguingly, if advanced civilizations exist and possess the capacity to manipulate dark matter, they could exert a profound influence over their environments. Theoretical frameworks nourished by advancements in physics propose that such beings may recognize and leverage dark matter to manage the orbits of their planets or terraform their atmospheres, further prompting us to consider the intricate connections between civilizations and the fundamental forces that shape the universe. These wonders fuel our imaginations and benchmark a compelling narrative at the intersection of science and speculation.

Although the potential for linking dark matter to natural phenomena and the advanced engineering of cosmological environments expands our horizons, the challenges of interpretation and empirical validation persist. Researchers must progress cautiously, ensuring that claims of dark matter manipulation or connections to terraforming efforts remain grounded in evidence and scientific rigor. The creative entanglement of theoretical implications alongside advances in our observational capabilities fosters a critical dialogue about the possibilities that dark matter holds within the broader narrative of life beyond Earth.

In conclusion, linking dark matter to natural phenomena underscores a significant aspect of our ongoing inquiry into the cosmos. As we uncover the intricate relationships between dark matter and the events that shape our universe, we inch closer to understanding the possibilities of advanced civilizations harnessing these forces for terraforming initiatives. The mysteries of dark matter beckon, inviting reflections on the interconnectedness of existence as we seek to chart a course among the stars—a journey laden with awe, uncertainty, and the pursuit of knowledge that animates our exploration of the majestic universe.

19.4. Impact on Terraforming Models

The exploration of "Impact on Terraforming Models" encapsulates the intersection of scientific principles, technological advancements, and ethical considerations that shape our understanding of how terraforming efforts might unfold across celestial bodies. As humanity grapples with the potential for life beyond Earth, the implications of terraforming and the methodologies employed provide profound insights into our cosmic aspirations. This chapter navigates the complexities surrounding terraforming models, emphasizing their adaptability, innovative strategies, and the responsibilities we bear as we embark on this ambitious journey.

At the foundation of effective terraforming models lies a thorough understanding of the environmental conditions necessary to support life. These models draw upon principles from biology, geology, and planetary science, allowing researchers to conceptualize the processes required to transform inhospitable worlds into vibrant ecosystems. Models elucidate the essential parameters such as atmospheric composition, temperature regulation, and water availability that function as cornerstones of habitability.

For instance, when exploring Mars as a candidate for terraforming, models spotlight the need for increasing atmospheric pressure and composition—potentially through the introduction of greenhouse gases and engineered organisms capable of supporting ecological stability. Researchers may design extensive simulations to understand the interactions between these elements, refining the approach and forecasting potential outcomes. The iterative nature of developing these models ensures that scientists continually adapt their methods based on new discoveries or data, leading to innovative solutions that align with the complexities of various environments.

However, flexibility and adaptability are crucial components of successful terraforming models. Each celestial body possesses unique characteristics, from atmospheric properties to geological formations, that dictate how terraforming efforts should be tailored. For example, while Mars may benefit from the infusion of greenhouse gases to promote warming and liquid water, approaches to terraforming might differ significantly on a moon like Europa, where subsurface oceans could present a different set of challenges. This variability underscores the necessity for detailed, location-specific models that account for the distinctive qualities of each target world.

The advancements in technology further bolster our capacity to refine these models. The integration of artificial intelligence and machine learning has the potential to revolutionize terraforming simulations, enabling researchers to analyze vast datasets and explore variables beyond human capacity to conceptualize. By employing predictive algorithms that can imitate ecological dynamics, scientists can significantly reduce the time and resources necessary to test various terraforming strategies.

While scientific rigor and technological innovation play critical roles in the development of terraforming models, ethical considerations remain paramount. As we venture into the realm of altering alien environments, the responsibility to preserve existing ecosystems becomes a guiding principle. Should we encounter life, even in the most primitive forms, our models must account for potential impact and risk to these ecosystems. Creating guidelines and ethical frameworks that prioritize the preservation of alien life will shape our understanding of what responsible terraforming entails.

The implications of these terraforming models extend into public discourse as well. As interest in space exploration grows, society must engage with the discussion around terraforming and its ethical implications. Education initiatives that inform the public about these responsibilities will foster a well-rounded dialogue and encourage respect for diverse forms of life. This understanding cultivates a collective sense of accountability as humanity seeks to explore and transform neighboring worlds.

In summary, the impact on terraforming models encapsulates the fusion of science, technology, and ethics that frame our aspirations for altering alien environments. Developing adaptive, location-specific models enhances our understanding of the complexities surrounding habitability while ensuring that our explorative endeavors reflect responsible stewardship. As we continue to chart our path into the cosmos, the insights gained from these models will serve as the foundation for our endeavors to understand, engage with, and thrive among the celestial realms beyond our own.

19.5. Advanced Civilizations and Dark Matter

In the absence of specific content for the subchapter "Advanced Civilizations and Dark Matter," the following detailed and comprehensive narrative has been composed based on the overarching themes of the book, "The Majestic Universe: Recognizing Signs of Alien Terraformation."

—

The exploration of advanced civilizations coupled with dark matter presents a captivating inquiry that traverses the realms of astrophysics, cosmology, and the potential for life beyond Earth. As humanity embarks on its quest to uncover the mysteries of the universe, it is increasingly recognized that dark matter, which constitutes a significant portion of the cosmos, may hold the key to understanding the processes governing these advanced societies and their possible interactions with their environments.

At its core, dark matter comprises an invisible substance that does not emit or absorb light, making it extraordinarily challenging to detect with conventional observational methods. However, its presence is inferred through its gravitational effects on visible matter, including stars and galaxies. The study of dark matter serves as a reminder of the limitations inherent in our understanding of the cosmos, illustrating that much of what exists is still shrouded in mystery. As researchers delve deeper into the nature of dark matter, they grapple with profound questions that may elucidate the role of advanced civilizations in the fabric of the universe.

One particularly intriguing speculation revolves around the notion that civilizations wise enough to recognize the properties of dark matter might harness its gravitational effects for their purposes. Imagine a technologically advanced society capable of manipulating dark matter to alter gravitational influences on their home planet or neighboring celestial bodies. Such capabilities could enable them to terraform inhospitable environments into flourishing worlds, creating habitable conditions by controlling not only their planetary atmospheres but also the trajectories of neighboring celestial bodies.

For instance, if dark matter can be manipulated effectively, it might allow advanced civilizations to stabilize the orbits of planets in binary star systems, aligning them in such a way as to maintain habitable climates despite the dynamic forces exerted by multiple stars. The idea of engineering gravitational interactions through dark matter introduces new paradigms of planetary adaptation, challenging our current understanding of what constitutes a viable environment for life.

The exploration of dark matter's relationship with advanced civilizations also invites contemplation about the potential for communication across the cosmos. If intelligent life exists that possesses the technology to manipulate dark matter, could they also utilize it as a medium for communication? The patterns of gravitational waves emitted by stellar events or engineered systems could very well represent a cosmic language, one that transcends the limitations of electromagnetic communication that we currently employ. This theoretical framework opens new avenues of exploration, urging us to redefine our understanding of interstellar communication.

Additionally, the intersection of dark matter and cosmic phenomena sparks a dialogue about the evolution of advanced civilizations in response to their environments. The gravitational influences of dark matter may determine how galaxies form, evolve, and interact, consequently shaping the conditions under which life may arise and civilizations may develop. The synthesis of dark matter's gravitational properties with the observable universe underscores the intricate balance maintained through cosmic forces, demonstrating that the emergence and survival of intelligent life hinge not only on biological evolution but also on the dynamics of the universe itself.

Nevertheless, the study of dark matter remains fraught with challenges. As advanced civilizations utilize their understanding of dark matter for manipulation, there looms the specter of unintended consequences. If civilizations inadvertently disrupt the intricate balance of their cosmic neighborhoods, the ramifications could echo throughout their ecosystems and extend to neighboring worlds. This realization compels us to reflect on the ethical responsibilities of such advanced life forms—preserving the integrity of other realms while striving to shape their destinies within the cosmos.

Moreover, the quest for understanding dark matter is an emblematic reflection of human curiosity—it mirrors our desire to transcend limitations and explore the unknown. As we endeavor to uncover its secrets, we deepen our comprehension of not only our own existence but also the potential for life elsewhere in the universe. The interplay of dark matter, advanced civilizations, and the possibilities for terraforming serves to remind us that the universe holds countless mysteries waiting to be unveiled.

In conclusion, the investigation into advanced civilizations and dark matter provides a unique vantage point in our quest for knowledge about the cosmos. As scientists continue to unlock the secrets of dark matter, we contemplate the interconnections between celestial forces and intelligent life, recognizing that as we pursue understanding, we also delve into ethical considerations that guide our engagement with the universe. The journey toward uncovering the truths surrounding dark matter embodies humanity's enduring desire to explore and connect—a testament to our collective curiosity and responsibility as stewards of life in all its forms, lighting the path as we strive to understand our place amid the magnificence of the cosmos.

20. A New Paradigm of Reality: The Multiverse

20.1. Conceptualizing Multiverses

In contemplating the vast cosmic canvas, the conceptualization of multiverses emerges as an intellectually stimulating endeavor that challenges our understanding of existence, reality, and the very fabric of the universe. This notion posits that our universe may be just one of many, forming a multiverse—a realm brimming with parallel realities, distinct laws of physics, and diverse manifestations of life. As the fabric of the cosmos unravels, the implications of multiverses redefine not only the quest for extraterrestrial life and terraforming but also our philosophical reflections on existence itself.

The foundational concept of multiverses spans multiple theoretical frameworks, including quantum mechanics and cosmological models. The ever-elusive nature of dark energy provides fertile ground for contemplating alternate realities that exist alongside our own. Quantum theories, such as the Many-Worlds Interpretation, suggest that every decision or random event may spawn an entirely new universe, each a branch in the endless tree of existence. The realization that different timelines can coexist presents a tantalizing perspective, allowing us to imagine the myriad ways civilizations might evolve or alter environments across distinct universes.

As scientists delve deeper into the possibility of multiverses, they also investigate potential evidence for parallel realities. Astrophysical phenomena—such as cosmic inflation, abrupt fluctuations in cosmic microwave background radiation, or observations of gravitational anomalies—might serve as breadcrumbs, hinting at the existence of universes beyond our perception. While definitive evidence remains elusive, theorizing about speculative realities challenges traditional views of celestial mechanics and our place within the larger cosmic framework. The notion that different physical laws characterize each universe spices the conversation surrounding the adaptability of life, further broadening the horizons for exploring terraforming possibilities in varied environments.

Terraforming across universes conjures up images of incredible possibilities, where advanced civilizations might possess the means to manipulate not just their planets but also the fundamental parameters within their entire realities. The harnessing of dark matter and energy could enable civilizations to traverse between universes, discovering and influencing worlds that mirror their own or diverge fantastically from their familiar landscapes. The sheer magnitude of these potential endeavors sparks wonder and curiosity about the extent of cosmic engineering capabilities—transformations that meld imagination with scientific speculation.

However, the implications of experimenting with multiverses beckon profound ethical considerations. As advanced civilizations seek to terraform realms beyond their own, questions arise regarding the rights of existence within those parallel realities. How do we navigate responsibilities when engaging with uncharted territories and the potential sentience inherent in alternate forms of life? The intermingling of ethical discourse with scientific innovations propels us toward a more thoughtful approach, urging a reflection on our values as we explore the cosmos.

The exploration of multiverses inevitably leads us to ponder the grand theory that could unify our understanding of existence. The search for a unifying framework—whether in physics, cosmology, or philosophy—characterizes humanity's enduring quest to make sense of the universe's intricacies. Futures filled with advanced technologies may one day allow us to test the boundaries of known laws and delve into realms that challenge our very humanity. The ultimate aspiration remains to connect the threads that bind these realities together, nurturing a deeper comprehension of our existence and our place within the tapestry of life beyond Earth.

In conclusion, the multiverse concept reframes the possibilities of life and terraforming within the cosmos, transforming the narrative surrounding existence itself. As we traverse this intricate landscape, contemplating the implications of parallel realities, the ethical responsibilities of cosmic exploration permeate our quest. The awe-inspiring journey unfolds before us, inviting us to embrace the complexity of existence, propelling humanity toward the embodiment of curiosity, innovation, and unity amid the multitudes of realms that lie beyond the veil of our comprehension. The conceptualization of multiverses enriches our exploration, guiding us as we seek to understand not just the wonders of the cosmos, but also the profound narratives that interconnect us all.

20.2. Evidence for Parallel Realities

In the search for extraterrestrial life and the transformative practice of terraforming, the compelling question of "Evidence for Parallel Realities" evokes curiosity about the cosmic landscape as we traverse not only physical realms but also the philosophical and scientific dimensions embedded within our understanding of existence. This subchapter delves into the intriguing possibilities associated with the multiverse theory, investigating the implications of alternate dimensions and their potential intersections with the aspirations of terraforming and the quest for life beyond our planet.

The concept of parallel realities suggests that our universe may coexist with countless others, each exhibiting its own distinct physical laws, configurations, and possibilities. This notion stretches the boundaries of traditional scientific thought, inviting us to explore the nature of existence beyond a singular reality. Quantum mechanics and the theories surrounding many-world interpretations lay the groundwork for envisioning a multiverse, thus framing a vibrant landscape where alternate timelines and realities intersect and diverge.

The implications of these parallel realities extend into the realm of terraforming—a transformative process that often takes center stage when considering the methods society might employ to make other worlds hospitable to life. If parallel realities exist, could they harbor planets uniquely suited to support advanced civilizations, each adapting in different states of existence? The vast diversity of worlds within the multiverse invites deep speculation about various evolutionary pathways, ecological balances, and the complexities that may arise from distinct environments.

As we consider the evidence for such realities, the intersection between dark matter, dark energy, and the cosmic phenomena we observe becomes vital. Astonishing anomalies in the laws of physics —whether pertaining to gravitational behavior, cosmic inflation patterns, or the cosmic microwave background radiation—hint at the possibility of realms beyond our perception. If such phenomena arise from influences exerted by neighboring universes or interdimensional interactions, we may begin to delve into the threads that connect the myriad realities within the cosmic tapestry.

Moreover, the act of terraforming itself serves as a metaphor for humanity's journey in navigating these multiple dimensions. When envisioning the alteration of environments to create habitable conditions, we grapple with profound questions about agency, responsibility, and the interconnectedness of life. The possible existence of parallel realities reinforces the notion that life, even in its most diverse forms, may have evolved in varied and intertwined environments— each uniquely tailored to its respective cosmological conditions.

While drawing connections between parallel realities and terraforming, the necessity for multidisciplinary collaboration becomes increasingly apparent. Scientists, philosophers, ethicists, and cultural advocates must come together to reflect on the ethical implications of exploring and altering planetary environments. As humanity seeks to understand the vast capabilities for existence, the broader questions surrounding the potential rights of life forms—whether terrestrial or extraterrestrial—must remain front and center as we navigate the multiverse and its implications for our own existence.

In summary, the investigation into evidence for parallel realities not only shapes our understanding of the cosmos but also encourages us to reflect on our place within it. As we explore the multiverse theory and its implications for terraforming and extraterrestrial life, we evoke a sense of wonder and inquiry fundamental to the human experience. This exploration invites us to engage with the myriad potentials embedded in the cosmic narrative, fostering a deeper appreciation for the interconnectedness of existence as we strive to uncover the mysteries that lie beyond our world and beyond our imagination.

In concluding this subchapter, we recognize that embracing the possibilities of parallel realities enhances our journey toward cosmic understanding. As we venture into the unknown, the prospect of diverse worlds and life experiences motivates our quest for knowledge, ultimately becoming a testament to the resilience of life, the complexity of existence, and our indomitable curiosity that propels us across the vast cosmic expanse. Each exploration serves as a reminder that the universe is rich with opportunities for discovery and connection, beckoning us to dream, to ask, and to reach for the stars in pursuit of understanding and belonging in the grand tapestry of the multiverse.

As we synthesize current evidence surrounding our aspirations for terraforming and the potential for parallel dimensions, the prospects grow brighter, beckoning us to remain open to the boundless possibilities that await us in the cosmic mystery.

20.3. Terraforming Across Universes

In the realm of speculative thought and scientific exploration, the potential for terraforming other worlds has captured the imagination of humanity, prompting a multitude of inquiries regarding the feasibility and implications of such endeavors. As we synthesize current evidence, consider predictions for future discoveries, and reflect on our natural curiosity, we can begin to outline the possibilities that lie ahead in our quest to transform inhospitable environments into thriving ecosystems.

The synthesis of current evidence regarding the potential for terraforming begins with a comprehensive understanding of the scientific principles that govern planetary systems. From the essential roles of atmospheric composition and temperature regulation to the delicate balance of ecosystems, our grasp of what constitutes a habitable environment has evolved significantly. The conversations sparked by the discovery of numerous exoplanets within the habitable zones of their stars exemplify this progress, as scientists ponder both the natural conditions required for life and the methods by which we might engineer those conditions effectively.

Predictions for future discoveries also encourage optimism and ambition. Advancements in astronomical technology, such as the James Webb Space Telescope and next-generation exploratories focused on astrobiology, will expand our ability to identify potentially habitable planets and study their atmospheric signatures. Ongoing missions to Mars and robotic expeditions to the icy moons of Jupiter and Saturn serve as vital stepping stones in our understanding of what it means to create favorable conditions for life. As researchers continue to unveil the mysteries surrounding these celestial bodies, the groundwork for terraforming initiatives will become increasingly robust.

The role of human curiosity is central to our exploration of terraforming and extraterrestrial life. This intrinsic drive compels us to seek knowledge and connection, propelling scientific advancement alongside cultural narratives that embrace the unknown. As public interest in the cosmos intensifies, educational initiatives that promote scientific literacy engage broader audiences in conversations about the ethical considerations surrounding terraforming. Ensuring a common understanding of the implications of our actions will guide future exploration efforts in sustainable and responsible ways.

Preparing for a terraforming revelation requires that we engage not only with scientific inquiry but also with philosophical reflections on our place in the cosmos. Each step taken toward unlocking the secrets of the universe serves as a reminder of our collective responsibilities as stewards of life—grounding our aspirations in ethics and a deep respect for all forms of existence. As we envision transforming distant worlds into habitable environments, we must remain attentive to the lessons of humility needed as potential cosmic custodians.

In concluding this exploration, the cosmic mystery of terraforming presents both astonishing possibilities and profound responsibilities. The convergence of scientific discovery, technological advancements, and ethical considerations reveals our interconnectedness with the universe as we strive to understand our place within it. As human curiosity and exploration lay the foundations for future endeavors, we prepare to unlock the doors to distant worlds filled with the promise of life. The quest for terraforming realized beckons us forward—a journey that transcends boundaries, illuminates the path ahead, and echoes the enduring human spirit to explore the vast and magnificent cosmos.

In this pursuit, we affirm our commitment to navigate with care and conscience, honoring all forms of life while daring to dream of futures colored by the vibrant richness of existence beyond our terrestrial home. Ultimately, the overarching narrative is one of hope—nurturing the aspirations of both human and alien life as we journey into the vast expanse of the universe.

20.4. Exploration and Implications

In the vast tapestry of cosmic exploration, the narrative surrounding alien terraformation is both intricately complex and profoundly hopeful. The drive to understand and potentially alter other worlds connects humanity with the very essence of existence, prompting reflection upon our responsibilities as stewards of both Earth and the distant environments we aspire to nurture. As we synthesize the current evidence surrounding terraforming, evaluate predictions for future discoveries, and consider the role of human curiosity, we pave the way for a broader dialogue about our cosmic aspirations.

Current evidence reveals that numerous exoplanets exist within their stars' habitable zones, raising tantalizing prospects for environments that might support life. The investigation of atmospheric signatures, geological characteristics, and potential biomarkers underscores the viability of these worlds as candidates for terraforming initiatives. Notably, Mars remains a prime focus, with ongoing missions exploring its surface, geological history, and signs of past water. Similarly, the icy moons of Jupiter and Saturn, such as Europa and Enceladus, present unique opportunities for study as scientists pursue the secrets hidden beneath their frigid crusts.

Predictions for future discoveries signal an optimistic trajectory for our understanding of terraforming. With advancements in technology—such as powerful telescopes and robotic exploration—scientists can uncover new details about exoplanet atmospheres, surface conditions, and possible biological processes. The anticipated launch and operationalization of next-generation observatories like the James Webb Space Telescope promise to yield unprecedented insights into the characteristics of distant worlds, refining our criteria for identifying potential habitats amenable to terraforming.

As we reflect upon the role of human curiosity, it becomes evident that our collective drive propels scientific inquiry and exploration. This intrinsic desire to uncover the cosmos encourages interdisciplinary collaboration, as experts from various fields—ranging from astrobiology to engineering—convene to address the multifaceted challenges inherent in terraforming. Ultimately, curiosity serves as the guiding force behind our endeavors to connect with life beyond Earth, urging us to engage ethically and responsibly with the mysteries that lie before us.

Preparation for a terraforming revelation necessitates a thoughtful approach—one that encompasses rigorous scientific methodologies, ethical reflection, and a commitment to preserving the integrity of ecosystems, both known and unknown. As we chart pathways toward transforming alien worlds, fostering inclusive dialogues that engage diverse perspectives will allow us to navigate the complexities of existence while remaining grounded in our responsibilities as cosmic custodians.

In conclusion, the aspiration of realizing terraforming opens avenues filled with both potential and uncertainty. The synthesis of current evidence, the anticipation of future discoveries, and the acknowledgment of our innate curiosity shape a narrative rich with possibility, binding humanity to the universe at large. As we progress in our cosmic exploration endeavors, we embrace not only the exciting challenges that lie ahead but also the moral imperatives that accompany our engagements with the vast tapestry of life. The grand theory connecting all of existence lies in our collective journey—a journey marked by discovery, reflection, and an enduring commitment to understanding our place among the stars.

As we encapsulate these ideas and reflect on the cosmic mystery, we find ourselves not only as explorers but as caretakers of the deeper narratives woven across the universe. In seeking to terraform and understand alien environments, we reaffirm our responsibility to uphold the values of curiosity, compassion, and ethical stewardship for all forms of life—both terrestrial and extraterrestrial. The unfolding journey into the cosmos remains a magnificent odyssey, inviting us to reach for the stars while cherishing the connections we forge across the boundless expanse.

20.5. The Grand Theory Connecting All

The exploration of the cosmos, particularly through the lens of terraforming and the potential for extraterrestrial life, presents humanity with a profound narrative that intertwines science, philosophy, and ethics. As we synthesize current evidence regarding exoplanets, atmospheric conditions, and the interactions between celestial bodies, we begin to form a comprehensive understanding of the mechanisms that may facilitate life beyond Earth. This synthesis is not merely a collection of findings; it reflects the cumulative aspirations and inquiries of a civilization eager to connect with the broader universe.

At the forefront of this synthesis is the realization that numerous exoplanets exist within the habitable zones of their stars, many of which exhibit characteristics favorable for sustaining life. Current research enables us to detect potential biomarkers in these environments and highlights the remarkable diversity of planetary systems. For instance, the Kepler Space Telescope's discoveries have unveiled thousands of candidate planets, offering tantalizing prospects for future exploration and the possibilities of terraforming. The ongoing missions to our solar system's celestial bodies—Mars, Europa, and others—provide essential case studies for understanding the prerequisites for habitability and environmental manipulation.

As we gaze toward the future, predictions for upcoming discoveries play a pivotal role in shaping our understanding of potential extraterrestrial life and terraforming initiatives. With advancements in technology—bolstered by projects such as the James Webb Space Telescope—researchers are poised to uncover previously obscured aspects of planetary atmospheres, climate systems, and potential biospheres. The continuing refinement of instruments and methodologies promises a new era of exploration, one in which the lines separating fact from fiction blur as possibilities manifest.

Central to this exploration is the role of human curiosity. It serves as the driving force propelling us to seek answers to profound questions about our place in the cosmos. Our innate desire to discover and understand the unknown fosters innovation and ingenuity across scientific disciplines. Curiosity does not solely motivate scientific inquiry; it invokes narratives that capture the human imagination, inviting broader public engagement and interest in space exploration. As we contemplate the ethical considerations surrounding terraforming and potential contact with alien life, curiosity must be tempered with responsibility, ensuring that our ambitions resonate with the values of compassion and respect.

Preparing for a terraforming revelation is not merely a task of scientific endeavor; it encompasses an intricate web of legal, ethical, and societal dynamics. As humanity pushes forward, the challenge lies in engaging a global audience in conversations about the responsibilities inherent in shaping new environments. International collaboration must yield frameworks that protect the integrity of extraterrestrial ecosystems, ensuring we approach cosmic inquiries with mindfulness and care. Establishing stratified regulatory measures enables us to set a precedence that reflects the shared responsibility we bear in the cosmic arena.

Conclusively, the vision of terraforming realized is not simply a fantasy; it is grounded in the potential of informed scientific inquiry, creativity, and ethical reflection. As we strive to understand the mysteries of the cosmos, the interconnected narratives of what we have learned and what lies ahead drive us toward coexistence with life—both terrestrial and extraterrestrial. The journey of exploration beckons answers to questions we have long pondered, while also inviting us to reflect on the broader implications of our presence in the universe.

The cosmic mystery remains a compelling adventure riddled with possibilities. As we reach for the stars and refine our aspirations of terraforming, we remain accountable to the lives we wish to create and preserve. This ongoing odyssey into the unknown is an enduring testament to humanity's spirit—where each discovery, each exploration, and each reflection fosters a deeper understanding of our collective existence, our responsibilities, and the remarkable journey that unites us across the vast expanse of space. As we seek to realize the potential of terraforming, the future of our cosmic endeavors stands at the crossroads of curiosity and ethical stewardship —propelling us into a future illuminated by the intersection of life, exploration, and the boundless wonders of the universe.

21. Conclusively Possible: Terraforming Realized?

21.1. Synthesis of Current Evidence

In today's cosmic exploration, the synthesis of current evidence surrounding the possibility of terraforming other worlds reveals a multifaceted tapestry of scientific inquiry and burgeoning insights. As researchers accumulate knowledge from exoplanet studies, atmospheric analyses, and the intricate dynamics of celestial bodies, they construct a foundational understanding of the prerequisites required to support life beyond Earth. The increasing prevalence of exoplanets detected within habitable zones encourages optimism and ambition, paving the way for innovative terraforming models that could enhance planetary environments.

As we amalgamate our findings concerning worlds like Mars, Europa, and various exoplanets, we also recognize the theoretical frameworks and methodologies that underscore our efforts. Recent technological advancements, including innovative telescopes and probing missions, bolster our ability to identify potential signs of life and unravel the conditions necessary for habitation. This growing repository of evidence fosters a rich dialogue regarding terraforming possibilities that challenges conventional notions of habitability and expands the horizons of our collective imagination.

Predicting future discoveries in this field becomes essential for shaping the trajectory of our cosmic initiatives. The ongoing development of instruments such as the James Webb Space Telescope promises groundbreaking insights into the characteristics of exoplanetary atmospheres, facilitating our understanding of their potential to sustain life. As astronomers and planetary scientists refine their methodologies, the prospect of uncovering those elusive signals or signatures becomes more tangible, paving the way for potential reconceptualization of existing models for planetary transformation.

The role of human curiosity remains central to our explorations of the universe; it is this innate desire to uncover the unknown that propels scientific inquiry and initiatives in terraforming other worlds. As humanity reflects on its existence, this curiosity nurtures a sense of responsibility for the environments we endeavor to modify. The desire to understand life beyond Earth fosters inquiry that resonates with our hopes for connectivity and understanding, driving our quest into the vast unknown.

Preparing for a terraforming revelation necessitates an adaptations approach, one that emphasizes the collaborative nature of scientific and ethical considerations. Engaging in interdisciplinary dialogue among scientists, ethicists, policymakers, and the public will be crucial for navigating the complexities of cosmic engagement and ensuring that our aspirations align with a broader commitment to stewardship and sustainability. Future endeavors should reinforce principles that prioritize the preservation and respect of existing ecosystems, fostering harmony amidst cosmic intrigue.

Concluding thoughts on the cosmic mystery encapsulate the moral imperatives and profound questions that accompany our search for extraterrestrial life. The quest to terraform other worlds invites contemplation not only about the practicalities of creating habitable environments, but also about the essence of existence itself. Each discovery illuminates the interconnected narrative that binds us as seekers and custodians of life in all its forms.

In summary, the potential for terraforming becomes ever clearer as humanity cultivates a deeper understanding of the universe. The combination of scientific rigor, the excitement of future discoveries, and the desire for connection lays the groundwork for a journey that transcends boundaries. The synthesis of current evidence surrounding terraformable worlds embodies hope and reflection, reminding us of our awe-inspiring place within the celestial tapestry that stretches far into the cosmos. As we navigate this mysterious frontier, we commit to approaching each new revelation with a sense of wonder and a dedication to preserving the delicate balance of life that exists in all its forms. The cosmic mystery beckons, inviting us to embrace the possibilities and forge our path toward a future filled with exploration, curiosity, and interconnectedness throughout the universe.

21.2. Predictions for Future Discoveries

Predictions for future discoveries in the realm of alien terraformation and cosmic exploration offer an exhilarating glimpse into the possibilities that lie ahead. As we stand on the precipice of scientific advancement, the convergence of technologies, theories, and a deepening understanding of the cosmos compel us to envision the myriad ways in which our searching efforts may soon bear fruit. This uncharted journey ignites an aspiration for knowledge, pushing researchers, engineers, and curious minds to daringly pursue the mysteries of extraterrestrial life and the potential transformation of hostile environments into flourishing ecosystems.

The advent of next-generation telescopes, such as the James Webb Space Telescope, presents a cornerstone for future discoveries. By peering into the intricate details of exoplanetary atmospheres, scientists will gain insights into the chemical compositions and potential habitability of newfound worlds. Observing atmospheric signatures indicative of life—such as oxygen, methane, or water vapor—will propel the dialogue surrounding targeted terraforming initiatives, allowing us to explore strategies for cultivating these environments for future colonization.

Additionally, the ongoing exploration of our solar system will provide essential case studies to inform terraforming methodologies. Missions to Mars, Europa, and Enceladus will investigate both the possibility of existing microbial life and the conditions required for sustainable ecosystems. The data collected will help refine our understanding of the biological and chemical interplay needed to create Earth-like environments. The lessons learned from these endeavors will not only establish precedents for future terraforming projects but also engender a sense of humility as we grapple with the complexity of life and the ecosystems that foster it.

As we prepare for a future where terraforming becomes a tangible undertaking, the emphasis on interdisciplinary collaboration will be paramount. Bringing together experts across a range of fields —including astrobiology, environmental science, engineering, and ethics—can yield optimizing approaches for launching terraforming efforts and engaging responsibly with other worlds. The merging of insights can sharpen methodologies, expand knowledge, and inform critical decisions regarding how to interact with potential life forms and ecosystems encountered during exploratory missions.

A key facet of this preparation hinges on the evolving landscape of public engagement and education. With growing interest in space exploration, it becomes imperative to foster awareness about the ethical dimensions of terraforming and the responsibilities associated with altering alien environments. Encouraging scientific literacy and promoting community discussions about our cosmic responsibilities will inspire future generations to take up the mantle of explorers, guiding them toward connecting scientific inquiry with ethical practices. The establishment of educational initiatives surrounding astrobiology, planetary science, and terraforming ethics will empower society to engage actively in discussions about the potential for life beyond Earth.

In reflecting upon the role of human curiosity, we recognize it stands as the very driving force behind our desire to comprehend the universe. This intrinsic motivation fuels innovation and discovery, prompting space agencies and private enterprises to invest in ambitious programs aimed at exploring distant worlds. As we reach deeper into the cosmos, the act of inquisitiveness must be coupled with a commitment to understanding the consequences of our actions, ensuring that our exploration is conducted thoughtfully and compassionately.

In conclusion, predictions for future discoveries surrounding alien terraformation and cosmic exploration serve as both a reminder and an invitation. They illustrate the potential awaiting us as we harness technology, collaboration, and curiosity to unravel the mysteries of existence beyond our planet. As we navigate this ever-expanding universe, we embrace the challenges and opportunities that lie ahead, holding fast to the morally grounded approaches that ensure our explorative journeys respect the delicate balance of life and ecosystems we encounter. The cosmic mystery beckons—a tapestry woven with threads of wonder and responsibility—inviting us to explore, adapt, and discover the extraordinary realms that await among the stars.

21.3. The Role of Human Curiosity

The Role of Human Curiosity is an integral part of our cosmic journey, driving exploration and the relentless quest to understand our place in the universe. This intrinsic characteristic of our species has propelled us to look beyond our immediate environment, pushing boundaries through innovation, creativity, and scientific inquiry. As we pursue knowledge about alien terraformation and the potential for life beyond Earth, curiosity not only fuels our ambitions but also shapes the ethical considerations that govern our engagement with the cosmos.

At the core of human curiosity is an innate desire to question the nature of existence. From early philosophical musings to contemporary scientific hypotheses, humans have sought to unravel the mysteries of the universe. The vastness of space, filled with unknowns, beckons an exploration that transcends the limitations of our terrestrial experience, inviting us to ponder profound questions: Are we alone? What might life elsewhere look like? How can we adapt distant worlds to sustain life? Each inquiry leads to deeper insights and further questions, creating a perpetual cycle of exploration.

The curiosity that drives us extends beyond the theoretical; it manifests in tangible actions. The pursuit of space exploration, including missions to Mars, the study of the moons of Jupiter and Saturn, and the search for exoplanets, embodies humanity's desire to grasp the complexities of the universe. Each mission serves as a testament to our willingness to invest time, energy, and resources in understanding what lies beyond our world. This commitment to exploration defines our role as active participants in the cosmic narrative.

Moreover, the marriage of human curiosity with technological innovation has ushered in a new era of discovery. Advancements in robotics, artificial intelligence, and materials science enable scientists to venture further and probe deeper into the cosmos than ever before. High-resolution telescopes, like the upcoming James Webb Space Telescope, provide unprecedented views of distant galaxies and planets that were once unimaginable. This synergy of inquiry and technology positions humanity to engage in transformative processes that could potentially reshape alien environments for the sustenance of life.

However, the spirit of curiosity is not without responsibility. As we consider the implications of terraforming and getting in contact with potential extraterrestrial civilizations, we must engage thoughtfully with ethical considerations. The lessons learned from our history on Earth, where explorations often led to the disruption of existing ecosystems and cultures, prompt us to reflect on our moral obligations to preserve the integrity of alien environments. This necessitates a mindful approach to exploration—one that seeks to understand, respect, and, whenever possible, protect the natural mechanisms at work on other planets.

As humanity sets its sights on the possibilities for terraforming and interaction with extraterrestrial life, it is essential to foster a culture of inquiry that emphasizes ethical stewardship. Educational initiatives must promote scientific literacy while also encouraging citizens to engage in discussions about the responsibilities accompanying our explorations. By nurturing informed dialogue, we can create a community that supports responsible exploration—one willing to consider the ethical ramifications of actions taken in the pursuit of knowledge.

Preparing for a terraforming revelation ultimately hinges on nurturing the role of human curiosity. As we contemplate the profound potential of transforming inhospitable worlds into life-sustaining environments, we must remain committed to ethical practices that honor the delicate balance of ecosystems. We are inspired by the wonders the universe has to offer and challenged by the responsibilities that come with such ambitions.

In conclusion, the role of human curiosity in the exploration of terraforming and the search for extraterrestrial life embodies the essence of who we are as a species. It drives our ambitions to learn, create, and engage with the cosmos. As we reach for the stars, we do so not only as seekers of knowledge but as guardians of the worlds we explore. This responsibility shapes our paths forward, inviting a future where exploration is informed by curiosity, ethical stewardship, and a commitment to nurturing the intricate tapestry of existence that connects us all across the universe.

21.4. Preparing for a Terraforming Revelation

Preparing for a Terraforming Revelation

As humanity stands poised on the threshold of an unprecedented era of exploration, the prospect of terraforming distant worlds emerges as a central narrative in our cosmic ambitions. These discussions tap into our innate longing to venture beyond the confines of Earth and reshape alien environments into thriving ecosystems. However, preparing for the realities of such transformative endeavors necessitates a thorough understanding of scientific principles, ethical frameworks, and the multifaceted interplay between ecological systems and technological interventions.

Understanding the foundational science behind terraforming is essential. A successful terraforming initiative hinges on our ability to modify atmospheric conditions, temperature, and resource availability on target planets. Each planet's unique characteristics demand tailored strategies; for instance, the challenges inherent in terraforming Mars differ significantly from those associated with transforming Venus or the icy moons of Jupiter. Comprehensive research into the geological, atmospheric, and biological realms of these worlds will guide the crafting of effective terraforming models that align with their specific environments.

Moreover, an essential aspect of preparing for terraforming lies in acknowledging the ethical implications associated with intervening in extraterrestrial ecosystems. The notion of altering alien landscapes prompts profound questions concerning our responsibilities toward any indigenous life forms that may exist. Such considerations compel us to adopt a framework that prioritizes respect and stewardship—recognizing the intrinsic value of any forms of life we may encounter.

The path toward responsible terraforming initiatives also emphasizes the necessity for international collaboration and public engagement. Space exploration is a collective journey, one that stretches beyond national borders and involves a global commitment to ethical practices and sustainable exploration. Developing international treaties and guidelines that govern terraforming efforts ensures that the sharing of knowledge, resources, and responsibilities extends beyond a singular perspective, fostering diverse engagement as we explore distant worlds together.

The exploration of potential terraforming also invites us to reflect on the broader implications for human society. As we set our eyes on distant planets, we should remain attuned to the challenges that our home planet faces, including climate change and resource depletion. The lessons learned from such trials remind us of the interconnectedness of life and reveal that the pursuit of terraforming must be paired with a robust commitment to sustainability on Earth.

Advancements in technology will play a crucial role in preparing for the terraforming revelation. Innovations in robotics, biotechnology, and life-support systems will be necessary to engineer environments that can sustain human life and perhaps support diverse ecosystems. The continuous refinement of these technologies, paired with a renewed focus on fostering biodiversity and ecological resilience, will ensure that our terraforming efforts are not merely focused on human habitation, but on creating vibrant environments capable of sustaining myriad forms of life.

As we contemplate the cosmic journey toward terraforming, the anticipation of discovery stirs our imaginations. Preparations must be accompanied by scientific rigor, technological innovation, and ethical reflection. The ideal of reshaping distant worlds invites us to engage responsibly with the cosmos as we strive toward profound discoveries that resonate with our innate curiosity.

In conclusion, preparing for a terraforming revelation embodies not just scientific ambition, but a commitment to navigating the intricacies of existence itself. Our quest for understanding and exploration must be guided by respect for life, empathy for potential experiences, and a desire to cultivate environments that embrace the rich diversity of existence. As we venture into the cosmic tapestry that lies before us, the journey offers not only the excitement of discovery but also the opportunity to shape our shared trajectory as guardians of life across the universe. Embracing the challenges inherent in terraforming requires an unwavering dedication to curiosity, sustainability, and responsibility as we seek our place among the stars. Thus, as we prepare for the revelation of terraforming, we fortify our commitment to honor the intricate connections that define us and the universe we seek to engage with.

Concluding Thoughts on the Cosmic Mystery

As we reach the conclusion of our exploration into the possibilities of terraforming and the quest for understanding extraterrestrial life, the narrative transforms into a contemplation of the cosmic mystery itself. Humanity's journey through the stars is marked by a rich tapestry of scientific discovery, philosophical reflection, and ethical considerations. This synthesis frames our understanding of how interstellar exploration shapes our identity as a species poised to transcend the boundaries of our own existence.

The cosmic mystery reminds us of both the brilliance and fragility of life as we investigate the conditions that might foster existence elsewhere. The search for alien life, the ambition to terraform distant worlds, and the complexities of encountering other civilizations underscore humanity's profound desire to connect and belong. This innate curiosity propels us forward, guiding scientific inquiry and igniting imaginations as we seek to understand our place in the universe.

Within the narrative of the cosmic mystery lies a call to balance ambition with respect for the unknown. As we explore the implications of altering alien environments, we must ground our pursuits in ethical frameworks that honor existing ecosystems and potential life forms. The lessons drawn from Earth's ecological challenges illuminate the critical need for responsible stewardship as we reach for the stars—an imperative rooted in the interconnectedness of all life.

Looking ahead, the advancements arising from understanding cosmic phenomena and the development of technologies to facilitate terraforming present abundant opportunities. We stand on the cusp of innovative exploration, where collaboration among diverse scientific disciplines and artistic expressions enriches our understanding of life and existence across the cosmos. The potential for discovering life beyond Earth beckons, urging a broader dialogue that intertwines science, philosophy, and ethics—enabling us to forge connections that transcend perspectives and foster inclusivity in our cosmic endeavors.

Ultimately, the cosmic mystery invites us to ask the essential questions: What does it mean to be part of the universe? How do we define our existence in the grand tapestry of life? As we delve deeper into the possibilities of terraforming and the cosmos, we are compelled to engage with these inquiries, recognizing that the journey of exploration is not merely about the discovery of other worlds; it is also about understanding ourselves and the responsibilities we bear.

In summarizing our exploration, we affirm that the pursuit of knowledge leads us into realms filled with promise, complexity, and wonder. The cosmic mystery is not solely a canvas of uncertainty; it is an invitation to embrace curiosity, compassion, and ethical engagement as we navigate our path among the stars. As humanity extends its reach into the universe, may we do so with an unwavering commitment to foster life in all its forms—nurturing the delicate balance that sustains the intricate web of existence. The journey forward is rich with potential; it beckons us into the vast unknown, igniting the spirit of exploration that has defined our species since the dawn of time.

21.5. Concluding Thoughts on the Cosmic Mystery

In the grand tapestry of our exploration of the universe, concluding thoughts on the cosmic mystery invite us to reflect on the profound questions that lie at the heart of humanity's quest for knowledge. As we have navigated through the complexities of alien terraformation, the search for extraterrestrial life, and the intricate relationships that define our existence, we find ourselves on the precipice of discovery —ready to engage with the unknown while remaining grounded in ethical considerations and scientific integrity.

The allure of the cosmos is defined not only by the potential for discovering life beyond Earth but also by the acknowledgment of our place within this vast and intricate universe. The cosmic mystery calls upon us to embrace curiosity as a guiding principle, propelling our pursuits into realms that stretch our understanding of existence. Each journey undertaken, whether through the lens of modern technology or the imaginative faculty of literature and art, offers insights that can reshape our perspectives, challenging us to embrace the richness of diverse forms of life and the responsibilities they evoke.

As we consider the implications of terraforming—transforming worlds to create habitable environments—we confront significant ethical dilemmas that resonate deeply with our historical narratives here on Earth. The lessons learned from our ecological challenges impel us to tread carefully into alien landscapes, ensuring that our endeavors reflect respect, stewardship, and a commitment to preserving the integrity of ecosystems, even those uncharted by human understanding.

Moreover, the ongoing advancements in technology expand the horizons of our explorations, equipping us with tools and methodologies that were once the domain of science fiction. The potential for future discoveries is vast, embodying hopes for identifying habitable exoplanets, deciphering cosmic signals, and revealing the wonders of planetary systems that may harbor life. In this pursuit, collaboration among international scientific communities reinforces the spirit of unified exploration, where diverse voices contribute to our shared understanding of the cosmos.

Yet, amidst the excitement of discovery, we must always return to the ethical frameworks guiding our actions. The potential for contact with alien civilizations heightens the urgency to engage in thoughtful discussions about the implications of such encounters. How should we respond when faced with the possibility of interaction? What responsibilities accompany the endeavor to terraform, explore, and engage with the unknown? The answers to these questions shape our societal discourse, urging us to consider the future we desire and the legacy we wish to leave behind.

Ultimately, the cosmic mystery represents a journey of exploration that transcends mere scientific inquiry. It invites us to ponder not just the nature of life beyond Earth, but the very essence of our humanity. As we reach for the stars, we must strive to foster a sense of interconnectedness that honors all forms of existence. The pursuit of knowledge inspires a consciousness that recognizes the delicate balance sustaining life and the vast potential for collaboration that lies within our grasp.

In conclusion, the journey through the cosmic mystery embodies humanity's enduring spirit of curiosity, creativity, and ethical reflection. As we stand ready to explore new horizons, we must embrace the complexities of existence that accompany our aspirations. The cosmos beckons us with the promise of discovery while reminding us of our responsibilities to honor the diverse tapestry of life that flourishes across the universe. As we venture forth, may we be guided by wonder, compassion, and the relentless pursuit of understanding —the essence of our shared cosmic journey.